ADVANCE PRAISE FOR *HIRE RIGHT, FIRE RIGHT*

"Every leader, no matter what kind of workplace, should have a dog-eared copy of *Hire Right, Fire Right* close at hand. Roxi's book fills a desperate need for employers all in one place—how to find, retain, and let go of the right people, the right way, at the right time, and for the right reasons. There's nothing out there that provides such a comprehensive road map like this book with its superb tools and step-by-step methods for success."

—Marshall Goldsmith, world-renowned business leader, executive coach, teacher, and best-selling author of *Triggers* and *What Got You Here Won't Get You There*

"Few leaders are taught the fine art of hiring and firing. What makes Roxi Bahar Hewertson an excellent writer of business material is that she does it with humor, grace, and with practical examples that move the reader from a state of ignorance and anxiety to competence and confidence. In *Hire Right, Fire Right*, Hewertson does what she does best—provide her readers with concrete, specific, and useful tools to address these ever-present business challenges and to raise the bar for any manager. This book is definitely worth your time."

—Rodney Napier, PhD; CEO of The Napier Group; founding father of organizational development; and author of numerous books including *Groups: Theory and Experience*

"As usual, Roxi delivers. This is a wonderfully readable guide to hiring and firing that is filled with voices of experience, good humor, and practical advice. If you have employees, you need this book."

—Deborah Hoard, CEO, Photosynthesis Productions

"Roxi certainly has a knack for communicating complicated ideas in a very accessible and directly applicable way. The book's checklists and worksheets alone are worth way more than the price of admission—thousands of dollars of consulting advice wrapped up in the modest price of a book."

—Dr. Lee Dyer, professor emeritus, ILR School, Cornell University

"Roxi Bahar Hewertson delivers sage advice that will save every manager time, money, and heartache. Her key message that hiring is 'relational, not transactional' applies to every stage of an employee's tenure. Besides making a solid business case for doing it right, Roxi provides a proven system for acquisition, retention, and closure that, if followed, ensures your success as a leader and your company's sustainability."
—**Dr. Nancy O'Reilly, founder of WomenConnect4Good, Inc.; author of** *In This Together* **and** *Leading Women*; **international philanthropist; and president of Take the Lead**

"We all say it: 'Our most valuable resource is our people.' Yet, if we truly believe that, we must master the crucial skills of hiring, developing, and (even) firing people the right way. And if you want the definitive road map to become a master in this pursuit, Roxi's book is it!"
—**John Rutkiewicz, facilitator and coach, Living As A Leader**

"Finally! A no-nonsense guide to hiring the right person in the right way. Thank you, Roxi, for expanding on the very definition of leadership—getting the right people to support and expand the culture needed for success."
—**Craig S. Evans, EdD, vice president for development, Rochester Regional Health Foundations**

"Brain drain can kill a good organization. So hiring—and keeping—top talent must be a key priority for leaders. But it takes know-how, strategy, and a relentless focus on clear-eyed principles. Roxi Bahar Hewertson shows the way."
—**Rodger Dean Duncan, best-selling author of** *Change-Friendly Leadership*

"Roxi's book is about hiring, growing, and keeping good employees at all levels. It's a well-written 'manual' in that it provides practical step-by-step and tested recipes for hiring the right people in the first place; building their confidence, skill, and motivation; and retaining them for the long run. You can't ask for more than that."
—**Tom DeCotiis, PhD; cofounder of Corvirtus, LLC; and author of** *Make It Glow*

"Leaders and HR professionals alike will find *Hire Right, Fire Right* to be of immense value. With wisdom and humanity, Roxi provides much-needed insight, practical advice and resources, and a strategic road map to more skillfully navigate the talent lifecycle."

—Natalia Rabin, MA, MS, PCC, Certified Presence-Based® Coach

"Given that, as Jac Fitz-Enz noted, 'People, not cash, buildings, or equipment, are the critical differentiators of a business,' *Hire Right, Fire Right* is a book every manager needs to own. In this practical guide to getting, keeping, and—when necessary—letting go of employees, Roxi Bahar Hewertson makes the business case that no organization can afford the cost of hiring the wrong people, failing to retain the right ones, or tolerating unacceptable performers. She provides pragmatic and specific advice and tools to improve results in all three areas—acquisition, retention, and closure."

—Roy V. H. Pollock, DVM, PhD; chief learning officer of The 6Ds Company; and coauthor of *The Six Disciplines of Breakthrough Learning*

"*Hire Right, Fire Right* is much more than a book. It is a road map of practical advice, insights, and resources filled with aha moments, and it is a fantastic read! Roxi Bahar Hewertson provides a handy and sensible road map for anyone tasked with hiring and managing people. She gives us an easy-to-follow practical guide to acquiring the best talent, retaining and growing that talent, and separating graciously, no matter the reason. She reminds us that all of our interactions with employees are relational, not transactional. *Hire Right, Fire Right* is a resource that you will return to again and again, and it will be covered in Post-it notes."

—Deborah Hall, vice president for finance and operations, LaGrange College

"In her new book, Roxi Hewertson offers a thorough and practical guide for something that's usually either fraught with difficulties or avoided altogether! This is a book to be read slowly and implemented carefully. My bet is you will enjoy this resource, which is full of Roxi's hard-won wisdom from her many years of experience and learning about this topic."

—**Beatrice W. Hansen, principal,**
Presence-Based® Coaching

"For frontline managers to board chairs, the most important role is to attract, hire, and nurture the right individuals for your team and organization. In *Hire Right, Fire Right*, Roxi Bahar Hewertson provides thoughtful, sophisticated, practical, and seasoned guidance on how to navigate that continuum successfully based on her significant professional and personal experience as an employee, leader, coach, and consultant."

—**Dr. Harold D. Craft Jr., vice president for**
administration emeritus, Cornell University

"Roxi Bahar Hewertson has been there and done exactly what she teaches us about in *Hire Right, Fire Right*. She takes the employer-employee experience out of the theoretical and puts it into practice, offering us insights and actions that will pay off immediately and for years to come. Thank you, Roxi!"

—**Dane Cruz, director,**
Cornell Interactive Theater Ensemble

"*Hire Right, Fire Right* is the easiest collection of best practices I have ever read! With the war for talent raging at a pace we have never seen, paying attention to the guides in this book is a guarantee you will win a lot of battles. If you want to be the smartest manager or HR professional, keep this book on your desk as an essential resource. Roxi Bahar Hewertson has provided a comprehensive recipe for every staffing area essential to managers. If you lead people, you will appreciate the checklists, templates, and scripts every time you need to recruit, retain, or let go of a staff member."

—**Chris Halladay, associate vice president for**
human resources, Lehigh University

"I wish *Hire Right, Fire Right* existed twenty-plus years ago! The principles of good management are presented very well, and what is particularly helpful is the road map that Roxi Bahar Hewertson provides. I'm grateful that she is sharing her many years of experience to help new and seasoned managers understand the importance of hiring right and firing right. As a senior member of a national career and search firm, I intend to spread the word: the best book on this subject is now available!"

**—Shelley Semmler, senior founding consultant,
Aspen Leadership Group, and former vice president
for advancement, Ithaca College**

"If you are looking to hire someone, develop someone, or bring closure to a relationship, *Hire Right, Fire Right* is a must read and a powerful resource. I was a fortunate recipient of what Roxi Bahar Hewertson writes about in this book having been hired, onboarded, and developed by her early in my career. I can attest that the how-to processes, questions, lessons, and solutions she writes about result in positive outcomes, and I apply them today. Roxi's wisdom is spot-on, timeless, time-saving, and, for me, life shaping."

**—Dr. Kathryn Burkgren, associate vice president for
organizational development and effectiveness,
Cornell University**

"This practical, easy-to-read guide is full of Roxi's sage advice, signature wit, and gold-standard best practices when building and cultivating highly effective teams. Read it cover to cover and then keep it close by as a handy reference tool."

**—Amy Kellestine, manager,
Leadership Academy, PCL Constructors Inc.**

"An essential book for any leader who wants to have a high-performing, cost-effective, fun place to work."

—Daniel R. Brown, executive director, Racker

"Sought-after leadership coach Roxi Bahar Hewertson has knocked it out of the park *again* with *Hire Right, Fire Right*! She is generous with her practical examples, scenarios, and questions—making it easy for any leader to hire in alignment with their company's core values. She shares timeless wisdom infused with fresh insights. This is a brilliant business book *and* a page-turner!"

**—Louise Phipps Senft, Esq.; CEO, Baltimore Mediation;
and best-selling author of *Being Relational:
The Seven Ways to Quality Interaction and Lasting Change***

Hire Right, Fire Right

A Leader's Guide to Finding and Keeping Your Best People

Roxi Bahar Hewertson

ROWMAN & LITTLEFIELD
Lanham • Boulder • New York • London

Published by Rowman & Littlefield
An imprint of The Rowman & Littlefield Publishing Group, Inc.
4501 Forbes Boulevard, Suite 200, Lanham, Maryland 20706
www.rowman.com

6 Tinworth Street, London SE11 5AL, United Kingdom

British Library Cataloguing in Publication Information Available

Library of Congress Cataloging-in-Publication Data

Names: Bahar Hewertson, Roxi, author.
Title: Hire right, fire right : a leader's guide to finding and keeping your best people / Roxi Bahar Hewertson.
Description: Lanham : Rowman & Littlefield, [2020] | Includes bibliographical references and index.
Identifiers: LCCN 2020008596 (print) | LCCN 2020008597 (ebook) | ISBN 9781538130629 (hardcover ; alk. paper) | ISBN 9781538130636 (epub)
Subjects: LCSH: Employee selection. | Employee retention.
Classification: LCC HF5549.5.S38 B347 2020 (print) | LCC HF5549.5.S38 (ebook) | DDC 658.3—dc23
LC record available at https://lccn.loc.gov/2020008596
LC ebook record available at https://lccn.loc.gov/2020008597

To every single person I've hired, helped to grow, and even had to fire. You have all contributed so much to my learning about human nature, the power of presence, and the meaning of empathy. You've taught me how to be tough and how to have compassion. Thank you!

And to George, who has unfailingly believed in this book and never let me stop believing!

Contents

SECTION C: CLOSURE = FIRE RIGHT **175**

Foreword

The "war for talent" is real, and it's escalating. We live in a time where new employee demands for work-life balance, telecommuting, and service to community are changing the way employers and organizations attract and retain top talent. In this increasingly competitive and complex landscape, organizations can ill afford a bad hire or, even worse, losing top talent.

As both a researcher and former Global Vice President of Talent for an international company, I can attest to increased pressures and demands for business leaders, especially those in Human Resources (HR), to "get it right." Sadly, until now, no one has produced a comprehensive road map to support the efforts of the entire employee life cycle, from recruitment and onboarding to retention and, ultimately, release.

In *Hire Right, Fire Right*, Roxi Bahar Hewertson provides a much-needed resource to help those on the front lines in the talent war. In sharing her vast leadership experience and expertise, Hewertson delivers an exceptional resource that provides a rare and insightful balance between tactical action and strategic reflection. For example, rather than just remind us that there is an increasing trend to use technology, especially social media platforms, to recruit top talent, she encourages the reader to adopt a proactive and positive mind-set to the task of finding top talent. Another example is her examination of bias—both conscious and unconscious—and how it can derail the most well-intentioned efforts in finding and hiring the right person.

A unique contribution this book makes to the field is addressing the entire "ARC"—Acquisition, Retention, and Closure—of an employee's experience. To do so, Hewertson provides us with the tools, worksheets, and checklists necessary to execute a successful talent strategy while probing deeper to allow the reader to understand the complex and often murky psychosocial factors that cloud our judgment and adversely impact our ability to be objective and, ultimately, successful.

Hire Right, Fire Right is divided in three sections. The first section focuses on attracting top talent as well as evaluating candidates on eight key factors, including emotional intelligence, to dramatically increase hiring success. Hewertson points out that knowledge, skills, and abilities are important but insufficient metrics in hiring the right person into the right position.

In the second section, the emphasis shifts to retention and engagement and provides the necessary strategies and tools to effectively keep your talent engaged, productive, and wanting to stay. In the third section, the focus is on closure and how to end employment relationships well, including when and how to "fire right" with the realization that saying "goodbye" correctly is just as important as getting your first "hello" right.

Along with the wealth of insightful and practical information provided in this book, there are numerous tables and charts (e.g., Hiring Right Search Map) to help more visual learners (like myself) quickly grasp the necessary sequential steps needed in the various components of the employee life cycle, such as recruitment and the onboarding processes.

Having sat on both sides of the "talent desk"—both as an internal leader and as an external talent consultant—I can absolutely understand and empathize with those of you charged with attracting, hiring, and retaining top talent as well as having to let someone go. In *Hire Right, Fire Right*, Hewertson provides an insightful road map to help you navigate this increasingly complex world within the "war for talent."

Hire Right, Fire Right is going to become an essential part of your arsenal. This book, through the wise counsel of Roxi Bahar Hewertson, will guide you through the process of the talent life cycle with a plethora of tangible assets and tools to help ensure that you, and your organization, are well equipped to take on this critical business challenge and win.

William L. Sparks, PhD
Dennis Thompson Chair and Professor of Leadership, McColl School of Business, Queens University of Charlotte
Author, *Actualized Leadership: Meeting Your Shadow & Maximizing Your Potential*
http://www.DrWillSparks.com

Acknowledgments

This book started rolling around in my head several years ago. Once I began telling my colleagues, friends, and family about the idea and heard their enthusiastic responses, it started to come to life. It does feel a bit like giving birth!

It's been a lifetime of experiences that have formed the stories and insights for this book, and I am grateful beyond measure for each one of those priceless relationships, as well as the guidance, wisdom, and hand-holding I've been given during the good times and especially during the tough times.

Dr. Will Sparks, who so kindly wrote the foreword for my book, has been and continues to be a never-ending inspiration, because of who he is as a human being and as a brilliant professor, author, and friend. My heartfelt thanks go to Leticia Gomez at Savvy Literacy Services who once again believed in me and found *Hire Right, Fire Right* such a good home with Rowman & Littlefield. My editor Suzanne Staszak-Silva has provided gentle guidance and great encouragement all along the way. These two powerful women took me under their wings. I am blessed!

I want to thank all the writers of blogs, websites, articles, and books whose insights and wisdom I share within these pages. They have added insightful perspectives and helped me get this all as right as I know how.

Two of my dearest friends have helped this book come full circle, from idea to reality. Rod Napier, my long-time mentor, someone who will never let me get away with anything short of my best and from whom I've learned so much about life, work, people, and, definitely, how to hire right. And then there's Barb Kathan, who read every single word of the first draft and gave me great feedback, encouragement, and love every step of the way. My daughter, Jenna, took time out of her busy life to edit many of these chapters and provided me with clear and insightful advice that I incorporated throughout the book.

Dear readers, thank *you* for picking up this book. It means you're curious and that you want to learn more. I hope you'll enjoy reading it as much as I enjoyed writing it for you. More than that, my overriding goal will have been achieved if *anything* you discover in these pages helps you succeed at the critical job of finding, developing, and saying goodbye to the right people at the right time in the right ways.

Introduction

You can take my factories, burn up my buildings, but give me my people and I'll build the business right back again.

—Henry Ford

When I mention to people I'm writing a book that includes hiring and firing right, the most consistent response I receive sounds a lot like this, "Oh, my God! Please let me know as soon as it's published—I need this right now . . . and (whispering in my ear) so does my boss!"

Acquiring and retaining talent, and eventually bringing closure when employees leave, is a *relational, not a transactional process*. In their best-selling book, *Being Relational*, Louise Phipps Senft and William Senft remind us of the importance of high-quality personal interactions for collective success. A transactional approach views interactions with others as a means by which to get the maximum value for oneself. In a relational approach, the goal is to maximize the quality of the interaction for both parties.[1]

This book guides you through a successful relational approach with each interaction you have with a candidate—the person you choose to hire and then develop, and the employee to whom you must say "goodbye"—for whatever reason. Author, teacher, and consultant Simon Sinek believes that "the trick to balance is to not make sacrificing the important things become the norm."[2] Acquiring and retaining employees, and bringing graceful closure when appropriate, are the important things.

When I'm discussing painful staffing issues with a person who supervises the work of others, this is what I often hear:

- "If only we'd hired right in the first place, I wouldn't have this awful mess now."
- "If only we'd paid attention and developed him more closely, we might have prevented his leaving."
- "If only I'd acted sooner. I have never lost so much sleep with any work problem as I have in firing her, and now it's cost us in so many ways."

Do any of these pain points sound familiar to you? If so, you're not alone! These are very real and present challenges for leaders everywhere, and we all seem to know it in our bones. We also see the impact on our teams' morale. This book aims to change all that.

Fact 1: No one can afford a bad hire!
Fact 2: No one can afford a bad fire!
Fact 3: Nationally about 50 percent of hires fail.[3] Of those that succeed, only around 20 percent are top performers.[4]
Fact 4: People rarely sue or hurt people they like and respect.

No leader in their right mind can ignore these realities, and yet plenty of right-minded people do. Hiring, retaining, and firing people into, through, and out of their jobs happens thousands, if not millions, of times every day all over the world. Without a doubt, it is in everyone's best interests to hire, retain, and fire very well. That's not the case today in far too many workplaces, but it can be the case for your workplace tomorrow.

This is a build-it-strong and keep-it-strong book, not a quick fix or silver bullet. I'm a big believer in *preventing the accident* rather than trying to stop the bleeding after it's happened. Preventing the "people problems" so many leaders complain about is at the heart of what we will explore together.

This book is for any leader who may have forgotten how, or has become too focused on "other important stuff," or simply doesn't have the right knowledge or tools to hire, develop, or fire people well. In my experience, the most successful leaders spend their valuable time recruiting the right people for the right jobs and then carefully guide their development.

When we hire well, firing is rarely an issue. When we fire well, lawsuits and violence are rarely an issue. In the life of an employee, like any good story, there must be an arc with a great beginning, a satisfying experience in the middle, and finally, an appropriate and meaningful ending—regardless of the outcome. All good stories also have underlying motivations, interesting characters, twists and turns, and conflicts that need to be resolved.

This book is focused on the three core processes experienced by the hiring leader and every employee: ARC—Acquisition (hire right), Retention (nurture right), Closure (fire right). My goal is to help you get the entire ARC done well and, by doing so, save a lot of money, lost opportunity, and heartache along the way.

Over several decades in increasingly complex leadership roles, with different enterprises including my own businesses, I've hired hundreds of people. I've fired my share as well. These have been union members, entry- to senior-level positions, and people in protected classes. I've not been sued once or lost a single union arbitration. When it has been *my call* to make the final hiring decision, believe it or not, I have *never* had to fire someone I hired. This book is my way of paying it forward by sharing my philosophy and methods. I would like to help others achieve at least a 90–95 percent success rate. While I can't live in your head or in your organization or promise the same rate of success, I can promise:

WHEN you follow my system of hiring staff, you will measurably and dramatically increase your success rate of hiring the right people for the right jobs.

WHEN you follow my system for developing your employees, you will increase the retention rates of those terrific people you just hired.

WHEN you follow my system for terminating employees, you will significantly lower your risk of lawsuits, arbitrations, and damage (unfair or not) to your organization's reputation.

Sounds simple, not easy, but simple, and it is, if you know how to do it. This book will give you the tools to execute all three of these critical leadership actions with consistent success. You'll have access to a full set of practical, easy-to-use tools and processes giving you a leg up in the marketplace for finding and keeping your best talent.

The first section of this book provides my Hiring Right Search Map and a well-tested toolbox for the (A) acquisition or hiring phase. Since we can't lead the wrong people to the right places, we need to find and choose the right people to hire and reduce the likelihood they'll leave too soon. To paraphrase Jim Collins in his book *Good to Great*, it is better to first get the right people on the bus, the wrong people off the bus, the right people in the right seats, and then figure out where to drive it.[5] The first section is the longest because getting the hiring right will prevent a busload of problems down the road.

The second section provides focused tools and insights to help ensure you are (R) retaining the terrific people you hired by nurturing and successfully developing them so they'll continue to add value and remain engaged and highly productive.

Finally, if a person is leaving or asked to leave, for whatever reason, the third section is about (C) closure and provides methods and checklists about how to end the employment relationship well. This includes why, when, and how to fire right—safely and with fairness, grace, and with the least amount of pain and drama for all parties. How you say "goodbye" is as important as how you say "hello."

Many organizations and their leaders spend too little time hiring right and as much as 17 percent of their time dealing with the fallout from failing to invest in hiring the right employees.[6] This is nearly a day per week, which is backward and costly. In my experience, this can be even higher. In fact, there was one case I remember vividly. The number of people involved in a senior leader's firing, including the lawyers, was six highly paid people. For close to three months, this case burned up to 50 percent of the firing leader's week and a significant amount of everyone else's time. It's truly a productivity killer when this happens.

Unfortunately, too many otherwise talented and smart frontline supervisors, managers, department heads, CEOs, and Human Resources (HR) departments have it backward and suffer chronic organizational migraines because of it—so let's remedy the problem together!

We need to mitigate this reality by spending most of our time hiring and developing great performers and running our businesses, and 5 percent, or less, of our time managing or creating an exit plan for the bottom 10–20 percent of performers. Poor and marginal performers need to be given clear expectations about what is expected of them and how their performance is not meeting those expectations. They need the opportunity to develop, turn a corner—perhaps in a different role—and come up to speed. We can lose good talent if we don't take the time to support the development of an employee. However, if in the final analysis, the employee won't or can't meet your expectations, it's time to say goodbye—gracefully!

Hiring, developing, and retaining great employees must be at the top of your organization's key strategy list. Think about it—can you imagine any other single strategy that matters more or is a better value proposition for long-term success than having the right talent on board?

One of the most jaw-dropping stories I've come across in all my years of consulting comes from the senior living industry, where I have coached dozens of executives and taught leadership courses to leaders at all levels in the organization. I was meeting with the CEO of one of the largest senior care companies in the country and, in the course of conversation, we began talking about the excessively high turnover rate within the industry. He said, and I am not exaggerating, "We budget annually for at least an 85 percent turnover rate." This didn't surprise me because I already knew the turnover rate in the nursing-home side of the industry ranged from about 50 percent to 100 percent. Hard to get your head around, isn't it?

When I asked him how much that translated to in his annual budget, he said around $25 million! More shocking was his deep conviction that this was an unchangeable line item and a normal cost of doing business. He was so adamant that I was unable to share with him how I believed he could cut that in half or more. I left the meeting feeling sick to my stomach. I couldn't stop thinking how much good that *huge* amount of money could do if it were invested in hiring, developing, and retaining good people or improving the facilities serving our elders or how much this company's residents would appreciate seeing a familiar face every day instead of a new one every couple of weeks or less. This is a classic example of disastrous decision making in hiring and retaining the caregiving staff the clients and taxpayers depend on and are charged for every month of the year.

Given that the national average turnover rate across all industries is roughly 15 percent,[7] and in some segments of the senior living industry it's 70–90 percent,[8] can you imagine if there were a law or a public outcry that resulted in client bills being reduced if the staff turnover was more than even 40 percent? I'm confident that senior living CEOs would demonstrate a rapid change of heart or be fired by their boards for clinging to a belief that 85 percent was acceptable, or as likely, the company would soon be out of business.

Everyone has customers, people who are served, who purchase, or in some way utilize and/or interact with your organization for mutually beneficial purposes. Every hire and fire will reverberate in some way that touches the people you are in business to serve. The impact could be minor, or it could make or break your organization.

For example, consider where you like to go for a good meal versus where you rarely or never choose to go. If your experience of the food was good but the service was bad, it is possible you might return. If the food was bad and the service was good, you probably won't return. If both the food and service were bad, it's a good bet you'll never return—and to top it off, your friends, social media, and restaurant rating sites will hear all about it! Of course the opposite is also true for great food and service. It's the same story for your organization. A leader's skills and behaviors, particularly in hiring, developing, and firing employees, ripples out into the world and to the stakeholders, like it or not.

We could all make up a list of hiring and firing failures we've observed in the news, from afar, or up close. My point is to remind us that these disasters were caused by people who were *hired* by someone or some group of people and, in most cases, not fired or held accountable in any way for a very long time even though many people knew of the wrongdoings. When nothing is done until it is too late, the human and financial consequences are immeasurable. One only needs to scan the world of big business, government, school systems, hospitals, religious organizations, and large nonprofits to see the huge negative impact bad hires and lack of accountability can have on individual lives, community health, and even a nation, for a very long time and, sometimes, forever.

It is estimated that at least 50 percent and, in some studies, nearly 70 percent of people working are dissatisfied in their jobs. That can't be healthy for anyone, or for any enterprise, public or private. Another 18 percent are actively disengaged and haven't yet been turned around or fired. That 18 percent is estimated to cost the US economy at least $550 billion every year.[9]

The first solution to these challenges is *prevention*—hiring the right person into the right job. The second solution is to *develop and grow that person so that great talent is retained*. Both solutions require deep *organization-wide commitment* and systematic *discipline* to carry out best practices that align with the organization's mission, vision, and values.

Furthermore, every one of these three processes—hiring, nurturing, and firing—requires meaningful conversations with employees, due diligence, and relationship building. *How* each person is hired (or not), nurtured and retained (or not), and fired (or not) really matters to any organization's *bottom line*, including the bottom line of the employer's *reputation.*

I'm convinced there are two things we need to *significantly improve* in our workplaces in the United States and around the world: (1) the quality of leadership and (2) the ways in which we manage the ARC when we acquire, retain, and close a relationship with each employee. My previous book, *Lead Like It Matters . . . Because It Does*[10] focuses on practical tools for leaders at all levels so they can master the skills needed to lead their people effectively and with purpose. This book completes the story I need to tell.

LET'S BEGIN!

Any journey worth taking must have a starting point, stops along the way, and an ending point. The Hiring Right Search Map provides all the steps in my system for getting to the finish line with that terrific new employee. In "Section A: Acquisition = Hire Right," we travel to chapters 1, "Call to Action" through chapter 5, "The Invitation." Once your new staff member is on board, you'll have the Retention Map to guide you through "Section R: Retention = Nurture Right," which takes us from chapter 6, "Welcome Aboard!" through chapter 9, "Growing Your People." On this part of our journey, you'll discover my system and tools for retaining the great talent you just hired. And finally, in "Section C: Closure = Fire Right," we come to the end of the road with chapters 10 and 11, "When It's Really Over: Parts 1 and 2." Here we learn about my system for saying goodbye the right way—with grace and dignity for all parties, regardless of whether it is an involuntary or voluntary exit.

As you can see, we have a lot of ground to cover, so let's get started. Drumroll please!

Section A

ACQUISITION = HIRE RIGHT

Chapter One

Call to Action

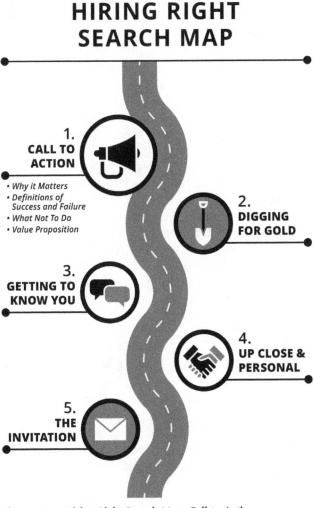

Figure 1.1. Hiring Right Search Map: Call to Action

The secret of my success is that we have gone to exceptional lengths to hire the best people in the world.

—Steve Jobs

WHY IT MATTERS

We're going to kick off our hiring journey at step 1 on the Hiring Right Search Map presented in figure 1.1. This call to action is intended to inspire you to keep going, even if the going gets a little slippery, you trip here and there, or a new path has to be forged from scratch. I have no doubt that you have some kind of hiring process in place already; the question is this: Is it working for you? My guess is you picked up this book because something's not working as well as you need it to, and you'd like to improve your results. To understand the "why" a bit more clearly, let's begin by looking into *your organization's wallet.*

As hard as it may be to believe, the hard data show us over and over again that the cost of a bad hire can be more than two times (2x) the person's annual salary . . . until you fire them or they leave. How much you lose depends on how much time, money, and productivity is flushed away in the meantime. Add the loss of morale among the team members before and/or after the person leaves. Then . . . add another two (2x) or three times (3x) or more of their salary to replace them. In Geoff Smart and Randy Street's book, *WHO: The A Method for Hiring*, their client research resulted in estimating that "the average hiring mistake costs *fifteen times* an employee's base salary in hard costs and productivity loss."[1] While theirs is mainly a single industry- and role-specific calculation, it still makes the point, right? *This hiring business is costly and important!*

And yet . . . we hire most people and positions the way "we've always done it" and based on resumes with thus and such degree and/or technical skills along with perceived or tested IQ. We now know that EQ (Emotional Quotient), or Emotional Intelligence (EI) as it is also known, is far more important for success in most jobs, and it's critical for success within leadership roles. We continue to hire and promote people, particularly leaders, by relying heavily on IQ and technical skill sets that they present on that all-important resume.

Have you heard anything like this in your workplace? "She's the best salesperson so she'll surely be the best leader of other salespeople." Or how about this: "I know he's a bit of a bully, but he's uber smart, so he'll do fine." We might as well say a brilliant scientist, who is deathly afraid of heights, should go up to the moon, or a known con man will make a great CEO because *he says* he knows how to negotiate. Assumptions as ridiculous as these happen every day and everywhere. Too often hiring managers operate on wrong, and even dangerous, assumptions about the knowledge, skills, and abilities that are truly needed for a particular position. We keep getting the same lousy results, and yet we have not substantively evolved and adopted best hiring practices in many, if not most, organizations.

DEFINITIONS OF SUCCESS AND FAILURE

I agree with Albert Einstein, "We cannot solve our problems with the same thinking we used when we created them."[2]

Success in hiring well is defined this way: *The newly hired person has been on board for at least eighteen months, is productive, and is doing exactly what he or she was hired to do, resulting in a satisfied, engaged employee and positive business outcomes.*

A successful hire means far more than avoiding failure. We can hide failure by allowing mediocre new hires to remain in place for far too long. A successful hire is what we need to work toward; an 85–90 percent, or more, hiring success rate should be expected.

The question is, are you prepared to invest in finding and wooing the cream of the crop for your team, or will you settle for "good enough for now"? Your answer to that question will determine your hiring success rate. And remember, it does not matter what business you are in. You could be the owner of a pizza franchise, the executive director of a local food bank, a superintendent of schools, a presidential candidate, a house cleaning service provider, COO of a trucking company, a bank manager . . . if you hire and fire people in your workplace, I'm talking to you.

I'd like to help you experience the task of hiring someone as positive and a lot more fun than you may have thought possible. Hiring right is an excellent opportunity to grow your organization in a mindful and productive way. You'll be amazed at the how much time and energy you can access when you aren't spending a huge chunk of your work life cleaning up personnel messes. And if that weren't enough incentive, it is so much *more work and expense* to get *hiring wrong* than to get *hiring right*.

Failure in hiring well is defined this way: *The employee voluntarily left or was asked to leave within the first eighteen months, and this exit has affected or will negatively affect business outcomes.*

Today, we are still seeing tired old hiring methods that result in at least a 50 percent failure rate in those we hire.[3] Recruiting firms score only around 10 percent better in their results—coming in on average at a 40 percent failure rate. That means that we face more difficulties in developing people and, too often, suffer the painful and costly results of having to either replace a fleeing or fired employee. It's no wonder hiring managers often have a "deer in the headlights" look and sometimes seem a little nauseated or just downright depressed, or even anxious, when they consider what might happen with the next hire.

WHAT NOT TO DO

Here are six common mistakes hiring managers regularly make with a success rate of *zero* in identifying the qualities you need to find in your best hire:

1. *Resume Blindness:* Without deep and reliable verification, you believe what you see on the page and assume no one lies (they do!).
2. *Group Grope:* You throw the whole organization at the candidate without well-communicated plans and coordination and just hope it works out. This is like playing "pin the tail on the donkey" and praying somebody hits the right target in another room.
3. *Fire Hose:* This is where no logic is applied. The hiring manager and/or Search Team members pump questions out of a hose waiting to see if the candidate chokes or swims, even though the job doesn't require swimming.
4. *Whack a Mole:* When you "test" for things that have nothing to do with the position or a person's ability to do it well, it's a waste of time and money at the very least. Whack 'em here and whack 'em there and see what happens is both insulting and useless. Mind

games, tricks, meaningless (vs. meaningful) social gatherings, and irrelevant off-the-wall questions like "Who—living or dead—would you like to have dinner with?" all demonstrate ignorance on the part of the interviewer and provide nothing of value. Great candidates will and should run away fast!

5. *Hug-fest:* This is when you talk about everything *but* the job and also do most of the talking. "How 'bout those Yankees!" Another hug-fest clue: you spend most if not all of your time *schmoozing* the candidate with nonstop chatter that is all about trying to sell them on your job offering.

6. *One-Trick Pony:* When an organization bets on only one or two metrics for measuring candidates, they lose time and time again. Whether it's an assessment instrument or someone's "gut" check, one metric or two are not nearly enough to tell you what you need to know. Some metrics may or may not help with early screening, but they will never give you the full picture. And even worse, you could lose some of the best people because the standard metric wasn't a good measure for what another exceptional individual could bring to the table. You need as much quantitative and qualitative data as you can get to win the "land the best" game.

Hiring isn't easy. Most things worth doing well are not easy, certainly to start with. It takes practice, patience, and undivided attention to become an expert in or even proficient at anything in life. We can think it's easy, wish it were, or pray for the hiring gods to help us. The bare-boned truth is this: it takes more than our belief that we can assess someone and get it right by using some combination of the tactics above. Instead, it requires a well-defined and disciplined process.

I hope we can agree that the cost of a bad hire is staggering no matter if the business is for profit or nonprofit, big or small. Just how staggering depends on the position, the salary, and whether the real costs are accurate or underestimated. The costs routinely calculated are often limited to the obvious such as advertising and/or recruitment, travel, relocation expense, and compensation package. Under the radar are the additional and very real costs of lower morale, onboarding time and expense, overtime, time wasted by the Human Resources (HR) staff and the Search Teams, the hiring supervisor's time, lost productivity, negative internal or external customer impact, as well as the impact on those who, in some way, utilize the skills of that position to do their own jobs well.

No leader, in any enterprise, would purposefully perpetuate these poor quality performance results *anywhere else*. The fact that high failure rates in hiring are tolerated—even expected and explained away as "the way it is," "a crap shoot," or "we just hope for the best"—is inexplicable and preventable.

This is a *call to action* for anyone who hires even one person a year. When we know bad hires costs the organization 2x to 15x the salary in direct and indirect losses, there should be a megaphone blasting out the *hire right* message to every corner of every workplace!

How do we change old habits? *When the pain of staying the same exceeds the pain of changing, we are more likely to change.* Another way to think about it is this: when we *reward what we do want* and *stop rewarding what we do not want*, things change much more quickly.

It makes good business sense to *reward best practices and results* in hiring when you want and need the best people in your workplace. If we want great staffing results, we have to communicate explicit hiring expectations to all levels of leadership (do not assume they know). Then we must reward people who meet or exceed our expectations and provide negative consequences to people who don't.

Management expert and twentieth-century business guru Peter Drucker famously said, "What gets measured, gets managed." If the quality of the hires was truly measured and rewarded, hiring well would receive the attention it deserves. When the real costs of hiring failures are communicated up front and a leader's hiring track record is tied to a performance review, the culture around hiring changes. It's so easy to do this, so why doesn't it happen more often?

One answer: *A history of institutionalized bad hiring habits, resistance to change, and failure to measure the true costs.*

When the top leadership accepts a low-quality hiring process and fails to insist that hiring well is the organization's—and therefore every hiring supervisor's—*top priority*, the result is bad business and bad *for* business, no matter whether we're talking about one employee in your small nonprofit office, fifty employees in your own business, or you are the CEO of hundreds of thousands of employees around the world. It's safe to say no one has created, or ever will create, a *great* agency, business, or company by settling for mediocre hires and performance.

The reasons hiring failures happen at such an alarming rate are all over the map. It is rare that leaders and their teams are coached or taught the skills to hire well, and fewer are aware of the true costs of failure. When I ask leaders what is preventing them from making a great hiring process a top priority, I hear things like this:

• We usually get more good than bad people in the door.
• It would take too long and waste too much of my (and my people's) time and energy.
• I'm a great judge of character so I know a good candidate when I see one.
• We are just replacing the person who left, so it should be a cake-walk.
• We know what we're looking for, so we don't need a protracted process.
• It's boring, mundane, and repetitive—not a good use of my time.
• I just want it to be over and get on with running my business.
• It's just an entry-level job.
• We can't really know until the new person is on the job anyway.
• My boss told me I had to hire _____ (fill in the blank).

These statements don't hold much water when hiring right is the one sure thing that can and will make the organization more successful. Consider for a moment that you just learned that 50 percent of your customers are dissatisfied. The first question should be: "What are we doing to fix our customer satisfaction problem?" It's unlikely that we would hear a similar list of excuses for a customer satisfaction problem that's costing the business dearly. If so, I wouldn't want to put a wager on how long that leader remained employed!

Expediency and distraction, and even workload, are common but not valid reasons to shortchange the hiring process. The true costs (human, time, and money) of poor hiring practices need to be clear to everyone involved. This is a choice *to pay now, or pay even more later*, and it is a choice. Here's another reason to consider: WIIFM (what's in it for me?). If no one "up there" in your organization is sending *you* the message to invest in hiring well, send it to yourself—it's by far one of the smartest things you can do for your own career, today and for the future. Hire the best people—including people who know things you don't, have skills you need, and are smarter than you—and watch your career rise to new heights. Great hires make you look good—really good.

If that isn't convincing enough, we also know that bad hires often lead to terminations of employment. These can and do devolve into nasty behaviors and sometimes very expensive lawsuits and arbitrations. They can even result in workplace violence where the health and lives of other employees can be at risk. Perhaps that is a wake-up call that will make it worth it for top management to invest the time and effort and insist that hiring right and firing right *is* a top strategic priority and provide the resources to make it a reality.

VALUE PROPOSITION

These are samples of questions you can ask yourself and your team to get grounded in the cost/benefit value proposition and give yourself and others an objective reality check:

- How much time and money did we spend to hire this person, including staff time?
- What worked and what didn't work—what did I/we learn?
- What are our percentages of great, mediocre, or bad hires over the last three years, and how do we know?
- How long will it take to get a replacement for the great hire I lost too soon?
- What did it cost us in time, money, lost productivity, morale, and customer satisfaction to hire that employee who didn't work out?

This is a sobering conversation, even if you just have it with yourself!

It is safe to assume that most people want a job that matches and can grow their career interests, talents, and skills. Let's also assume that most people want their work to be meaningful, to be part of an enjoyable workplace, and to work for a leader and with coworkers they respect. And finally, let's assume that no one (employee or supervisor) enjoys the "we're letting you go" conversation.

Great talent does not want to or have to work for an employer who hires, develops, or fires poorly. This is a *call to action* to take an honest look at your current hiring practices. You have or will have a job opening to fill soon, no doubt. Let's get a jump on it now!

In chapter 2, "Digging for Gold," we'll begin this important journey in earnest. Think of it like a treasure hunt; you might get your hands dirty and your feet wet, but it will be worth it when you find that nugget of talent you've been searching for. You'll have a checklist to help you dot your i's and cross your t's *before* you launch your search, as well as one to guide you if you choose to use an outside search firm. We will explore the world of options so you can make well-informed decisions as you move forward.

Let's get digging!

Chapter Two

Digging for Gold

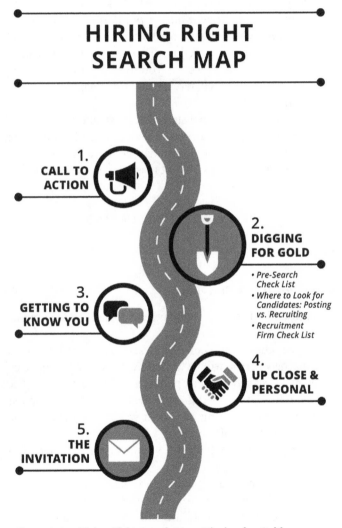

Figure 2.1. Hiring Right Search Map: Digging for Gold

Give me six hours to chop down a tree and I will spend the first four sharpening the axe.

—Abraham Lincoln

As we continue to step 2 of the Hiring Right Search Map, "Digging for Gold" (see figure 2.1), we'll focus on readiness preparations for your search journey as well as how and where to look for the best candidates. If you're *promoting or filling a lateral position with a unionized employee from within,* you're bound by the rules of the contract and may want to skip over to the next section, "Retention = Nurture Right," and focus on development. However, if you're hiring for new bargaining unit positions or from a civil service list, this chapter and those that follow are still for you.

There are a number of crucial steps that must take place *prior* to any job posting or recruitment effort. For the odds to be in your favor, this checklist is the starting point. There may be more things you want to add to your customized checklist, but these will get you started.

PRE-SEARCH CHECKLIST

Complete *each* item.

Create the Position's Storybook

This is the essential first step and may take some time to complete.

✓ Review the current job/position description carefully, including people this new person will be working with and/or serving. Get input from as many stakeholders as possible, including any direct reports and Human Resources (HR) if appropriate. Make no assumptions that anything is staying the same as you answer at least these questions:
  • Why do you need this position?
  • What do you need in this position now that has changed from the past?
  • What impact does this position have on others' work?
  • What are the absolutes for education, experience, and KSAs (knowledge, skills, and abilities) that you *know* are essential for any candidate to succeed?

- What are the "nice to have's" you would like to see and why?
- How should this position fit within the organizational chart?
- Final check: What, if anything, is still missing or should be removed from the new position description?

✓ Imagine you're a candidate reading the job description. Does it describe what success looks like? Is it welcoming and inclusive? Is the language explicit enough? Are all the expectations and requirements clear, including any values-based expectations?

✓ During the review, consider the wording and anything else you believe would make the position attractive to the kind of candidates you want to attract. The more diverse your intended pool, the more you need to pay attention to wording that is inclusive and not biased.

Scorecards

✓ Determine all requirements you have of all your candidates from writing samples to presentations, any testing you will require for this position, and the scores you are looking for and why. Think of creative ways to remove barriers versus erecting them without weakening your ability to assess.

✓ Be certain of the objective value of any assessments and ensure they are legal instruments authorized for use in hiring and not biased by gender, age, race, religion, or ethnicity and do not violate the Americans with Disabilities Act (ADA).

✓ Do not use 360 assessments or self-scoring personality or style instruments for the purpose of hiring. If a candidate knows you are using these, be aware that these can either be "gamed" or biased, telling you nothing of value. No candidate is going to hand over a negative 360 report, and clever ones will know how to answer self-scoring instruments to match what they think you want.

✓ Include any Industrial Psychologist interview requirements.

Pay to Play

✓ Identify your pay range, or state that you pay competitively, and include extras such as signing benefits, bonuses, moving, housing, visits, and such that you are willing to offer.

✓ Create a budget for getting the results you want. Include, for example, your search plan costs of recruitment, advertisements, yours and/or candidates' travel costs, staff time investment (this is an indirect but real cost to the organization), testing, all likely perks, recruitment firms, and dual career couples costs/options. Then, do your best to stick to that budget!

Your Team and Your Strategy

✓ Establish your Search Team and your search process plan. These are the people who will each have important roles in the selection process. (More on this in chapter 3, "Getting to Know You.")

✓ Define your search strategy and identify your most promising means and methods for attracting the candidates you want to have apply by posting (advertising, listing, etc.) or recruitment (active reaching out) or both.

When you're clear about exactly who and what you need, you're well on your way to letting the world know about this job opening. When you hire right and retain those great hires, and when everyone *believes* it to be a *top business priority*, you will likely see an increase in people who will volunteer to serve on Search Teams and actively participate in onboarding activities. This happens when you, the hiring supervisor, make hiring right a top priority and prove it by establishing expectations and accountability throughout the process.

Pitfall: Not enough time. Need this position yesterday!

Solution: Remember it is real money in the bank to get this right. A fast hire is too often a slow fire, and you can't afford it!

You and your organization's mind-set and attitude about recruitment and filling positions with the best people can be, and usually is, a significant differentiator in attracting the best people. The ways in which you present your organization to your most desirable candidates matters—a lot. It is often the little things that make you stand out from the crowd—the first impression with the first human contact, the wording of the job description, the organization's description of itself, its web presence, and the personal touch and tone of the invitation to apply. All these are clues that send important signals to prospective candidates.

Sharing what you are proud of—your mission, services, products, vision, values, and your culture—is fair game and important to convey. I suggest you refrain from boasting, bragging, or demonstrating hubris in any way, no matter how big or fancy your organization happens to be at this moment. Top candidates do their homework before an interview and know a great deal about your organization already. How you treat your candidates, from the very beginning to the finish line of the search process, will have the greatest impact on attracting the people you want to work for and with you, and not insignificantly, affect your reputation as a prospective employer out there in the world of social media.

On the flip side, one of the most off-putting things you can convey to a prospective candidate is that they are somehow "lucky" to be considered by your enterprise. If a candidate wants to know the ratio of applicants to hires, they will ask.

WHERE TO LOOK FOR CANDIDATES: POSTING VERSUS RECRUITING

Let's look at the options you have to choose from to find those desirable candidates.

There is a big difference between posting a job versus recruiting and attracting the right person for that job. Advertising it inside and outside the organization is generally a reactive approach (you react to those who apply); recruiting is generally a proactive approach (you reach out to encourage various people to apply). Posting may appear to be fast and efficient, but it can be a crapshoot; recruiting, however, is more precise and strategic and may take the same, less, or more time. Posting is like a potluck supper, where you might get a nice smorgasbord, or, more often, there are too many salads and not enough of anything else. Recruitment is more like choosing your menu carefully and going only to restaurants with a good rating that offer exactly what you want.

Choosing to post should be the result of a strategic thought process for the hiring leader; it should be chosen as the smartest method for the right reasons, not out of habit or with the false assumption that it will save you time and money. It often won't in the long run and, perhaps, not even in the short run.

There are smart and compelling reasons to post a job internally and/ or more broadly. For instance, you may know from experience that your internal or local/regional pool contains many good candidates whom you know will apply, and you want to save your resources for the screening and interviewing process and other important expenditures. Perhaps you've had layoffs and you need to post internally first to give those folks an opportunity to be reemployed. It makes sense if you believe you have one or more internal qualified candidates for whom this would be a growth or promotion opportunity, and/or you prefer to fill the job from within. Of course, if you know of people, inside or outside your workplace, whom you want to encourage to apply, you can certainly recruit them to be candidates as long as you make no promises about the search outcome. In all these examples, posting is a choice that makes good business sense.

Pitfall: Subjectivity, plus or minus, with internal candidate.

Solution: A rigorous, objective process that measures all candidates against the same criteria.

Online platforms are one proactive approach to search for and recruit great candidates. The ground is constantly moving in the techno-recruitment world, so there are no easy answers about how to and where to recruit your best candidates for a particular position. The plethora of internet companies that promise you the best and the brightest list of job seekers through their screening algorithms can be a useful tool, but it is *not* the toolbox. Sifting through which dot.com company does what well is not the purpose of this book, but I will give you some options to review because only you can judge if it is a good option for your situation. A current (as of this writing) list of online resources that have a good history and good ratings by users (both job seekers and employers) can be found in the Resources section for this chapter at the end of the book.

Before you venture there, though, let's look at the rest of the story. Many companies have entire teams of people that show up on college campuses every semester. Others scour their competition for high-potential candidates they might be able to lure away from another employer. Internal recruiters use a multitude of methods including recruitment sites; job posting sites; social media, including LinkedIn, Facebook, and Instagram; and discipline-specific professional networks. External recruiting firms specialize in finding just the right person for just the right job using many of the same tools as their internal counterparts. They work in virtually every field of expertise: sales, marketing, C-Suite, college presidents and faculty, science and research, school superintendents, HR professionals, fundraising professionals, and IT whiz kids, to name a few.

Nearly all mid- to top-level positions in any enterprise can find a recruitment company that specializes in their target job market. There's no question these companies exist, but you should ask these questions: How good are they? Is this the best firm for your organization? Can you afford their fees? In considering hiring a talent acquisition, search, or recruitment firm (all three terms are used in the industry along with the generic term, *head hunters*), there are a number of things to discuss with a firm before you sign on.

Here's a checklist of starter questions that are important to ask.

RECRUITMENT FIRM CHECKLIST QUESTIONS

✓ Cost: Most recruiters will charge a percentage of the annual salary. Ask what they charge exactly and by what method.

✓ Timing: What is the firm's turnaround time to present at least three or four high-potential candidates? It is a good indicator if the firm can provide you with at least a few viable candidates within two weeks. The national average of a completed search is 90–120 days, so the faster a firm can respond, the better.[1]

✓ Quality: What is the firm's specialty and the ratio of candidate slates offered versus candidates who are acceptable to the client? You'll want to see that at least 75 percent of the candidates presented are acceptable to the firm's clients and invited to interview.

✓ Offer acceptance: Just as when you do your own posting and search, the rate of acceptance of an offer should be around 95 percent in most jobs and about 80 percent in IT jobs if the search was done well. This kind of success rate will indicate the firm has presented the right people for the job.

✓ Sustainability: What is the average stay-on-the-job time for the candidates who have been hired from this firm's slate of candidates?

✓ Pool potential: How difficult (or not) do they say it will be to find high-potential candidates in today's market for this job? What is their vetting process?

✓ Inclusion: What do they do to attract a diverse pool of candidates?

✓ Relationship: Who works with the client on the search, and how much time do they typically spend getting to know your culture and the hiring leader?

✓ Guarantees: What *exactly* do they promise in return for your check—particularly in the event the hire does not prove successful?

For additional resources in helping you select recruiting firms, check the Resources section for this chapter at the end of the book.

There are two predominant types of outsourced (vs. in-house) recruiters, and there are differences in their fee structures.

Retained: In this case, and the most predominant method, you pay the recruiter a fee based on a percentage of the salary for the position you want to fill. Of course they have to successfully fill the job to get paid! The range today is from 20 to 35 percent. It is generally at the higher end with harder to fill position titles, and the fee fluctuates based on what's happening in the real-time marketplace. The fee may also be applied to any bonuses or commissions you pay the candidate in that first year, so it is important to have all the details and obligations clearly defined and agreed upon before contracting with a firm. The firm may agree to only charge you once you've hired a candidate, or you may be asked to pay a percentage at the beginning, another portion during the process, and the rest at a successful conclusion.

Contract: This refers both to the way some recruiters are paid, and it can also relate to the type of job you need filled. For instance, a contract recruiter is paid by the hour and the range can be from $15 to $250 or more an hour depending both on the recruiter and the job they are trying to fill for you. This arrangement can be easily abused without written iron-clad expectations and controls over how they use their time and your money. It is also important to know your guarantees, including one that you pay nothing if they are not successful!

When it refers to the type of person you're hiring as an "independent contractor" versus a regular employee, it means the recruiter charges you a percentage of the contractor's hourly rate for the entire time the person is employed with you. Whatever your arrangement with a recruiter or recruiting firm, always ask for your guarantees in writing before you agree to or sign anything. You can ask for and often get contingencies such as a new search at no cost to you if the hired person leaves or is fired within the first thirty days, or if it's in the first quarter, the firm may be willing to do another search for a discounted price. Good firms want repeat business and will work with you to ensure success.

You can always negotiate rates, particularly if you have gained frequent-client status. Take note that recruiters do not have to take you on as a client, and they won't if you have a history of people they've placed leaving your organization in less than a year. That's a big red flag to a recruiter. It could indicate that something particularly dysfunctional is happening in your workplace, and they won't want to place others in the future without changes and improvements.

The key advantage of using a recruiting firm is the ability to reduce or completely eliminate your need to internally manage the candidate *screening* process. If you are partnering with a firm where the screening includes things that matter to you like testing or specific written materials, and you have confidence that the firm is carrying out that process responsibly, it is a very tempting option. You will need to make your own cost-benefit analysis. Dollar for dollar, it may be worth it so that you can invest your valuable time and resources on the internal stage of the process with just a few top-notch candidates.

Here is a summary of a search study that might interest you as you make your decisions about how to find your ideal candidates. I am not recommending any one or combination of strategies. I am suggesting that you learn from the wisdom of paid recruiters and explore their methods, particularly if you are going to rely on internal resources to find the best of the best for your open positions.

A 2016 SilkRoad study of thirteen million applicants and three hundred thousand hires at twelve hundred companies revealed that the post-and-pray strategy still is the most popular way of hiring candidates. That is, 42 percent of hires came from posting roles on job boards and company websites. Recruiter-sourced candidates represented only 10 percent of hires.

While job postings have some benefits, hoping that star performers will fall into your lap is not advisable. Successful recruiters help organizations by building a repeatable and a scalable formula for finding and engaging star performers. For some roles, e-mails to candidates that do not include a job description are 27 percent more efficient than those that do. This could be because candidates have more trust in e-mails without a link or attachment, or it could be that e-mails with job descriptions are longer. Personalized e-mails are about 75 percent more effective than generic ones. LinkedIn messages are about six times (!) more effective than e-mails for parts of the candidate pool.[2]

We've explored the post-and-pray option and the professional recruiter option. There is a *combo approach*. Today, many organizations do both posting and recruiting in one form or another. Depending on your internal staff resources and skill sets, the job at hand, the difficulty in attracting preferred candidates, unique state mandates, and your financial resources, different combinations of recruitment options should be considered.

A combo approach opens up the position to the local and regional pool and simultaneously posts in national publications that serve the appropriate industry. Professional networks, your Search Team's networks, alumni networks, word of mouth, referral bonuses, user-friendly organizational job posting websites, and using social media effectively can all enhance an internal search process beyond simply posting a position. Internal recruiting and networking with people to encourage them to apply can make very good sense. At the same time, contracting with a search firm will broaden your pool and could speed up the process. It doesn't have to be a choice of either/or; it can be both/and. Whatever your search strategy is, it has to work for you and the position you need to fill. The key is to thoughtfully develop your search strategy each and every time.

In my final position at Cornell University, I was promoted to the role of Director for Administration, Facilities and Finance as a result of a combo search effort. The job was posted internally, regionally, and nationally in print media and higher-education professional publications. There was no search firm. This was a high-profile position with dual responsibility for operating budgets of $250 million and overseeing the HR activities for roughly two thousand employees (professional, administrative, and bargaining unit). The man who would become my boss asked me to lunch to discuss the job and encouraged me to apply. The incumbent called me as well and urged me to consider his job. I felt honored and courted; the encouragement had everything to do with my decision to throw my hat in the ring. This is a good example of combining recruiting with posting for a job. The process was extremely rigorous, and the competition was fierce. When I was offered the position, I was certain it was a great match for me and for them, and it was.

My system may seem like a lot of work to you right now, and you would be right; the setup and decision making at the front end of the search process requires your time and due diligence. The good news is that once you have a consistent, well-considered system in place, the next search will take less time to set up correctly, and the next time, less again. The even better news is that proper preparation will likely shorten the total timeline of your searches. You'll also have established a precedent and a process, one that can lend itself well to delegation of many of the pieces and parts. The first time, though, the hiring leader needs to be fully immersed in getting it right, just like you would for any important new project.

In chapter 3, "Getting to Know You," things get more exciting! You have your pool of viable candidates in front of you, and it's time to introduce them to your organization and the position you are offering.

Let's open the door!

Chapter 3

Getting to Know You

Figure 3.1.   Hiring Right Search Map: Getting to Know You

We don't see things as they are; we see them as we are.

—Anaïs Nin

THE SEARCH TEAM

We have arrived at step 3 of our Hiring Right Search Map (see figure 3.1), and it's time to take a deep dive into our pool of candidates. In this Anaïs Nin quote, there is a caution for us in hiring. If you replace her word *things* with the word *people*, you'll understand what I mean. There is a real danger in seeing what you want to see and ignoring patterns, oddities, and biases. I alert you to this because too often bad hires are a result of hiring leaders and their Search Teams making mistaken assumptions without due diligence. A well-selected Search Team that is committed to the process and represents your organization well will go a long way to prevent poor results.

In chapter 2, we created your Pre-search Checklist. On that list was the task of creating your Search Team. I promised to tell you more, so here we go!

No matter what type of position or what method you choose for seeking out candidates (posting, recruiting, or combo), you will need to create a Search Team. I offer suggestions of Search Team members for each of the five general levels of positions. It is imperative that more eyes and ears beyond the hiring supervisor are involved in the vetting process regardless of the position. The old saying "Haste makes waste" was never truer than in hiring right! Be as serious in choosing your Search Team as you are in choosing your candidates. You can, and should, establish your Search Team before—or at least during—the time you are waiting to receive potential candidates' materials.

The Search Team members list gets longer and more complex as the jobs get more complex and expensive.

Keep these two points in mind all the way through:

1. One person can fill more than one role when they serve in a dual capacity—like a peer who is also an internal customer.
2. Search Teams should not be too big or too small. Too big and they are unwieldy and less effective with too many people to inform and

keep track of. Too small and group-think can set in with a higher risk of hearing fewer perspectives and/or choosing "someone just like us" or other biases that can seep into a small closed group.

Both of these extremes are a danger to due diligence and a great hire. The players and minimum and maximum numbers are, of course, guidelines. You're the best judge of your positions and must decide based on the situation at hand.

Sample Makeup of Search Teams

Nonexempt:* building and maintenance trades, bank tellers, waitstaff, administrative support, customer service reps, teaching assistants, reception, sales clerks, certified nursing assistant, etc.

- Hiring supervisor
- Immediate work team member(s)
- One or two key customers (internal and/or external)
- Minimum three; maximum five

Exempt Entry Level: project coordinator, first-level IT engineer, first-year teacher, account manager, site manager, sous chef, recruiter, etc.

- Hiring supervisor's supervisor (optional)
- Hiring supervisor
- Immediate work team member(s)
- One or two peers not in immediate work team
- One or two key customers (internal and/or external)
- Minimum four; maximum six

Exempt Mid-Level and Mid-Level Technical: project manager, business analyst, tenure-track teacher, nursing supervisor, safety manager, IT operations manager, building trades supervisor, etc.

- Hiring supervisor's supervisor (optional)
- Hiring supervisor
- Immediate work team member(s)
- Two to four peers not in immediate work team
- Two to three key customers (internal and/or external)
- Minimum six; maximum ten

Exempt Senior Level and Senior Technical: regional manager, senior operations manager, head of nursing, IT director, health and safety manager, senior human resources (HR) officer, etc.

- Senior-level leadership but not necessarily C-Suite (optional)
- Hiring supervisor's supervisor
- Hiring supervisor
- Immediate work team member(s)
- Four to six peers not in immediate work team
- Three to five key customers (internal and/or external)
- Minimum ten; maximum fifteen

Exempt Top Management and Top Technical: executive director, chief operating officer, chief information officer, chief financial officer, chief HR officer, CEO, SVP, VP, etc.

- One to three board members (optional)
- C-Suite, owners, partners
- Senior-level leadership
- Hiring supervisor
- Immediate work team members
- Four to six peers not in immediate work team
- Three to five key customers (internal and/or external)
- Minimum twelve; maximum twenty

*The Federal Fair Labor Standard Act (FSLA) requires most employees, unless specifically listed as not subject to FSLA, to be classified as either nonexempt from overtime rules or exempt from overtime rules. One of the exceptions to this is an independent contractor. This is someone, or some entity, you contract with for a specific amount of time and money to do specific work for your organization. This type of hire is not an employee. For example, independent contractors might be an outside consultant presenting a program or training, a project consultant, an architect, a lawyer, or an accounting firm. In addition, some states have their own labor laws that must be followed in classifying the work people do. Fair Labor Standards Act, "FLSA Coverage," FLSA Homepage, https://www.flsa.com/coverage.html.

Each job category needs your full attention. For instance, entry-level nonexempt jobs are the most frequently experienced "face" of your organization for your customers, internal or external. These are the people who create that important first impression representing your entire enterprise. You're not going to need as extensive a search process for a cashier as you would a store manager because the job requirements are fewer. However, it is important to pay very close attention to hiring the right people in your frontline jobs. We are, as consumers of products and services, interacting with frontline folks far more often, and generally much longer, than with a leader or anyone else more senior. These folks are your organization's ambassadors to the world.

To illustrate just how big a small experience can be with your frontline staff, I'll share two case stories.

Case 1: Ellyn drove to a chain store to buy some simple white pillowcases because she had purchased them there in the past and it was close to home. After looking at every linen shelf and endcap and seeing none, she tried to find a store clerk. No luck. She waited in a checkout line to ask her question. The cashier told her to look in the linen section. Ellyn said she'd been there and couldn't see them. She asked if the cashier could call someone to help her. The cashier said, "We're probably out then," and looking past Ellyn, said, "Next in line." Ellyn left, went to her car, checked online with her phone, and ordered what she needed. It came the next day. Sound familiar?

Case 2: Sam purchased a large piece of furniture from an online seller. It arrived with one piece of glass broken. He called customer service and, in less than five minutes, the problem was solved. Apologies given, no need to send a picture of the damage, and "Please look for your full refund within twenty-four hours unless you would like us to send another one right away," the customer service representative said. "Thanks so much for the refund. I'll just keep the piece you sent, no need to replace it," said Sam. "I am sure I can get someone to fix the broken glass." They thanked each other, and Sam continued to shop from that company.

According to Jonah Berger in his book *Contagious*, "word of mouth is the primary factor behind 20% to 50% of all purchasing decisions."[1] This is true whether it's a service or a product. As for the end game— the business in case 1 went bankrupt, closing hundreds of stores and eliminating thousands of jobs. The business in case 2 is thriving, hiring more people, and moving ahead of their competitors. Word does get around. No real surprises in these outcomes, right?

Search Team Checklist

When you, the hiring supervisor and leader of your team, are selecting your Search Team members, the first step is to answer at least the following questions *before* asking anyone to join your team:

✓ How much is this person affected by who gets hired?

✓ Has this person been involved in any searches before?

✓ Does this person have a good performance and accountability history?

✓ What have you noticed about any biases this person may have about people and/or your organization? How inclusive are they?

✓ How well does this person collaborate with others right now?

✓ What skills, perspectives, knowledge, and attitude does this person bring to the team?

✓ Does this person reflect your organizational values in his/her behaviors?

✓ Does this person contribute to diversity on your team (e.g., gender, race, age, skill sets, personality, experience, perspective, and current role)?

While a Search Team member may not tick all the boxes on these questions, you should be satisfied with the answers to most of them. Select people who care about the position and are prepared to invest their time and effort to reach a successful outcome. Choose carefully; a diverse team that works well together makes better hires together.

The second step is to train the Search Team members. Yes, train them! Serving on a Search Team is rarely, if ever, someone's primary role, and people tend to forget things like what is and isn't legal to ask or say or do. It is in *your* best interest to have a well-informed and or-ganized team where each person knows the plan, the rules of the game, and their specific role in the process. Typically, different people play different roles along the way. Some may review candidate materials and select who moves forward; others may conduct phone or video interviews; and still others may participate in on-site interview roles.

Once you've gathered your team together, it's time to discuss what matters in the search at hand, even if they have served on other Search Teams in the past. It is best to assume nothing and create a shared awareness and understanding about the following:

1. The position description with a clear picture of everything you've determined the ideal candidate needs to bring to the table as a result of your Pre-search Checklist work.

2. The search plan with each step defined, including the timeline for each step.

3. Each person's strengths, interests, and role on the Search Team so everyone knows who is working with whom on what and when.

4. How and by whom the final decision will be made (the hiring supervisor, the next level up, the team, people with veto power, etc.).

5. All the rules around questions: what is legal or not legal, what is and is not appropriate, and any special training for evaluating the answers you'll be receiving in different steps of the process from the pool of candidates. (See examples in the Resources section for this chapter.)

6. How to ask open-ended powerful questions—with examples and even specific scripts. How to listen deeply, how to reflect back what they hear and see, and how to use interview time to the best advantage. (See examples in the Resources section for this chapter.)

7. How to recognize bias in themselves and in the candidates. (See examples of bias in the Resources section for this chapter.) Your first look at submitted resumes should be "blind" to help prevent unconscious or even conscious bias from causing problems early on. That means names, pictures, any identifying gender, race, age, and ethnicity information are redacted by someone who is not on your Search Team.

To illustrate how training the Search Team members works, we will walk through a relatively straightforward example for an Administrative Assistant to a Vice President for Human Resources position and answer the seven questions.

Administrative Assistant to the Vice President of Human Resources

Question 1

Must-haves: three to five years' prior experience in a complex or senior level office; excellent oral and written communication skills; positive attitude and proven history of diplomacy; proven history of keeping sensitive information confidential; excellent working knowledge of computer programs XYZ; high school graduate; ability to type at least sixty words a minute.

Preferred: has worked in HR operations in the past and/or in a confidential setting; more than high school education; has led some projects; known to be calm under pressure.

Question 2

Posted on January 15 by HR; resumes received and vetted (see question 3); top four or five selected for next step by February 5; written questions and answers due from vetted candidates by February 15; phone interviews of top two or three by February 20 (see question 3); finalist on-site interviews completed by February 28 (see question 3).

Question 3

Team members are VP Sallie; coworkers Tom, Natasha, José, Dorothy, Rashaad, and Mae; and divisional customers Doug and Mary. Sallie will weigh in after written questions are received and vetted and be involved in finalist interviews and weigh in on any "maybe candidates." Tom and Mae have skills in resume vetting and will screen all candidates; everyone on the team will have access to all the resumes and the cover sheet reviews by Tom and Mae stating the reason a resume was screened in or out. Natasha and Rashaad have interviewing skills and will sit in together on the phone calls with one of them asking questions and the other with follow-up if needed. They will create the questions to ask all candidates and review with the team, then conduct the phone/video interviews and provide a cover sheet of their rating of the answers as well as any additions or new information the candidate provided. José, Dorothy, Mary, and Doug will create the questions and format for the on-site interviews, organize people and logistics, and keep the team well informed. Everyone will be involved in the on-site interviews in one way or another.

Question 4

Sallie has the final hiring decision, but she will not hire anyone the team does not recommend. Any team member can question if a candidate should have been screened in or out at each step of the process, and the team will confer with Sallie if needed.

Question 5

Team members will read and ask questions about the illegal questions sheet (see example in the Resources section for this chapter) as well as questions that are deemed inappropriate for this position. For instance, the team members will not ask the candidates what they've heard about the VP, her office, or what they didn't like about past bosses. While these are not illegal questions, they are not appropriate in a professional search. The candidate may offer this information, but do not ask for it.

Question 6

Create questions for the candidates that are open-ended with sentences beginning with words like *what*, *how*, and *when* instead of close-ended "yes" or "no" questions. Put your proposed interview questions to this test. If possible, mock up a practice training session with the team to demonstrate allowing for silence and letting the candidate fill in the silences.

Question 7

Have an open discussion about the team's biases to watch out for, such as wanting to hire someone who is just like themselves; preferring one gender over another, one race over another, one personality type over another, or one age over another; and having a certain level of familiarity with the candidate (i.e., nepotism). Examine the interview questions through a lens that demonstrates bias: stereotyping, labeling, and prejudging. Discuss how to identify undesirable biases in the candidates' answers.

* * *

As you are sifting through candidate files, keep in mind that there is a living, breathing human being connected to that file, a person who was interested enough in working with your organization to put their name forward. This is the beginning of the relationship phase of the hiring process.

Assuming your due diligence in seeking great candidates for your open position is completed, you now have a number of names, resumes, and cover letters on your desk. I often think of this process to be like a blind date because, especially today, with online virtual meeting space and a growing number of employer/employee matchmaking companies, it really seems much like a professional blind date. We're all trying to find the right match! In whatever ways your applicants were reviewed and winnowed, the next step is to vet this initial group before any other steps.

This is the moment in the book where I have to burst any balloons you may have about candidates and their resumes. According to an article by Monster.com, almost half of workers (46 percent) polled by one staffing firm said they know someone who included false information on a resume.[2] Other surveys have reported even higher percentages. The survey research tells us that the three most common lies people put on their resumes are the following:

- Education embellishments
- Date deception
- Skill stretching

Here are three commonsense ways to lower your risk:

1. **Skills assessments.** Test for the skills required before hire. The appropriate assessment can measure specific abilities, for example, typing speed for an administrative assistant.
2. **Social media research.** It is common practice today to check for inconsistencies and outright lies on social media sites like Facebook and LinkedIn and professional networking sites that are relevant. If you have kept past applications and resumes on file, check to see if this person has applied before and if the facts have changed in material ways. If any version of a candidate's resume or work history is online, compare it to what you receive.
3. **Reference checks.** Before you hire, it is essential to contact a candidate's references and as many former employers as reasonable. Check educational institutions to verify the accuracy of the resume. You will need the candidate's permission to contact a current employer prior to making an offer. Making an offer *contingent* on your reference checks is a wise thing to do. To take a deeper dive, ask for additional references beyond the initial candidate-friendly ones. While you may get only date of hire, job title, and date of departure from some references, you often can get more if you ask the right questions. For instance: "Would you hire Joe again and if so why?" If they loved that employee, they'll usually say, "Absolutely!" Even if they say nothing, listen to their phone or body language. Hesitation

and silence is at least a yellow if not a *red* flag. It is one more nugget of data to help you vet candidates.

4. **Background checks.** Employers can also outsource background checks to specialty firms who do this routinely, and some choose to run a credit check and/or legal checks. In most cases, you must ask a candidate's permission to request a credit report. If the position does *not* involve financial risk, ask yourself if there is a real justification for this; many people have been damaged through no fault of their own with credit reports due to hacking and identity theft. In addition, class, social status, and other biases are concerns to be considered prior to asking a candidate's permission to run a credit check.

Post-hire reference checks are too little too late as you can imagine. On the other side of the coin, if you are the reference, please don't lie when someone asks you about a candidate. Giving a false positive reference is downright wrong. Neither you nor anyone else deserves to be on the receiving end of a lie. People have been known to do it to get rid of a problem employee. If you haven't experienced this yet, you will eventually. When they don't know how or don't want to deal with a firing, some people will just pass the problem along to you and breathe a sigh of relief. The old saying, "If you can't say anything good, say nothing at all," holds true. Hopefully, you're able to be 100 percent honest about the strengths and weaknesses of the person in question, but if you can only give the bare minimum of facts due to internal policy or for legal reasons, do your best as a reference giver to find a way to give subtle hints in hopes the reference checker is discerning enough to notice.

The quality and commitment of your Search Team is a cornerstone to making a great hire. When you choose members carefully, prepare the team well, and create a well-considered plan together, including all the steps for due diligence, the process should be both enjoyable and effective.

FIRST IMPRESSIONS

From the moment you announce to the world you have a position open, you are making some kind of an impression—good, bad, or neutral.

It's a bit like that blind date. You want the position to sound attractive without overdoing it; what you print needs to be welcoming and sound professional.

Have you ever read a job ad in a print publication or online that excited you? How about one that put you off, maybe even offended you? What was it about either of those situations that caused your reaction? For me, the ad's a killer when it says little of value and is boring. On the other end of the spectrum is an ad with a long list of expectations that are, shall we say, ridiculous for anyone to take seriously.

Writing job postings, whether crafted internally or with the assistance of a paid recruiter, needs to be done with intention. You want to attract the best candidates, *and* you are putting your workplace, and you as an employer, in a public-facing forum every single time. You need your opening to sound attractive, no matter what the job is. If you want to stand out, begin at the beginning. Here are some points to consider:

- Are the essential must-haves for education, experience, attitude, and such clear?
- Is what you need for the position to accomplish crystal clear?
- Is it too short, too long, or just right? (See examples 4a, 4b, 5a, and 5b.)
- Is it too open-ended, too rigid, or just right? (See examples 4a, 4b, 5a, and 5b.)
- Does it pass the "would I find it readable and interesting" test?
- Is it welcoming to all, or does it feel exclusive to a category of people (i.e., gender, race, location, ethnicity, only able bodied, etc.)?
- Does it talk about your mission, vision, and organizational values?
- Does it abide by your internal policies as well as state and federal laws? If you don't know, ask your HR professionals or legal counsel.

To illustrate, with some exaggeration, the importance of tone and approach in your job postings, I offer two different job types, each with two sample ad options for the same employer. The first one is for a Director of Technology Operations position at a health care service company; the second is for three entry-level job offerings at a fast food franchise.

Example 4a

Ad Option #1: Happy Health Care Company

Position: Director, Technology Operations:
Corporate Information Systems Department

MAJOR DUTIES AND RESPONSIBILITIES

- Technical operations: 40 percent
- Networking and telco infrastructure: 20 percent
- Software maintenance: 20 percent
- Helpdesk and PC support: 20 percent

REQUIREMENTS

- Bachelor's degree in IT management, business administration, or equivalent required
- Five to ten years' experience in managing computer systems and teams
- Apply online at www.happyhealthcarecompany.com or e-mail Careers@HappyHealthCareCompany.com. Cutoff date for application is DATE.
- We are an Equal Opportunity Employer.

Example 4b

Ad Option #2: Happy Health Care Company

Director of Technology Operations:
Corporate Information Systems Department

POSITION SUMMARY

We are a values-based, mission-critical provider of web-based systems for long-term health care facilities serving more than three million patients. The person in this position will lead our computer operations group and team of technical experts to outcomes of 99.9 percent reliability. Experience in running a data/service center that operates 24/7 is critical. Salary for this position is highly competitive and commensurate with education and experience. Benefits include superb health care, matching 401K up to 8 percent, workout center, on-site cafeteria, free parking, and amazing people to work with!

MAJOR DUTIES AND RESPONSIBILITIES

- Technical operations: 40 percent
- Networking and telco infrastructure: 20 percent
- Software maintenance: 20 percent
- Helpdesk and PC support: 20 percent

REQUIREMENTS

Job Specific: Proven leadership skills; deep knowledge of business computer systems; customer-service focused; excellent project management skills.

Organizational Characteristics: Strong work ethic; high initiative; flexible; able to manage multiple priorities and able to work well with different generations of staff and customers; values integrity, teamwork, and excellence.

Minimum Qualifications: Bachelor's degree in IT management, business administration, or equivalent; five to ten years' experience in managing computer systems and teams with a customer focus.

To apply for this or another position with our company, please visit our website at www.HappyHealthCareCompany.com. You can e-mail application questions to: Careers@HappyHealthCareCompany.com (FAX 555-XXXX) or mail your credentials to (Career Center at ADDRESS).

We are an Equal Opportunity Employer.

Example 5a

Ad Option #1: Fast Food Franchise Posting

Our FFF Kitchen Cooking Team needs you! We have three full-time positions open:

- Assistant to Chef: works with Head Chef to cook meals ordered by customers
- Preparation Wizard: works with Head Chef to prepare all necessary ingredients
- Road Runner: ensures all meals are delivered on time and at proper temperatures

Each position starts at $15 per hour for the first thirty days and can move up to $20 per hour after six months of great performance.

We are a family-owned, community business. Our mission is to feed our neighbors good food every single time and encourage our team members to excel and grow. We believe in paying a living wage to all staff. We are looking for team members who enjoy eating and making good food, will work hard, and can grow with us. Ask us about eligibility for free meals, health insurance, GED assistance, college scholarships, disability and life insurance, flexible schedules, and training for leadership positions. Please contact XYZ at XYZ@gmail.com or by calling 555-XXXX by DATE to make an appointment or come into FFF at ADDRESS to apply in person.

FFF is an Equal Opportunity Employer and believes everyone who wants to work deserves a job. We welcome anyone with a question about any ability to talk to us about accommodations we may be able to make. We look forward to meeting you!

Example 5b

Ad Option #2: Fast Food Franchise Posting

FFF Current Job Openings

- Full-time Assistant Cook: reports to Head Cook
- Full-time Prep Worker: reports to Head Cook
- Full-time Runner: reports to Manager of Front of House

$15 hour with opportunity for an increase if performance is judged to be excellent after six months. May be eligible for free meals, health insurance, GED assistance, college scholarships, disability and life insurance, flexible schedules, and training for leadership positions. Contact XYZ at XYZ@gmail.com by DATE to fill out an application or come in and ask for an application at ADDRESS. FFF is an Equal Opportunity Employer.

What does each ad communicate about each employer? Which of these ads for the exact same jobs for the exact same employer is going to attract the most and best applicants? Obvious, isn't it? It only takes a few minutes to be mindful about what you put out there. That investment is likely to save a lot of wasted hours down the line. Yes, the best ads are a bit longer and cost more. It's worth it to make sure your ads are clear and enticing and keep people reading. It's not worth it to write paragraphs of history, mission, vision, or every little thing that could be in the job.

ADVERTISING CHECKLIST

✓ Explain the job well enough so those reading the ad can decide whether they are interested and qualified. Regardless of the job or ad or where it is placed, this is essential. Know your audience.

✓ List the job title along with a brief description and a few examples of duties.

✓ List the minimum education, experience, and skill levels that are required and/or acceptable, if applicable. Point out any special criteria such as extensive travel or relocation that will weed out applicants who aren't interested in those requirements.

✓ Don't use jargon or abbreviations and acronyms that make it difficult to understand. Do use proper grammar and spelling.

✓ Be specific about any specialized skills or equipment that applicants should know how to use or operate.

✓ Always check with your HR professional or legal counsel if you have questions about the legality of your ad. Federal laws generally apply to employers with fifteen or more employees and prohibit discrimination against any protected class of individuals. These laws dictate what you can and cannot say in a job advertisement. Check your state's laws for additional requirements that may apply to the same or smaller employers. Generally, federal law prohibits you from making statements or implications about not wanting people from federally protected groups (i.e., members of a certain race, color, ethnicity, national origin, religion, gender, age [over forty], disability, or veteran status).

Pitfall: Know your audience. Ad language written for the wrong audience will attract the wrong people or no people.

Solution: Test the language on people currently in the job or a similar one to gauge whether it hits the right buttons and is written in a way that someone in that job both understands and believes those who apply will understand.

While the law does not keep you from using gender-referent words and titles, the federal Equal Employment Opportunity Commission (EEOC) will not permit the use of the phrase "Equal Opportunity Employer" if you do. You must, in that case, choose one or the other. You also have to be particularly careful not to use language that will discriminate against potential applicants for your job because of their age. The EEOC gives policy guidance on how job advertisements may violate the Age Discrimination in Employment Act (ADEA). It's safer and smarter to avoid any reference to any definition of any protected class. For specific dos and don'ts, check your state's and the federal employment websites.

You've announced your job to the world and have begun receiving cover letters, resumes, applications, or CVs (curriculum vitae). As a point of reference, resumes are generally one to two pages long, but a CV can be any length. A resume (from French, *to sum up*) is a short, concise summary, used in both the United States and Canada, that provides a brief overview of a candidate's work history, education, specific courses, awards, certifications, and licenses relevant to the job at hand. A CV (from Latin, *course of life*) might be two pages or ten pages plus as it contains many more details about education, professional career, publications, awards, honors, and other achievements. In the United States and Canada, a CV is used primarily for academic positions.

This is your second opportunity to make an impression. Best practice is to get a short note out to all your candidates *acknowledging receipt* of their materials. When your Search Team is certain that a candidate *is not moving forward* in your process, let them know immediately. You don't need to wait to see others' materials if you know that a candidate is not appropriate for this position.

If you are not yet certain who is moving forward, send a different note acknowledging receipt of their materials. These can be plug-and-play templates until you've moved to the next phase, so all you have to do is fill in the name and job. It makes a world of difference to people to be informed about their status, in or out. When and how you do it will convey a lot about you and your organization.

My team had nicknames for each kind of letter we sent at the beginning of the process. Here are four samples you can copy or customize as appropriate.

The First-Round "Ding" Letter

Dear Name,

Thank you for your interest in our Administrative Assistant to the Vice President for Human Resources position. In reviewing all candidates, we have identified those who will be moving forward in our search process. While your application is not moving forward at this time, we would like to keep your resume on file should anything change or in the event another position comes open that would more closely match your experience.

I wish you the very best.

Sincerely,
Team Leader Name and Title

The "Hang in There" Letter

Dear Name,

Thank you for your interest in our Administrative Assistant to the Vice President for Human Resources position. We are reviewing all candidates now and will complete that process by DATE. As soon as we have determined who will be moving forward in our process, we will contact you.

Again, we appreciate your interest and look forward to being in touch again soon.

Sincerely,
Team Leader Name and Title

The Second-Round "Ding" Letter

Dear Name,

Thank you again for your interest in our Administrative Assistant to the Vice President for Human Resources position. In reviewing all candidates, we have identified the few who will be moving forward in our search process. While your application is not moving forward at this time, we would like to keep your resume on file should anything change with our current pool of candidates.

I wish you the very best.

Sincerely,
Team Leader Name and Title

The "Yes" Letter

Dear Name,

We are delighted to invite you to participate in the next phase of our search for our Administrative Assistant to the Vice President for Human Resources position. Your materials are impressive, and we'd like to get to know you a bit better before we begin to schedule interviews.

As you know, this position requires interactions with the public within a confidential office, and a wide-range of situations arise. Please answer the attached # questions within a three-page typewritten document by 5 p.m. on DATE. E-mail your answers to XYZ@gmail.com at any time prior to that time.

If you have any questions about our process or our request, don't hesitate to contact XYZ@gmail.com or call 555-XXXX. We are looking forward to hearing from you soon.

Sincerely,
Team Leader Name and Title

Pitfall: "I don't have time to send out letters to everyone. Can't I just write to the people who are moving forward in the search process and keep the ball rolling?"

Solution: No! You must find the time to notify every applicant of their status in your search. It's easy enough to delegate this task to someone you trust such as an administrative support person or a Search Team member. The timeline for these letters should be part of the search plan, and this task *must* be part of your search plan or you risk getting a reputation as an unresponsive and disrespectful employer.

Our "blind date" is about to get interesting! You've introduced yourself in at least three ways: you posted your position, sent a letter upon receipt of all the candidates' materials, and sent a "ding" letter or, for those moving forward, informed each selected candidate of their status. If you have a recruiter involved and/or you've done your own recruitment, you now have additional opportunities to make an impression. What matters is that you take each opportunity seriously because, when you do, the best candidates will notice and your chances of keeping each person engaged greatly increases. Now it's time to get to know your candidates at a deeper level.

BEYOND THE RESUME

Getting to know your top candidates beyond the constraints, truths, and (possibly) fiction of their resume will go a long way in finding the person you need. This is a step I always consider and frequently use in my system of hiring because it saves wasting time and resources on people who can't or won't communicate well in writing. Of course there are jobs that require little reading and writing—like the data entry clerk who sits alone in a cubby all day, or perhaps the night custodian who sees no one unless there is an emergency, or a line cook in a restaurant. Even so, custodians need to read product labels and names on doors, data entry clerks need to read instructions, and cooks need to read recipes.

I have also made reasonable accommodations for people with severe literacy challenges where appropriate and necessary. Depending on the job at hand, your screening may require a set of metrics that are specific to those positions, like timeliness, accuracy, or safety history. The important thing to keep in mind is to apply whatever metrics make sense before you hire.

Most positions need an individual who can communicate adequately, both verbally and in writing. You are the best judge of the degree of communication proficiency you need for each of your positions. An application, resume, or CV will not give you the answer to this question. People can and do hire professionals to write polished materials; even applications that are filled out online can only tell you about the person filling it out, not necessarily the applicant.

Do not assume anything about the first materials you receive. They could be true or not and written by your candidate or not. If this matters to you, create an appropriate screening for the necessary communication skills *before* you start to interview candidates. Because needs vary by job, evaluate the candidates' skills in concert with the kinds of communications they must read, write, and understand in their new job. If the person in the position only needs to verbally communicate well, you may decide to skip the written portion and plan to address those skills in your face-to-face interviews.

Craft your Beyond the Resume questions to get the most information you can about the candidates who have made it this far. I tend to err on the side of collecting as much and as varied information about a candidate as I can; it saves my team a lot of time and effort and helps us winnow our candidates more effectively. In fact, for mid-level and higher positions in the organization, this requirement will weed out the people who are unable or unwilling to answer written questions.

You may experience some people who will not submit answers for a myriad of reasons. I've heard these and more: "Could you extend the deadline? I'm really tied up right now." "I need more than three pages to answer your questions." "I don't see what this has to do with the job I applied for." "No thanks!" Even the no-shows tell a story.

There are questions that arise for me immediately: Is this someone who cannot or will not step out of their comfort zone? Is this someone who cannot or will not write, or perhaps someone who cannot or will not follow directions? Do I want that kind of person on my team? There can, of course, be extenuating and important life circumstances that should be taken into account when you want to keep a particular candidate in your pool. In that case, adjust as you see fit but not to an unfair disadvantage to the other candidates. For instance, I've extended the deadline in special circumstances that were both reasonable and well explained by the candidate.

I value this step for the rapid weeding out of folks who are not really serious but landed on your desk anyway. If seriousness matters to you, this is a highly effective approach. The following sample questions apply to our fictional Administrative Assistant to the Vice President of Human Resources. I recommend *at least three and no more than six* questions.

Please complete these questions within three typewritten pages by 5 p.m. on DATE and e-mail your answers to NAME at E-MAIL. Thank you!

1. In your career, when have you been *most* energized and engaged? Please be specific.
2. In your career, when have you been *least* energized and engaged? Please be specific.
3. Describe a conflict in which you were involved. What was it, and how did you respond to it? (No names, please.)
4. Have you ever felt uncomfortable with a request from a peer, supervisor, or another person at work that you deemed illegal or unethical? If yes, please describe how you handled it. If no, describe how you would choose to handle such a situation.
5. Describe how you would handle someone crying at your desk.
6. What do you think would be helpful for us to know about you that *is not* related to work?

Pitfall: I don't know how many or which questions to ask for different jobs.

Solution: This is determined by how complex and high risk the position is. Three questions may be appropriate for positions that are straightforward and are low risk. Up to six questions make sense for mid-level and higher positions with higher complexity and risk. What do you need to know about, for example, the character, approach, service orientation, or experience of the candidates that you cannot see in the resumes?

Your team's evaluation sheet needs to list the highlights they are looking for overall and in each question you are asking. Those sheets will track what the team's readers noticed in each candidate's answers. In our Administrative Assistant case, let's say we are looking for the following:

- Is the candidate able to follow directions and write coherent sentences with correct grammar and spelling?
- What energizes and bores each of the candidates? Are there any red or green flags?
- How direct is each candidate with answers about conflicts, ethics, and emotions?
- What does each candidate choose to reveal, and what might that indicate?

- What does each answer tell us, and/or what questions do the candidates' answers raise that we would like to know more about?

It is often powerful information and provides fodder for the live interview. For instance, if the candidate didn't share a lot in the written responses, you might later ask, "Tell us more about how you felt and what you did about your feelings when you were in the conflict you wrote to us about." Each answer tells you something different and something more. It all helps you get to know the human being who may become part of your team.

LET'S CHAT

Now that we know which of your candidates can write and answer questions that matter, and assuming you like the way a few of them answered the questions, it's time to get to know each of these stand-out candidates more fully. Regardless of the decision to chat via a video or telephone conference call, you have an opportunity to hear and feel the live human being beyond a flat piece of paper or e-mail.

In the case of employee candidates who are physically on-site, this conversation could be in person at your site, over lunch, at the candidate's workplace (if agreed to by the candidate), or a neutral location.

For some positions, you might decide to skip this step and move on to chapter 4, "Up Close and Personal," for the on-site formal interview. For key positions and certainly for senior positions, I highly recommend keeping this short interview step in place. It will, more often than not, save you the cost and time of bringing the wrong candidates onsite. While nothing is failsafe, this quick chat is a powerful tool in your toolbox to help you make better decisions. It's your first real "date" with your candidates.

Video calls are more revealing than the phone because you can see and sense more about the person on the other end of the call. You'll be able to better observe body language, tone, and energy. This is useful to gauge how aligned the real person is with the materials they sent.

I mention energy because each of us is sending and receiving energy 24/7. The energy you sense from the candidate in front of you matters on both a conscious and an unconscious level. Pay attention to your own body's reaction to the person—are *you* feeling tense, relaxed, excited, nervous, curious, drawn in or pushed away, annoyed, or happy? If you notice how this person impacts you, ask yourself "why?" and check yourself for both emotions and biases. In any case, noticing gives you more data so don't ignore what you are feeling.

Neuroscience has proven that our bodies know and respond more quickly and *before* our head can sift and edit, and then tells itself a story the head chooses to believe. Trust that all of us pick up signals faster than tuning into a radio station frequency. It's instant. And as we fiddle with that dial, things become more clear when we are paying close attention to the person in front of us and to our own emotional and cognitive responses.

There is a caution about the first live connection you are about to have. Be alert to interviewer biases on these calls. When your interviewers stay focused on what the candidate says and does, and pay little or no attention to social, cultural, generational, and stereotypes, you lower the risks of creating a "halo effect" or a "reverse halo effect" around the candidate.

For example, if you have a dress code for your workplace, and the candidate happens to dress that way for the interview, there is a risk of making erroneous assumptions such as thinking the candidate will fit in to your culture nicely—the halo effect; the reverse is also true. You would be creating a reverse halo effect by judging them negatively if they dress differently than you. Candidates may have no idea about your dress code; they may have religious, generational, or cultural preferences that can be respected and accommodated; or they may just be interviewing from a home office. You can't know what dressing for a virtual meeting means to their suitability for the job. And, this is just a small example of how biases can contaminate the selection process. Hiring the wrong person or losing the right person because biases were in play is not in your best interests. Keep focused on the whole person in front of you versus some piece or part of the whole. The point is to get as much information as you can on that "first date."

The candidate has an opportunity to demonstrate how they interact with other people in this conversation. It won't tell you everything, but if you're tuned in, really listening with your whole body, and are keenly present in the moment, you'll learn a great deal. Just remember not to make assumptions without justification—otherwise it's probably a bias getting in the way of objectivity.

This step in the vetting process should be no more than an hour. It takes very little time and money, and it can produce powerful results that benefit all parties. I recommend you assign two Search Team members to conduct these interviews. The appropriate key questions will already have had a Search Team review and will be asked of all candidates. Deeper-dive resume questions will vary among candidates but should be known ahead of time. This is not an ad hoc chat; the questions need to be crafted to discern which of your candidates should move on to the next step. (See this chapter's Resources section for sample first-interview questions.)

Having two people share this role is helpful because one person can ask questions while the other person observes and takes notes. The second person can also ask follow-up questions of the candidate that might have been missed by the main interviewer. This also allows the main questioner to take a break if needed. Finally, the two can compare impressions and notes after the conversation has ended. Even if they feel very differently about a candidate, it is revealing and should be part of their team report.

In this session, and in all live interviews, make sure to leave time for the candidates to ask any questions they may have of Search Team members in the room. Interviews are a two-way exchange and should be a dialogue between the candidate and the Search Team members. It should *never* be, or even perceived to be, an interrogation of the candidate. It is quite illuminating to sit back and see what happens when you ask, "What questions do you have for us about this position, our organization, or anything else?" This form of live chat is the final vetting before bringing candidates to your site, unless you have the candidate's permission to get a head start on your reference-checking process.

Employers who are conducting national searches may choose a location central to the first-round candidates to bring them all in for interviews, one at a time, with two or more members of the Search Team. Generally, these last longer than an hour, but these sessions rarely replace on-site interviews.

Another option for this live chat is three dimensional, in that your selected Search Team member(s) go to the candidates rather than, or in addition to, calling or video conferencing with them. This is a strategic decision that weighs costs versus potential value. Visits to candidates for high-ticket positions can make good financial sense if you want to see the candidates in action on their home turf, in a restaurant they choose, or in their car, for example.

I have conducted this type of vetting several times and found it to be immensely informative. In one case, the assumed informality of the situation led the candidate to tell me far more than he normally would have and resulted in a friendly goodbye with no further interviews. In another case, the phone interview didn't go particularly well, but we had so few qualified candidates we risked the cost of an in-person visit. While he didn't shine on that one phone call, in person he was superb! We invited him in for two days of on-site interviews where he outshone his competition by a good margin. After deep reference checking, he was hired and proved our investment worthwhile.

Now that we've initially met our candidates in one way or another on our first "date," we are going to get even more up close and personal in chapter 4.

Let's start shaking the branches!

Chapter Four

Up Close and Personal

HIRING RIGHT SEARCH MAP

1. CALL TO ACTION

2. DIGGING FOR GOLD

3. GETTING TO KNOW YOU

4. UP CLOSE & PERSONAL
- The On-Site Visit
- The A-H Factors
- Interviews
- The Scenario Interview

5. THE INVITATION

Figure 4.1. Hiring Right Search Map: Up Close and Personal

Plan your work and work your plan.

—Napoleon Hill

When someone shows you who they are, believe them the first time.

—Maya Angelou

We've been on our hiring journey for three chapters now (see the Hiring Right Search Map in figure 4.1), and it's all about to pay off. Planning, preparing, and thoughtful decision making has brought you this far— exactly where you need to be along the path to a great hire. We're at step 4, and it's time to get personal.

Let's take an inventory of where we are with the top candidates right now. If you're following my system, you will have completed the following at this point:

1. Defined the job carefully by including all relevant stakeholders.
2. Thoughtfully established your Search Team and each member's role.
3. Determined what you can offer the successful candidate, for example, salary range, benefits, any bonuses or perks, and where you will be flexible.
4. Determined your budget for the search.
5. Clarified decision maker(s) for the candidate offer.
6. Strategically determined your search process and timeline including interviews/research of any recruiters should you be using a firm.
7. Announced your job opening based on your search strategy.
8. Trained your Search Team in unbiased and legal vetting and interviewing.
9. Received and vetted cover letters and resumes including checking for resume inconsistencies on the internet, in your files, on social media.
10. Chosen up to ten candidates to receive your Beyond the Resume three to six questions.
11. Evaluated the answers to those questions and identified the top four to six people or more if necessary.

12. Designed your core questions and conducted up to sixty minutes, two-member-team video, live, or phone conversations with the top four to six people or more if necessary.
13. Met as a team to identify the top candidates from your larger pool.

Yes, there are a lot of steps, and yes, they take some time and attention. I hope I've convinced you to hang in here with me because you agree that doing this hiring thing well at the front end will save you so much *more* time and heartache over the tenure of each new employee. You'll be moving your organization forward instead of having to pick up all the painful pieces later and (yikes!) start over.

To ease your mind a bit, many of these steps can, and arguably should, happen in concert with one another, taking less time than you might expect. For instance, steps 3 and 4 are related to funding decisions; steps 2 and 8 are choosing and training your Search Team; and much of question design for written answers and phone interviews can be done at the same time.

When you've created a solid Search Team whose members take their roles and responsibilities seriously, you can delegate many of these steps. Your role, as the hiring leader, is to be clear with everyone about when (and how often) you wish to check in, where along the way you want to have input, and which steps you want to oversee directly. Delegating to your Search Team members will also continue to develop their skills while liberating you from some of the work. This is an opportunity to let your Search Team be creative and collaborate within the clear parameters you have established.

Now the real fun begins! It's time to bring your top three to four candidates on-site and find out what makes them tick—for real. If you believe that you have seen and heard enough about your candidates thus far in the process and know them pretty well, you'd be wrong.

Here's the reality of what you are facing with candidates. They are either talented actors who have expertly manipulated the entire process to date, or they are *mostly* who they appear to be. At this moment in time, you still *do not* know what's real and what's not, so keep a wide-open mind and assume nothing. You need to experience your candidates in ways in which they cannot fool you, and in ways any biases that show up within the Search Team, or the candidates, can be observed and addressed by you and your team members.

The story I'm about to share is true, just the names are changed. It illustrates the power and importance of a well-executed search process as well as the value of the Search Team.

Maria's team invited a well-qualified candidate on-site to interview for a very senior position. Brian had passed each step of the process to date. When he arrived on-site, a new picture began to emerge. During informal settings like the ride from the airport and dinners with Search Team members, he seemed aloof and consistently ignored or made no eye contact with waitstaff. He did adequately well in most of the on-site interviews with various stakeholders, but not so well with the Search Team members. His last interview was with Maria, his potential new boss. She said, "Brian, in the last two days we've spent a lot of time together. As we sit here today, I know what work you've done and I've observed you in interviews. Even so, I am still unclear how you would interact and work with our team." This was Brian's opportunity to talk more about himself and the team. Brian's response was curt and icy: "What you see is what you get, and I have all the credentials and then some for this job and I'm sure I'm your best candidate." Maria's response was, "I'm sure you believe you are. Thank you for coming to meet us, Brian. We'll make sure you catch your flight on time, and we'll be in touch."

When the evaluations from the Search Team and other interviewers came in, the raters were split. Those who wanted to hire him focused on his deep expertise and experience; those who didn't focused on his manner, attitude, and their inability to read him. While Maria was the final decision maker, her last step was to discuss the situation with her Search Team. No one on the Search Team backed this candidate; only other interviewers with less to gain or lose had supported him. Brian's lack of interpersonal skills and his arrogance were not a fit for the job or their workplace culture. Maria called Brian to thank him for coming to interview and shared that she was offering the position to another candidate. He told her she was making a *big* mistake in not hiring him and she'd regret it because no one was better for the job than he was! Maria shared his response with the Search Team and a collective sigh of relief filled the room.

THE ON-SITE VISIT

When you invite a candidate to your site for a series of interviews, it's a lot like inviting that "blind date" out for dinner. There are a number of logistics to consider that will make some kind of an impression on the candidate, and naturally, you hope that impression will be positive. If the candidate is from out of town, it starts with travel arrangements (possibly flights, accommodations, meals, and tours) and providing more information about the position and the organization ahead of the visit. For instance, these might include a more in-depth position write-up, organizational charts, past employee satisfaction or culture surveys, nonconfidential but relevant business facts and figures, or signing a nondisclosure document, among other things. If, for example, you have a tour planned of your workplace (or your city), or if the candidate requests a meeting with a real estate broker (or dual-career assistance for a partner), these should be arranged well in advance of the visit.

Whoever is working with the candidate to orchestrate all of these logistics is a rich resource and can provide input about each candidate based on this experience.

My executive assistant was in charge of all the logistics for three traveling candidates. After years of working together, I knew her to be smart, kind, levelheaded, flexible, and intuitive. I casually checked in with her about how the logistics were coming along. She told me two of the candidates were a pleasure to work with and everything was going smoothly. Then she told me about the third. "Gabriella has been e-mailing and calling me nonstop," she said. "She wants us to use a particular airline so she can get her points, even though it's far more expensive. She wants a hotel room that has windows that open and face west. She wants access to private office space when she's here so she can work when she's not in interviews. What should I do?"

I listened carefully and asked her if she would want Gabriella on our team. Her response was immediate. "Well, I really don't think she would like it here, and honestly, she doesn't seem to be flexible or much of a team player." I decided to call Gabriella. First, I asked her to help me understand her requests. All she could say is she travels too much to be uncomfortable, and her requirements will prevent that so she can be fresh for the interviews. When I explained our logistical decisions about her flights, hotel, and office space (we could provide a desk in a cubby but that was all), Gabriella decided, on the spot, to withdraw her application. The candidate we saw on paper and in the short video interview was not the person I heard on the phone. She could sprint, but she wasn't capable of going the distance with us. I doubted she was serious about our position after all. Whew! That saved a lot of time, aggravation, and money.

Dig deep, my friends! Asking our administrative staff about their impressions of candidates became a regular part of our search process from that day forward.

When out-of-town candidates arrive in your city, you (preferably), or someone from the Search Team should meet each candidate at the airport, or at least provide transportation and meet at the hotel. This is an important "first in-person date" opportunity, and you don't want to miss it or blow it. Candidates will either feel welcomed and well treated or they won't—it's up to you.

From the moment you meet, you'll be able to observe how the candidate deals with being tired and, perhaps, stressed or excited about the upcoming interview plan. In Search Team training, we ask everyone to pay close attention to the way our candidates treated our administrative staff, waitstaff, desk clerks, and bellhops. Smart candidates know how to put on a great show, short term, for known decision makers and can behave quite differently with people who "don't count" to them. If you see disrespectful behavior toward anyone, it should be a *huge red flag*!

Preparing your additional on-site interviewers (other than your Search Team) is also critical. They didn't receive the Search Team training, they will spend less time with candidates, and they may be somewhat less invested in the outcome. Each interviewer, in advance, will need to receive an organized packet with full candidate information, the job description, the legal and illegal questions list (refer to the Resources section for chapter 3), and the desired focus of the questions for one or more interviewers. Don't leave it to chance. Here's an example of why . . .

The dean, two peer faculty members, and an associate dean were interviewing a brilliant and accomplished female faculty candidate at dinner. One of the faculty members asked this question upon noticing the candidate's wedding ring: "So is your husband going to follow you here, and will you want help with a dual-career spouse?" The question may have been well meaning, but it was illegal. The candidate's answer: "I'm not sure why that matters to you or for this position, but no, *my wife* works from home and cares for our children." Beyond being an illegal question, it was also inappropriate and assumptive. The result: they lost their top candidate; she withdrew from consideration immediately after dinner and left the next day.

Before we delve deeply into the on-site interview section of this chapter, which might seem the logical next step, we need to back up a bit and ask these questions: What do we need to know about each candidate, and why? The answers will help you save on-site interview time and increase the likelihood of weeding the *actors* out of your pool.

In our original "blind date" analogy, things have changed. We are now on our second or third "date," and it may be beginning to feel like this could get serious, maybe even become a permanent relationship. It's time to discover if the candidate possesses the characteristics and attributes you believe will match your needs and your culture. What will tell you enough to keep this person at the top of your list? What will help you learn about the brains, heart, *and* soul of the person in front of you?

THE A–H FACTORS

We have established the fact that a resume, the Beyond the Resume questions, and a short live interview can get us part of the way to knowing the top-tier candidates, and still we have a *lot to learn* about each one.

Jack Welch, the famous and former CEO of General Electric, shared a great deal in his books and online about big business, including hiring right for senior leaders. He talks about the two must-haves—*high integrity* and *high IQ*—and the six definitely should-haves: *energy*, the ability to *energize* (others), *edge*, *execution*, *passion*, and, the game changer, the *generosity gene*.[1]

While I very much agree with Mr. Welch's criteria for big business CEOs and their senior leaders, I wrote this book for *everyone who hires, develops, and fires employees at any level* of your organization. The eight factors and examples you'll see here include virtually everything Mr. Welch points to in ways I believe make it much easier and more practical for you to apply within your search process for any job in any enterprise.

In our "blind date" analogy, this is your team's opportunity to really get to know each candidate by asking well-considered probing questions that will expose the truth, good or bad. These are the questions behind the questions; another way to think of it is that you are finding out what's behind the candidate's interviewing "mask." The eight A–H factors are *attitude, brains, character, drive, emotional intelligence, fit, gut,* and *heart.* You will find more sample questions for each of the eight factors in the Resources section for this chapter. You can use the questions as they are, or as starting points to customize for your situation.

You will likely have discovered some of the answers within these factors during the initial screening of the resumes, written questions, and the interviews. And . . . I can guarantee you haven't yet touched upon others and may even need a deeper dive in all of them.

A = Attitude

Is the candidate passionate about the work and about helping others on their team succeed? Is their attitude one of abundance and a can-do, solution-oriented approach to work and challenges, or do they focus on scarcity, blame, and obstacles?

Notice whether the candidate talks about solutions or about problems when you ask for examples of stressful situations that have arisen at work. You want to discover what the candidate thinks of the people who were involved. You want to know if they throw people "under the bus" or work with colleagues to find solutions.

For example, you might ask a few somewhat leading questions to see if they fall into a blaming mode. "Tell me about a failure you experienced." Then ask, "And whose fault was that?" If the candidate goes into people-blaming mode, you know you've got a problem. If he or she goes into solution mode, speaking more about the situation and lessons they learned rather than about people who messed up, you have a potential winner.

Frame your open-ended questions to probe what, where, how, and with whom the individual has addressed the challenges in his or her career and life. Don't limit the discussion to work examples. It's important to ask people about non-work-related challenges they have faced and learn how they have responded. As long as they get to choose the examples, and you don't ask about personal matters, they can talk all they want—and they usually will if you let them. Both the examples cited and the approach taken will tell you far more about the candidate than well-practiced pat answers.

B = Brains

Is the candidate capable of doing the job, or can the candidate learn how to do the parts of the job that are new in a reasonable time span? Can the candidate combine brainpower and execution? What is the depth of experience the candidate brings?

To paraphrase Jack Welch, "you can't train IQ," and most organizations judge IQ fairly well anyway. In fact, many rely heavily on this single factor without enough digging and context. While technical knowledge and IQ combine as the candidate's ticket to get in the door, neither should be the only metrics that let them stay. Some organizations use standardized quantitative tests or indicators, psychological testing, or job-fit testing.

Pitfall: Beware: testing can be manipulated and biased—plenty of smart people have learned how to fiddle with just about any test thrown at them. In addition, bias can be subtle and still be a barrier that may eliminate great candidates.

Solution: Put any metric you wish to use through a tough screening for fallibility and bias. If you can easily manipulate it, so can someone else. Ask your Human Resources (HR) professionals and Search Team to look for bias in the questions.

If all candidates undergo the same tests, you may indeed collect some useful information for your screening purposes. What testing data will not tell you is *whether or how* those candidates have *applied, and will apply, their brains (knowledge, skills, and abilities) to the job at hand.* Can they go beyond knowing to executing? An overreliance on knowing how technically smart a person is without the context of execution is risky business. Brains alone won't get the job done. *Brains plus the ability to execute* are both baseline qualities.

Knowing is the easy part; knowing plus doing is much more important and difficult, regardless of the role, the job, or business. Lots of people know—or think they know—*how* to do many things. That's not the point. Has the candidate truly experienced and executed well and long enough to reasonably understand the nuances, challenges, and the life cycle of the job you need to fill? What has the candidate learned from mistakes, and how were those mistakes responded to and managed?

Reading a dozen books about swimming without ever getting wet will get one drowned. Being able to discuss what it was like to dive in, flop around, swallow some water, and learn from mistakes is what you need to hear from the candidates. With this in mind, you have to determine whether your candidates have the right, and enough, experience *in life and work*—in other words, street smarts—to bring the necessary maturity, judgment, attitude, and skill to the job at hand. If little experience is needed, that's fine, but if you require someone who has a depth of knowledge and experience in specific areas, don't assume anything—dig and then dig some more!

C = Character

What are the candidate's core values? Is the candidate trustworthy?

People make decisions based on their personal values and belief systems. Even the little things like deciding to brush your teeth or arrive at work on time are based in your core values relating to hygiene and work ethic. Consider carefully exactly which core values you must see demonstrated in the person you are hiring for this position.

A quick internet search will give you laundry lists of "good character" traits. Here's one example of a list of character-related words: *integrity, honesty, loyalty, respectful, responsible, humble, compassionate, fair, forgiving, authentic, courageous, generous, persistent, kind, optimistic, reliable, conscientious,* and *self-disciplined.*

I am certain you can make a great list of important character qualities that fit your culture and organizational values. The bottom line for you is to define for yourself and your workplace the character traits you need to see in candidates you can trust. While no one is perfect, and no one can be perfect in every circumstance, a handy litmus test is this—do you trust this person to *say what they mean and do what they say?* I believe being trustworthy is a *bedrock quality*, and you need to *know, not assume*, your candidates are trustworthy. In order for me to consider a candidate trustworthy, the character trait I look for every time—regardless of the job at hand—is integrity.

People either have integrity, or they don't. In my experience, there is *no such thing as a minor lapse of integrity*. Poor judgment, yes, but people who operate fully in integrity admit their mistakes even before being asked. *We can't teach integrity*; it is hardwired into each person's moral value system. Every smart leader knows this as it plays out in the workplace and in the world. For instance, without a firm belief from your stakeholders that you'll tell the truth and that you and your services or products can be trusted to deliver what you promise, your business will fail; the same applies to each of your employees. Lack of integrity damages your enterprise and demoralizes your people.

Business ethics are also integral to success. Fortunately, *we can teach people about ethics*. We can be clear about our organizational ethics, guidelines, or principles, particularly as it pertains to a specific enterprise and the kind of business at hand. There are codes of ethics for virtually every profession—teachers, doctors, executive coaches, bankers, politicians, and lawyers, for example. Whether people live by those explicit ethical standards in their profession, or not, depends on their integrity.

Oprah Winfrey once said, "Real integrity is doing the right thing, knowing that nobody's going to know whether you did it or not."[2] I agree with Oprah and offer a bit more expansive definition of integrity as *doing the right thing, every single time, whether or not it is popular, profitable, convenient, comfortable, or known.*

It takes courage to stand firm in one's integrity.

You may be wondering, "How do I assess this person's integrity and trustworthiness?" Good question! You could ask a candidate to list the top five values that drive decisions in their life and work, but frankly, most people don't have that list on the tip of their tongues. More relevant is to probe the individual's responses to questions based on your own organizational values. For instance, let's say integrity is one of your values. You could ask, "Tell me about a time your integrity has been questioned. How did you feel, and what did you do?" Or, "Tell me about a time when you had to make a choice about a situation or a person you believed was unethical. What choice did you make and why?" Create your questions around the core values of your organization, and you'll get some important insights about how well aligned the candidate is with what character traits you want and need.

Character truly is a "go or no-go" factor in making good hiring decisions. If you have doubts, that's a bright red flag. If you are not sure, probe until you are sure, because it's just not worth the risk to shortchange the character factor.

D = Drive

Is the candidate self-motivated to achieve both personal goals and the goals of this position?

No one can motivate another person. We can inspire, encourage, demand, beg, order, and pray, but motivation is personal and intrinsic, not extrinsic. Before you hire, you need to know how high or low maintenance this person is going to be, and whether that reality fits your needs. For instance, you may want an initially higher maintenance rookie whom you can develop, coach, or mentor into a fine professional. Or, conversely, you may need someone who can finish your sentences and anticipate your needs and the needs of others—someone who will simply "get it done." Determine how self-starting and self-motivated the new hire needs to be in order to be successful, both for your and the individual's well-being. Once you know that answer, you can gauge the reality of the person in front of you, not his or her potential.

Potential is the hope side of the coin, not the production side. For instance, you may ask the candidate to describe a project they were not specifically asked to do but believed was important and proceeded to do it. You might also ask how they began it, managed it, and what were the final results.

There are clues to help you assess drive. Does the candidate ask you good questions, offer suggestions to a dilemma you've posed, offer to provide you with more information about a topic or themselves, show up on time, meet or beat all your deadlines, send a thank-you letter after the short phone/video interview, ask to meet various stakeholders, and appear confident without arrogance? All these behaviors indicate attributes of a person who is proactive versus reactive and who is a learner, is curious, and is self-motivated. These are all *driver attributes versus spectator attributes*. Every employee needs to be somewhat self-motivated, and all effective leaders need to demonstrate some degree of drive to inspire others and produce results.

A great question to ask that will separate the "driver" from the "spectator" is this one: "What are the three things you want to learn in your first three months on the job?" If the answer focuses primarily on proactive learning, discovering, or exploring, you probably have a driver. If the answer focuses primarily on the details of their employment, you may have a spectator.

Pitfall: Be alert to those who sound like "drivers" without a well-informed sense of where they're going. Candidates like this will often focus on the "what" and not the "why" or the "how." If they want to jump in too fast, too hard, too anything without first getting to know the people and the organization, the result is likely to be *crash and burn* with casualties along the way. These aren't true "drivers"; they are "slashers" in a driver's disguise. Where there is a slasher, there is pain—and a lot of it.

Solution: Notice the questions candidates ask you. Is there a balance between "how" and "what" questions? Ask questions related to how they envision beginning the new job. Are answers focused on the "what" (matters that serve the candidate) or the "how" (how a candidate will serve the organization)?

E = Emotional Intelligence (EI)

What is the candidate's degree of self-awareness, and how well do they manage their own emotions? What is the candidate's social awareness and ability to manage relationships?

A lot of smart people fail at work and in life. There is one reason that looms above all others—a shortage of emotional intelligence (EI) competencies. Here are some facts to consider:

- IQ, knowledge, and technical expertise are threshold capabilities *not* differentiators for success. This is covered in the "Brains" factor.

- EI is *twice as important* for success as IQ and technical expertise *combined.*
- EI is *four times as important* for overall success.
- Ninety percent of the difference between outstanding and average leaders is linked to EI. Only one cognitive ability, pattern recognition, differentiates outstanding leaders.[3]

Since top professionals are typically in the top 10 percent of raw intelligence, IQ itself offers relatively little competitive advantage. *Being smart does not prevent failure.* Therefore, it makes no sense to hire, reward, or promote people based on cognitive and technical competencies alone without assessing and giving significant weight to emotional intelligence competencies.

To assess emotional intelligence, you need to ask questions that require a candidate to demonstrate self-awareness of his or her emotions, how that person is able to self-manage those emotions when they arise, how socially aware and "tuned in" the candidate is to people and organizational clues, and finally, how the candidate manages relationships.[4]

Questions that dig into a candidate's emotional intelligence are often considered "behavioral interview questions." In creating these questions, all four quadrants—*self-awareness, self-management, social awareness,* and *relationship management*—need to be considered. There are twelve competencies within emotional intelligence, and each one can help guide you in developing your own questions. Here are the twelve competencies we want to assess:

1. Emotional self-awareness: *recognizing how your emotions affect your performance, knowing your inner resources and limits, open to feedback, sense of humor*
2. Achievement orientation: *striving to meet or exceed a standard of excellence*
3. Adaptability: *flexibility in handling change, resilient in times of stress*
4. Emotional self-control: *keeping disruptive emotions and impulses in check*
5. Positive outlook: *persistence in pursuing goals despite obstacles and setbacks*

6. Empathy: *sensing and understanding others' feelings and perspectives, taking an active interest in their concerns*
7. Organizational awareness: *reading emotional currents and power relationships*
8. Conflict management: *negotiating and transforming conflicts*
9. Coach and mentor: *taking a proactive interest in others' development and needs*
10. Influence: *having a positive impact on others*
11. Inspirational leadership: *inspiring and guiding individuals and groups*
12. Teamwork: *working well with others toward a shared purpose or goal*

Each of these is important to an individual's overall success. For example, consider someone you know or perhaps have observed in the news—a person who consistently demonstrates low or no empathy for others. Empathy is defined here as *the ability to understand, or the desire to understand, the feelings, experiences, and perspectives of another person.* A shortage of empathy breaks down trust between people. When only my point of view or my experience makes sense to me, then everyone else must be wrong, right? I have often observed that people who score low on the empathy scale tend to have low self-awareness as well.

I hope this demonstrates how significantly missing even one of the twelve EI competencies can contribute to a less productive workplace at best, and a highly toxic workplace in the extreme. Depending on the position you are filling, some of these will be more essential than others. For instance, a frontline employee may not need to be a competent coach and mentor or an inspirational leader, but any employee will be far more successful if they demonstrate the other ten competencies. Leaders need to demonstrate some level of competency in all twelve or at least be self-aware enough to know where they need to grow.

The great news is that emotional intelligence competencies *can be learned, practiced, and enhanced.* Self-awareness is the starting point. Without it, there's little to no hope of becoming fully competent in the other eleven. Here are competency examples for each quadrant. Additional information about these competencies is located in the Resources section for this chapter.

- Self-Awareness: When did you *first* trust your own voice? (self-awareness)
- Self-Management: What boundaries do you create for yourself to keep your integrity? (emotional self-control)
- Social Awareness: Describe a time when you demonstrated empathy for someone. (empathy)
- Relationship Management: How would a child you've known for a while describe you? (coach and mentor)

As we continue through the alphabet, you'll notice that emotional intelligence indicators are present in assessing *all but one* of our eight A–H factors—and that one is brains.[5] And just like in our "blind date" example, you wouldn't marry or go into business with someone just because they were smart, would you?

F = Fit

Will the candidate be a fit within your mission, vision, values, and culture?

"It was just a bad fit," is an all-too-common lament from leaders who find themselves in the unfortunate position of having to fire someone. You'll find out sooner or later whether or not the candidate embraces your organizational values, is committed to your mission, and is excited about your vision. The goal is to discover the truth *before* you hire.

For instance, if your mission is to publish *All the News That's Fit to Print*,[6] everyone in the organization, regardless of position, needs to be committed to delivering on that mission versus, say, winning a Pulitzer Prize. If your vision is to cure cancer but your candidate is more interested in working on Parkinson's disease, then the individual won't fit regardless of his scientific brilliance. If your organization declares *Safety First* as a top value, and your candidate is focused on fast results, even if it means taking short cuts, then it is not a fit. You need to know all of this *before* you hire.

A workplace with a diversity of ideas, backgrounds, gender, education, experience, race, ethnicity, personalities, and preferences makes every organization stronger, wiser, and more likely to succeed. Fit and diversity are *not opposites* or in conflict with one another. Many different people with an array of backgrounds and perspectives can and do fit into the same organizational culture.

You're falling into the trap of bias if you use "fit" as an excuse not to hire or promote someone who is simply different from you. Fit is not about sameness; it's about being a good match for the job at hand—can this person do the job well for your organization, or not?

None of the diversity considerations play into determining fit. What really matters is whether the candidate is on board with your mission, vision, and values. Is she able to be a productive member of the team who helps advance your goals? Is he genuinely excited to be part of what you are doing and how you are doing it?

Your organization's unique mission, vision, values, and culture must drive the questions you ask for determining fit. For example, if you run a company called the Widget Company, your mission is to make widgets. Your vision might be to become the number one widget company in the world. One of your top values might be integrity. Questions about your mission, vision, and values—such as (a) why this candidate is attracted to the Widget Company and widget making, (b) what the candidate thinks this particular position can do to help the company become number one, and (c) how this candidate demonstrates integrity—are all relevant questions no matter the job. Every person being hired into a job with the Widget Company can and should be able to answer these fit questions.

G = Gut

What are your instincts telling you about this candidate?

Our brains are hardwired to survive and to seek safety among other humans. We often know when a threatening person enters the room; the hair stands up on the back of our necks and our blood "turns cold." Some years back I attended a presentation by a national figure I knew very little about. As soon as the man began to speak, all my alarms went off! It wasn't what he said, it was how he said it and how he moved; his entire presence radiated a sense of doom. My skin felt prickly and hot, and I felt a pit in my stomach—the one I always feel when in the presence of a highly negative or evil-intentioned person. I left the room as soon as I could and wished I could rush back home and take a long, hot shower—that's how creepy he was. I won't mention his name here but, unfortunately, he had a long, controversial career in government. I came to understand and trust my visceral reactions.

Conversely, on some level of our being we know when we're feeling safe in someone's presence and can relax and be our authentic selves. Pay attention. This is your gut speaking. Let's not dismiss or short-change the importance of this factor for even a moment.

If you or your Search Team responds with phrases like "We have concerns" or "We can't tell" to any one of the eight factors, *do not hire* that person until and unless you fully address the concerns. Trust the answers to your questions *and* trust your instincts by paying attention to your gut. Once again, be alert to conscious and unconscious bias to make sure this isn't an excuse to exclude someone because you have made assumptions without checking them out.

When a person *feels right*, that's a good sign. When a person *does not feel right* to you or others in the search process, he or she *probably* isn't right. In either case, make sure you have connected all the dots, conducted your due diligence, and given *all* the factors the attention they deserve. You may be confusing the gut factor with personal preference or bias and could eliminate someone who deserves to be considered. And . . . it is rarely worth the risk to you and your team to invest in a candidate who doesn't sit well with your team after an honest gut check.

The gut factor is only one out of the eight factors. It is important, *and* it should carry the appropriate amount of weight.

Pitfall: The gut factor becomes a problem when hiring leaders rely on it to the exclusion of other factors, saying things like, "I trust my gut, and I don't need to know/hear/see/ask anything else."

Solution: The questions for this factor are for you, *not the candidate*. Examples might be, "Do I trust this person? What was my first and last impression? Are there any yellow or red flags anywhere along the process that we need to explore more deeply? Am I feeling positive or neutral or uneasy, and why? What more do I need to know to make the right decision about hiring this person?"

H = Heart

What kind of a human being is this candidate? How grounded, other centered, well balanced, compassionate, and humble will this person be in the workplace?
Each person is a complex human being with a boatload of life behind them, no matter their age. The heart factor shows up in the ways in which candidates choose to navigate life and relationships with the people they touch. Teddy Roosevelt is often attributed with some version of the phrase, "People don't care how much you know until they know how much you care." This is the heart factor.

The candidate's heart factor impacts all of his stakeholder relationships. When I ask my client groups to list best leader and worst leader or best and worst team member qualities, attributes, or traits, there is rarely more than one or two that involve the brain factor. All the rest are about *how* the leader leads people—factors A, C, D, E, and H show up every single time. I've conducted this exercise with thousands of people from a vast range of roles and professions—from CEOs to mail handlers. Every group I've asked, regardless of role or profession, arrives at the same conclusions time and time again. *It's all about our relationships—* it's the *how . . . not the what!* Heart plays a big part in the *how.*

In the emotional intelligence factor, we talked about *empathy.* Heart is about *compassion.* They are closely related behaviors but show up differently. Empathy is demonstrating that you want to understand or actually do understand what someone is going through, feeling, and saying. You might not care deeply about the situation, but you are truly listening and are genuine about trying to walk a mile in their shoes. Compassion, on the other hand, is demonstrating that you care about the person whether you understand them or not, agree or not, or can imagine anything they are feeling or not. A candidate who demonstrates both empathy and compassion for stakeholders in your organization is a fortunate find and one you'll likely be placing at the top of your list.

I believe the heart factor is what Jack Welch meant by the game-changing "generosity gene."[7] This is a person who is all about others' success, who celebrates members of the team when they accomplish difficult tasks, who feels fantastic about rewarding deserving employees, and who never takes credit for others' ideas. When authentic "heart" is demonstrated consistently, trust, loyalty, commitment, and productivity increase dramatically. These are people you want on your team. I often remind my clients that it is *important not to confuse kindness with weakness.* Humility and kindness result in increased team cohesiveness, productivity, and organizational strength.

The questions you can explore to get a greater and more accurate sense of a person's heart are personal in nature, still perfectly legal, and appropriate; for instance, "Tell us about a time you celebrated your team." "What has helped you most when it comes to building your confidence and self-esteem?" "What do you expect from employees you lead?" "What do you know to be true?" "What makes you feel alive?" "What gives you the most joy at work?"

An invisible but measurable energy exchange happens between human beings even though we may or may not be aware of it on a conscious level. It is definitely whirling around on a subconscious level. Our bodies react to stimuli before our minds can compute the experience. For example, consider what happens when you are watching a horror movie like *Jaws*, *Psycho*, or *Scream.* With any version of the classic scary film setup, your reptilian brain does not know or care that the frightening thing you are watching is a fictional experience. Your pulse rate rises, pupils dilate, adrenaline increases, sweat glands activate, and your stomach flops. You might even stop breathing for a moment. And all that happens when it's not even a real person or thing scaring you! It's only when your logical mind sorts all this out that your automatic reflexes relax a bit. When it's a real person or thing, it matters a lot more.

I demonstrate this human energy exchange with a simple children's toy—an energy stick you can buy in toy stores or online for around $10. Imagine being inside a room, with at least two and up to hundreds of people standing in a circle, either holding hands or simply touching the hand of the two people immediately on their left and right. When the circuit is complete, the tiny stick lights up. When one person, anywhere in the loop lets go, the stick goes silent. We can stop the tangible indicator, but the flow of energy remains ever present.

This is a simple and visible wonder that gets everyone's immediate attention and generates a lot of ooh's and ah's. The lesson people take away is that our human energy is always present and moving invisibly between and among us. I ask them to notice that we are all connected, knowingly or not. Then I ask people to take responsibility for the energy they each are sending out into the world.

In choosing a candidate to hire, it's important to notice the energy radiating outward from them and see how the candidate does or does not take responsibility for it. I first noticed this phenomenon in an interaction with a former boss. He was a nice enough guy, but not an honest one, and he had, for his own gain, purposefully thrown me "under the bus." One day at a restaurant lunch with friends, he approached the table and offered to shake my hand as if nothing had happened between us. This was apparently an "if looks could kill" moment because all I did was look at him. His face went pale, his body recoiled, and he turned and left. The two people with me at lunch said in unison, "What the hell was that?" I asked, "What was what?" They both told me that not only did my former boss seem to jump away from the table, but they each felt as if a hand had physically pushed them to the side as well. We all knew there were no hands involved. Mine had remained in my lap the entire time. That was a wild moment I cannot and do not want to forget; it was humbling to see how powerful one's energy can be!

None of the eight factors should carry the day, *and* every one of the factors has the potential to create a "go or no-go" decision. Of course, within the brains factor, you are looking for the right knowledge and experience that speaks to the job at hand whether it is fundraising, customer service, sales, project management, teaching . . . you name it. That's where the first screening happens for all candidates. After that, the rest of the A–H factors come into play.

For instance, if you are satisfied with someone's attitude and brains, but not comfortable with character and fit, that's probably a no-go. If everything has been superb so far and late in the game you discover this candidate takes credit for everyone else's work, you may have to revisit your conclusions. On the other hand, if you expect this is a learned behavior and could perhaps be adjusted with coaching, you might make a different decision. I'd still not make that hire without sharing my concerns with the candidate and taking a deep dive into reference checks to uncover what we may have missed or see what else we can learn.

That's it! Our eight A–H factors cover the critical aspects of the person in front of you. If there are other factors that are singularly unique beyond these, I have yet to experience them after more than thirty years of hiring people from many walks of life and cultures.

While this may seem complicated or even overcomplicated, it doesn't have to be. Once you create the interview framework and have a good selection of questions for each of the factors, you can quickly tweak them for each position until it becomes "the way we do things here." Since you will have to create interview questions anyway, why not create questions that will serve your best interests? I promise, it gets so much easier the more you do it, and just like any new skill, it takes practice. And . . . I've provided plenty of questions to get you going in the Resources section for this chapter.

INTERVIEWS

There are two kinds of on-site interviews I recommend: (1) meetings with various stakeholders, and (2) the scenario interview. These are two very different approaches and utilizing both well will give you and your Search Team a deeper and richer understanding of your candidates.

The first kind of interview plan is common practice in most organizations and, when done well, yields great information. The candidate meets with several groups and/or individuals for some part of one or more days. Everyone involved has some stake in the success of this person for this particular position. Depending on the position's level and complexity this could be a relatively small or larger undertaking.

The planning for these meetings should have taken place well before the candidate arrives on-site. Interviewers will have been preselected, are well informed about expectations for the position and the candidates, have the paperwork about the questions you want them to explore (and what's legal and not legal) in hand. Times and places have been scheduled to allow them to conduct each interview. Stakeholders will have an evaluation form, either hard copy or electronic, and have a deadline for returning same to a specific person on your staff or on the Search Team. Yes, the devil is in the details when it comes to interviews. Don't leave it to chance; plan far enough ahead to allow for the inevitable changes in people, times, and places.

Ask your interviewers to cover specific topics based on their own expertise and needs as well as questions from any of the A–H factors you deem appropriate. For instance, let's say you are hiring for a Business Manager position that will serve all your operating departments. It makes sense to ask a representative(s) of each department to be on the interviewer list. To prevent having the candidate bombarded with the same questions in every interview setting, preplanning is key. It does not help your learning, or the candidate's view of your organization, if everyone asks, "So why do you want this job?" You get the idea, I'm sure, and I expect you've seen this problem pop up more than once.

To prevent useless and redundant questions, you can assign which group or person gets particular questions based somewhat on their expertise as well your perception of their sensitivity to factors like character and drive or emotional intelligence and fit. It helps to be mindful about who would do the best job at assessing various and important aspects of each candidate. And . . . interviewers need to have the ability and time within the interview to be fluid enough to allow for impromptu follow-up questions as well as questions from the candidates.

Candidate questions can be illuminating so always allow time in every session for this. Watch for clues. If the candidate asks few or no questions, you can make an open-ended offer, "What questions do you have?" This is when silence is *your friend*. If you allow even a few seconds of space, most candidates will feel the need to fill the airtime. If they talk nonstop or interrupt you, it may indicate nervousness or a lack of good listening skills and a shortage of self-awareness. In any case, there may be reason for concern. If the candidate asks thoughtful and relevant questions, seeks clarification, and listens carefully to your answers, you have a positive indicator for good listening skills, awareness, and comprehension.

THE SCENARIO INTERVIEW

The second kind of interview is the scenario interview. I relish this process because it has a high success rate for *separating the best from the rest*.

A founding father of organizational development, thought leader, and author, Rod Napier, who is also my mentor and dear friend, wrote a little book about this process called *The Power Interview* in 1990. He plans to update and publish it again in the near future.[8] Rod broke important new ground with his approach, and in 1992, I was the first person at Cornell University to be hired into a position of leadership using Rod's "Power Interview" process. I've been a champion of it ever since. It is Rod's right and privilege to give you a more detailed description. He has given me permission, in this book, to share what I experienced when I was a candidate.

This two-part interview process generally takes place over one and a half to two days. The second day, and last set of formal interviews, is for scenarios. By the time the candidates come on-site for the scenario interviews, they will have met many people and had plenty of conversations. Each candidate should, by now, have a solid sense of the organization's culture and the position at hand.

Several members of your Search Team are going to have roles that may or may not be their real jobs. The planning for the scenarios needs to happen long before your candidates show up on-site. I recommend a dry run by the team nearer the time candidates arrive to provide enough time to make any needed changes but not too much time to risk people forgetting their roles.

My own experience as a candidate is typical of the right way to set up the scenarios with your Search Team. I invite you to walk in my shoes as a candidate for a moment.

Before coming on-site, I was informed about the two-part process, the people I would meet in the interviews and their relationship to the position, the locations, and who would be my guide to each location. I was also informed about the half-day scenario interview process. Someone on the Search Team explained the structure of the scenario interviews to me a few days prior. I would be given the opportunity to "be the director" for three real situational scenarios with members of the Search Team including the hiring leader in attendance. It would take three to four hours, and there would be a break after each one. That was it. I had never heard of or experienced anything like this for any of my positions—and, yes, I was nervous.

At the appointed time, I was warmly welcomed into a conference room for this half-day interview by my potential new boss, as well as the rest of the Search Team including the person serving as the facilitator. Outside the conference room was a small private office where I would be given twenty minutes to review one of the three scenarios prior to having to return to the conference room and interact with some, or all, of the group for a maximum of fifteen minutes.

I was guided into the private office by the facilitator, offered refreshments, and left at the desk with a piece of paper and a pen in front of me. The paper described an adaptation of one situation I, as the new director, would likely need to grapple with in real time. I was given a list of the names of people and their positions that I could choose to interact with—or not—my choice. They explained that I was either (1) making a report to my boss about my recommendations, (2) giving a short presentation, (3) managing the situation and people, or (4) some combination of these. When I reentered the conference room, I noticed that some of the Search Team members had new name cards in front of them. Each person who was being made available for the scenario had the name of a specific character in the scenario. Everyone else in the room was serving as observers and sat away from the conference table. This is when the real fun began!

It was my job to assess the situation they provided, decide who needed to be in the room with me, and when. Did I want several conversations or one? Who would I meet with first and last? Talk about a challenge!

After each fifteen-minute scenario was played out, we all stretched and relaxed, and the facilitator debriefed what happened with the group and me. Each time they asked what I believed I did well, whether I would do anything differently, and what questions I had about the situation after playing it out. They gave me positive comments about things they appreciated, and they asked what I was thinking during certain parts of the scenario, or why I asked this or that person to meet with me. They kept any negative feedback to themselves.

While I was reading the next scenario, the Search Team members were filling out their written evaluations of my recent performance based on the criteria they had predetermined, as well as anything meaningful that had popped up during the scenario. Again, all of this preparation was a team effort and completed before candidates arrived on-site. Each candidate was measured against the same criteria for each scenario. I learned later that they did not discuss their evaluations of the scenarios with each other until I left for the day.

We began at 8:30 a.m. and ended around 11:30 a.m., with each full cycle, including brief breaks, lasting about forty-five minutes. After all three scenarios were completed, the Search Team thanked me graciously and encouraged me to relax and enjoy the rest of my day. That was good advice because *I felt like a wet noodle!* Never in my life had I experienced such a think-on-your-feet, rapid series of events. Although it felt positive, I had no idea how well I had done in their eyes, but I knew they experienced the real me.

There had been no room to game the system; I had to show up, speak up, and do the best I knew how to do. I walked away with a lot of respect for the work and preparation the Search Team had invested in me and in the process and felt confident that if the real me wasn't the right fit, then that was okay and best for all of us.

Well, I expect you know the ending to this true story. As the top candidate, I learned I was offered the job over several people who had more experience and education. It turns out I was the unanimous choice of the Search Team with no close second—but *only after the scenario interviews*. Happily, I thrived and spent nearly thirteen years loving my job, my leader, and the great people on our team. We continued to use some version of the scenario process in our searches for a wide variety of positions and the "full monty" for our leadership positions. I continue to advise my clients—as I am advising you—to invest in it as a key part of your due diligence.

While no process can ever be fail proof, your well-written and well-planned scenarios offer a powerful method to differentiate among candidates. As a leader, I've seen a candidate drop out of the running because he didn't want to take part in such an intense process. Another turned to jelly before the third scenario and asked to be excused. Still others have tried to game the process only to see it backfire big time.

Yes, on rare occasions I have witnessed a bad hire despite the scenario process. Common causes for sad outcomes are a hiring leader who is feeling desperate and hires too fast and/or ignores valid concerns raised by others on the team. If we add the likelihood that bad hires often provide references who will only say positive things about them, it's a surefire disaster when we shortchange the process.

Our "blind date" isn't such a mystery anymore! We're about to enter into a serious and, hopefully, successful relationship. In chapter 5, "The Invitation," you'll complete your due diligence with reference checking, choose the winner of this marathon, and make an offer. Assuming all goes well, one person will be invited to become part of your team and your work family, and this person will help you create a positive future for your organization.

OK, it's time to pick up the phone!

Chapter Five

The Invitation

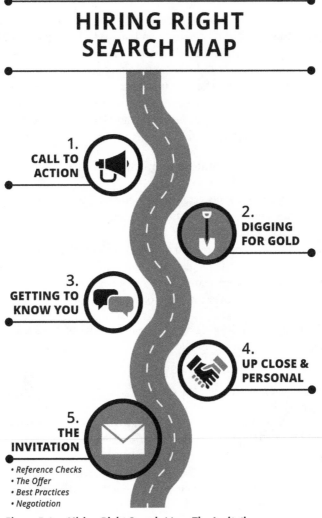

Figure 5.1.   Hiring Right Search Map: The Invitation

Most people do not listen with the intent to understand; they listen with the intent to reply.

—Stephen R. Covey

REFERENCE CHECKS

We're arrived at step 5, "The Invitation," on the Hiring Right Search Map (see figure 5.1). You've asked a zillion questions, listened, observed, and assessed the behaviors and answers from your candidates since the beginning of the search. One or more of them has risen to the top of your list. It's time to listen some more. As tempting as it may be to rush in and make an offer, the next critical step is to begin your reference-checking work and listen carefully to the answers you receive.

Reference checking is *very important*, and I strongly recommend that you, the hiring leader, *make all the calls yourself*. Here's why:

- You have the most intimate knowledge of what you need in this person and position.
- Because you are the closest to the job at hand, you can speak specifically to any concerns or questions you may have about the candidate better than anyone.
- The likelihood of getting good information increases when the person on the other end of the phone knows you'll be the candidate's leader.
- You'll hear the information directly, not second hand.
- You'll have control over the questions and can follow up as necessary.

This is *the* time for seeking verification (or not) of the facts *and* the manner in which the candidate showed up for you within the A–H

Pitfall: If you're excited about the candidate and/or are in a hurry to get this hiring thing done, you are more susceptible to *confirmation bias* and/or another opportunity for the *halo effect* to distract you from asking about important information you need to know.

Solution: Remember, no candidate is perfect, and that's fine. You still need to have a good idea where the person's growth edges and opportunities for development are. Keep digging until you have a full picture.

factors and during all your interviews. You are also seeking new or nuanced information from the candidate's references that can fill in gaps or reassure you.

Giving lip service to reference checking might check the official due diligence box, but it won't get you a great hire. I'd like to share two reference failure stories about the *same* employee as an illustration of *what not to do*.

A bright, knowledgeable, and accomplished employee, we'll call her Pam, had become untrustworthy in her highly sensitive and confidential position. Michael supervised her though he had not hired her. After delivering substantial constructive feedback, counseling her, giving her a formal warning, and then moving to a final disciplinary action, it was clear Pam was not willing or able to turn her behaviors around. Trust was completely destroyed. Michael allowed her to continue to do some basic parts of her job, but all sensitive duties were removed. Because of her long tenure, he gave her two months to find another job.

She found another job within a few weeks within a different division of their large organization. The hiring leader called Michael; he assumed it was to ask him for a reference. Instead, she said this, "Hi Michael, I am so sorry to be taking Pam away from you, so I just wanted to call and say thank you for encouraging her to apply for our position. We feel so lucky to get her!" After taking a deep breath, Michael volunteered to provide a full and contextual reference, but the hiring leader said she had hired Pam already so a reference was unnecessary.

It gets worse. Pam failed at her new job as well and applied for a third position. On behalf of the new hiring leader, a colleague asked Michael to provide a reference. Michael acknowledged Pam's strengths and provided several examples of the trust issues that caused him to terminate her. His colleague said the hiring leader was too keen on Pam to listen, and sure enough, they hired her anyway! The newest job blew up for exactly the same reasons. Pam was forced to leave the organization and was *finally* listed as an unacceptable candidate for any role in the future. What a waste of human energy and resources that could have been prevented if good reference-checking protocols had been used.

Great and poor character traits cast long shadows. I love this quote from Abraham Lincoln: "Character is like a tree and reputation like a shadow. The shadow is what we think of it; the tree is the real thing."[1] In reference checking, you're looking for *the tree*, and you'll discover more of the positives and negatives of the person you're hiring by exploring the kind of shadows they have cast.

A study by Robert Half International claims that senior managers report removing 34 percent of job candidates from consideration after a thorough reference check.[2] That's one in three!

It's safe to say we've explored the *why* we must do reference checks, so it's time to look at *how* to do it well. These checks help you confirm information on the candidate's application form and resume. You'll also gain greater insights into the candidate's skills, knowledge, and abilities from someone who has actually observed the candidate perform.

Here's the *what*:

- Tell candidates you will be conducting reference checks and be specific about what kinds of relationships you want them to provide, for example, past supervisors (more than one is better), peers, customers, and direct reports, if applicable. If the candidate's current supervisor does not know about the candidate's application for your position, require at least one past supervisor; two is better. Ask for the name, title, contact information, and relationship. You may also want to call people you know—people who also know the candidate but didn't make it to the preferred list. These folks may or may not answer your questions, but you can always ask.

- Most finalists understand the next step is to check references. No one worth hiring will have a problem with that. If there is only one person in the running for your position, you can choose to make your offer contingent upon your reference-checking process. Checking *before* you make an offer will speed up the time it takes to make an offer, but *only do this if your candidate agrees*. It could damage the candidate's current situation or create competing offers to yours. This is a situational judgment call, so consider the timing and context for each candidate.

- Make a solid list of job-related questions that you ask each candidate's references if you have more than one outstanding choice. Include specific questions that may have arisen from interviewing each candidate. The legality of the questions follows the same rules as interview questions. (See the Resources section for chapter 3.)

- In your conversations, be engaging and positive about the candidate with the person providing the reference.

- Thank each reference for being willing to chat with you to help gauge the candidate's suitability for the position.
- Provide a brief overview of the position at hand and then ask open-ended questions instead of yes/no close-ended questions.
- Focus on the facts and opinions the reference gives you more than on the delivery. You often will have no idea who the person is on the other end of the phone, how their day is going, or if they always speak in a strange-sounding voice. Notice hesitations, and how specific or vague the answers are. To stay focused, you'll need to really listen, don't interrupt, take notes, and allow as much time as needed for the conversation.
- Thank the person again for taking the time to help you get to know your candidate better.

You may already have a good reference-checking system in place and a list of powerful questions. If not, here's a checklist with examples of *what to ask*. If you apply rigor to questioning, your hiring success rate will increase. You'll want to put these questions into your own words and add, delete, or change anything that is missing or doesn't quite fit for you. Nevertheless, you'll be headed in the right direction. These questions will help confirm, or not, the information you've gathered so far on your candidates and will help you gain greater insights into the candidate's skills, knowledge, and abilities from people who've observed the candidate in at least one other position.

Reference Check Sample Questions

- Verify references' relationships and how well they know the candidate by stating what you believe and asking, "Is that right?" (Examples: How closely did you work with Morgan? How would you compare your working style and Morgan's? What is/was it like to supervise Morgan? What would direct reports say about Morgan as a leader? What would peers say?)
- What are/were the candidate's primary responsibilities? (Examples: Could you share some examples of the work Morgan performed? What kinds of work did Morgan prefer to do? Prefer not to do?)
- What does success look like in your organization, and how do you think Morgan measures up to that standard? (Examples: On a scale of

1–6 with 1 low and 6 high, where would you score Morgan in overall performance? Why?)

- What are the candidate's most impressive skills or qualities? (Example: Where did Morgan shine? What is Morgan passionate about?)
- What was the candidate's most significant accomplishment? (Examples: What did Morgan do to help you do better? What stands out about Morgan?)
- How well developed are the candidate's emotional intelligence competencies? (Examples: How self-aware is Morgan about personal and professional strengths and weaknesses? How open is Morgan to change? How savvy is Morgan about the culture of your organization? What leadership competencies have you seen Morgan demonstrate?)
- How does the candidate respond to constructive feedback? (Example: What have you noticed about how Morgan responds to constructive feedback particularly when it's about something that needs improvement?)
- What are growth and development areas? (Examples: What do you think Morgan could learn that would make him/her stronger? How well does Morgan integrate the skills learned?)
- How does the candidate respond to having to do necessary but less desirable work? (Example: When was a time Morgan had to slog through something to get it done?)
- What kinds of situations have you seen the candidate go above and beyond? (Examples: When specifically has Morgan gone the extra mile? How has Morgan involved others in doing so?)
- What is the candidate looking for in a new role? (Examples: What insights do you have about what would be Morgan's ideal job? How well does this job seem to suit Morgan?)
- Who else would you suggest I speak with?
- Would you rehire the candidate? (Example: Why would you want to rehire Morgan? Why not?)
- Open question: What haven't I asked that you think I should have asked or should know?

On the other side of the coin are several things to watch out for during your reference-checking process.

Reference Check Cautions

- Do not take reference letters too seriously. While they can be illuminating, it's good to remember that the letter writers knew the candidate was going to read them.
- Wonderful qualities matter more when there are also quantifiable results behind them.
- Do not delegate the reference-checking process.
- If the reference will not provide answers to open-ended questions, get as many yes/no answers as you can, including: "Would you rehire this person if you could?"
- It is a red flag if the reference had no idea you were going to call.
- It is a red flag if you hear: "I'm not the best person to talk to you about 'Morgan.'"
- It is a red flag if all you hear are positives about the candidate—no one is perfect.
- Do not rely on only one or two of the A–H factors in asking your questions.
- Do not supply the reference giver with the answer you want to hear.
- Do not hesitate to circle back to the candidate to clarify discrepancies. If at any point during the reference check a reference tells you something that doesn't align with what the candidate said or provided, that is a warning.
- Do not interrupt—leave space for references to elaborate.
- If references refuse to offer you anything valuable, it may or may not be a warning—it could be a policy—ask why.
- Do not hesitate to seek out informal references by getting in touch with people in your network who also know the candidate, such as professional associations, past colleagues, or employees, as well as LinkedIn.

If you are concerned about the references' information, and you have checked in with the candidate about those concerns, and you still feel uncertain—*do not hire that person!* People giving references generally err on the positive side in their descriptions, so any hesitation or disconnects must be dealt with. One of the fatal flaws hiring leaders can make is to convince themselves that it's more important to hire someone with "a few" known issues quickly versus starting over. The fallout from this choice is nearly always far more pain than gain. Once in awhile you might get lucky, but don't count on it. Starting over may seem overwhelming but it's nothing compared to making a bad hire you will have to manage and then fire. The result is the same—you still have to start over, but in the meantime you've lost much more time, money, and productivity.

THE OFFER

Assuming you are satisfied with the results from references, you have verified the candidate's information, and there are no other show-stopping concerns, you are ready to make a formal offer to your top contender. Who makes the offer and how and when the offer is made are critical questions to get right if you want that great candidate to accept your offer and not back out or accept another offer from someone else.

Some hiring leaders and their organizations believe making an offer is like buying a car or a house. It is nothing like that—believe me! This is a relationship, not a simple transaction, and the way you do it will set the tone for the entire relationship—if there is to be one.

Paying attention to best job offer practices will increase your odds of getting that top candidate to agree to work for and with you. There are, of course, no guarantees, but putting your best foot forward is the right place to start. Making an offer is more like a partnership proposal. You are offering a position with a number of pieces and parts, and the person is offering everything within their A–H factors that they are willing and able to share with you. This is a relationship you both want to see succeed and one you believe will add value to your organization. It is not a one-way street where you are in the driver's seat, particularly when the skills you need are in high demand in the marketplace. The offer conversation needs to be a dialogue between the hiring leader and the candidate. So let's take a look at some best practices I believe will give you the best shot at landing a deal that will satisfy both parties in this partnership. Once you've made your initial offer, you may or may not find it necessary to negotiate with your candidate. We'll take a look at that next.

BEST PRACTICES

First I'm giving you a sequential list of my seven best practices followed by detailed explanations of each. You now have a short checklist from which you can select topics to explore or skip based on your own knowledge and experience.

* Pre-work
* Candidate expectations and requirements
* Using the "golden" and "platinum" rules
* Always call
* Make the offer
* After the call follow-up letter
* Staying connected

1. Pre-work: At the beginning of a well-organized search process, you'll have
   ✓ created the job description with all the requirements and preferences you need;
   ✓ defined a competitive salary range based on your organization's policies and market research for this skill set;
   ✓ determined any benefits, stock options, perks, bonuses, moving reimbursements, etc. you're willing and able to offer;
   ✓ received all preapprovals to hire within agreed upon expectations and boundaries; and
   ✓ established the timeline for the search process, including optimum offer date.
2. Candidate expectations and requirements:
   ✓ discuss, during interviews, the salient points about reporting, salary, benefits, culture, duties, and responsibilities, and answer candidate questions;
   ✓ gauge how aligned (or not) you are with candidates' expectations and requirements;
   ✓ share any nonnegotiable items upfront: if you *never* pay for a move, tell them; if you offer a signing bonus to offset expenses, tell them; and
   ✓ share your timeline so candidates know what to expect and when.

3. Using the "golden" and "platinum" rules—treat others as you would want to be treated (golden) and treat others as *they* wish to be treated (platinum)—because
   - ✓ it demonstrates compassion *and* empathy for the candidate in a high-stakes situation;
   - ✓ it is the right thing to do and the right way to do business;
   - ✓ top candidates will appreciate your openness and understanding; and
   - ✓ candidates who feel respected, heard, and understood are more likely to accept your offer and often with fewer negotiations.

4. Always call because
   - ✓ as the hiring leader it means more coming from you than anyone else; you have spent a fair amount of time with your top candidate and will likely be this person's direct supervisor; if you aren't the direct supervisor, make sure that person is in the room with you or makes the call;
   - ✓ it's personal and you're able to convey your excitement in both words and tone;
   - ✓ e-mails and letters are impersonal and waste time;
   - ✓ a call helps you gauge the level of enthusiasm of the selected candidate and quickly assess whether the candidate is delighted about the news or hesitant; and
   - ✓ even if an outsourced recruiter extends the offer, a call from the recruiter saves you precious time particularly if a candidate withdraws from the hiring process then and there versus waiting for a written response.

5. Make your offer . . .
   - ✓ as soon as possible after your due diligence because every delay risks having top candidates go elsewhere or wonder where they stand with you.
   - ✓ attractive to your top candidate at the outset so it is clear you are serious. Make your best offer after considering internal equity and the candidate's value within your range; allow for some negotiation if necessary. *The employer-employee relationship begins with the job offer, so make it positive and memorable.* When you make the offer, highlight the points that will appeal to your candidate immediately. Do not hold back, particularly if your top candidate is considering multiple offers.

✓ honestly—do not sugarcoat, be vague, or imply something you are not fully prepared to deliver. If you fail to deliver what you promised, you'll likely lose or demoralize your candidate *after the hire* and will have wasted resources while damaging your reputation as an employer.

✓ more than about the dollars. Today, many candidates are concerned with an array of benefits beyond salary, health, and retirement benefits; consider learning and development opportunities, title, relocation packages, signing bonuses, career advancement expectations, work/life integration, stock options, flex time and flex place, on-site amenities, paid time off (PTO), dress code, and community.[3] It pays to get to know your candidates before you make the offer: for instance, someone who needs to relocate will care more about moving expenses than someone who is local.

6. The follow-up written letter includes the following:

✓ all elements of the offer as appropriate: job title, base salary, benefits, overtime exempt or nonexempt status, pay dates (weekly, biweekly, monthly), vacation, holidays, perks, office space, equipment provided, and anything else you agreed to offer the candidate.

✓ terms and conditions on which the job is being offered, including any policies and conditions with which the candidate must comply before you will hire (i.e., any probationary period, US employment eligibility form I-9, background check, drug screening, nondisclosure agreements, non-compete agreements, intellectual property agreements, etc.).

✓ starting date and, where relevant, work schedule for this position.

✓ the location (division or department) where the candidate should report on the first day of work, and what the candidate should expect, such as formal paperwork, benefits enrollment, security considerations, keys, and such.

✓ clarity of "at-will employment." In every state, with the exception of Montana, employees are presumed to be at will, meaning they or the employer may terminate the employment relationship at any time, for any reason.[4] This does not apply to certain employment situations, like a formal contract for specific work and time period, or for some collective bargaining agreements.

✓ the statements you made in the verbal offer. You must ensure that you have included in the letter everything you have offered verbally.

✓ the name of the candidate's immediate supervisor/s and contact information.

✓ the deadline for a signed acceptance; two to three days for a response is typical for many positions. The time frame for an entry-level job may be a day or two, and for a mid- or senior-level candidate in a competitive market, or for a position that involves relocation, a week is not excessive.

✓ a review of your organizational values, culture, and work environment, and how these align with the stated goals of the candidate.

✓ signature space for both the hiring leader and the candidate signifying acceptance to the terms offered.

✓ More on the follow-up written letter: everything you verbally offered is sent in a high-priority e-mail (make sure you get notification when the e-mail is opened), or a printed letter that you mail with same or next day delivery. The terms of a job offer letter or contract are usually final. If the candidate decides to reopen the negotiations and make a counteroffer after receiving your letter, beware unless there is a very good reason—such as a misunderstanding of your verbal offer that can be cleared up quickly, or an extenuating circumstance that impacts a start date. If you suspect your offer is being used as a bargaining chip to get more from another employer, you may want to flat out ask, "I'm curious, is our offer in competition with others?"

7. Stay connected because

✓ you should have been well connected and communicating with the candidates throughout the process, so don't stop now at the most crucial time.

✓ you need to be readily available in case your candidate has questions, or in the event that you have to follow up on your offer. Stay in touch so it is clear you are genuine in wanting the candidate to join your team.

✓ it may differentiate you from other employers and help seal the deal.

✓ you want to be enthusiastic and, at the same time, avoid being pushy or appearing desperate.

✓ there are only two possibilities after you have made the call and sent the letter to the candidate; the letter or contract is signed and returned or not. If the deadline lapses without the candidate responding to the offer, it usually means your offer has not been accepted, and you may want to call to verify this is true.

A well-formulated letter template will help make sure you hit all the salient points of the offer and welcome all new hires with the right tone. I've drafted a sample for you to use as a starting point; it is included in the Resources section for this chapter.

NEGOTIATION

Before entering into negotiation with your top candidate, ask yourself these two important questions about your Best Alternative to a Negotiated Agreement, or as we fondly refer to it in labor negotiation terms, BATNA. Answering these two questions can prevent falling into the win/lose mind-set trap.

1. What will you have if you *don't* reach agreement?
2. Will what you have if you *don't* reach agreement *be better than* what you have if you *do* reach agreement?

A job offer also falls neatly into the category of *interest-based negotiations*. This is a process by which we separate people from the problem and focus on interests—not positions—to arrive at a mutually agreeable solution. I've included relevant parts of the framework I often use in *preparing for negotiations* with top candidates, even if it turns out to be unnecessary.

Separate People from the Problem

- Understand and discuss each person's point of view and perceptions—*know and be able to articulate yours.*
- Make proposals consistent with each person's values—*know and be able to articulate yours.*
- Seek to understand the other person first by listening carefully and acknowledging what is said.

Focus on Interests, Not Position

* Acknowledge each side's multiple interests.
* Be firm and flexible.
* Be hard on the problem, not on people.

Invent Options

* Brainstorm together; look at both the specific and general parts of any disparities.
* Identify shared interests, values and goals.
* Do what you can to make the other person's decision easy for them.

Still, negotiations with candidates are rarely predictable for either party. Preparing for this conversation and knowing what you will and will not do can make it more productive. In the end, though, how far you'll stretch depends on what is possible and how much you want this person to work for you. How far the candidate will stretch will depend on how much they want the job and what will work best for them. Candidates know that it's a lot easier to get the goodies upfront than to ask for them once they are on the job, so you shouldn't be surprised to hear some requests that are different from your original offer.

To help prevent some back-and-forth negotiation, be as clear as possible from the start about your pay range or your "not-to-exceed" salary budget while emphasizing any great benefits or perks, including quality of life amenities that are less tangible. This will weed out applicants early on who will not or cannot accept even your top dollar. Doing this results in fewer surprises and often prevents wasted time and effort on everyone's part.

It is common for candidates to expect a pay increase of at least 10 percent when changing jobs; when the job is a significant promotion, a lot more. Few top candidates will change jobs for the same or lower salary (barring unusual circumstances). A signing bonus is often offered by larger organizations, particularly to external candidates. If this is not an option for you, look for other ways to make your offer more attractive, like a performance bonus after six months or a base salary bump in one year.

Pitfall: It is a bad practice to pay internal candidates less than you would offer an external candidate. They will likely find out and resent it and you. Besides, it is a lousy thing to do.

Solution: If an internal person is your best-qualified, top choice, they deserve a salary that reflects that. Don't go low with people who are already on your payroll. Pay them what you would pay an outside candidate with similar qualifications and experience.

If you know a candidate's current salary, do not offer a salary below that unless there are truly compelling reasons to do so—and even then, think long and hard about it. If you have another good candidate in the wings that you know will accept less, perhaps it makes sense. Generally, though, a few thousand dollars in salary or perks is not going to make or break you over the tenure of this employee when they are a great hire. I'll say it again: don't be cheap—it just doesn't pay.

You will have made the timeline clear in the verbal offer and follow-up letter. People often need some time to think, as well as talk with family, friends, colleagues, and their current employer. If it's a formal contract, they may need to review it with an attorney. They also may not accept immediately because they don't want to appear too eager. In any case, you can still ask questions during your offer call like, "I completely understand . . . and still, would you mind sharing what you are thinking or what comes to mind right now about our offer?" If there is hesitation or you sense uncertainty, ask questions, without being pushy, to tease out any objections and/or to help you provide additional information that may make acceptance more likely.

To demonstrate empathy as well as helping your candidate think through next steps, you might ask about how they are feeling about leaving their current job. "How do you feel about giving notice after working there for the last few years?" "How do you think your current leader will react?" "What will be the easiest and the hardest parts of making this move for you?"

Even if the candidate is enthusiastic about your offer, change is difficult and will create some stress and anxiety. A new boss, new role, new everything makes changing jobs one of life's most stressful transitions.

If you are seriously concerned about the candidate's level of interest, or if they've asked for more time to decide, you might choose to ask this question: "We interviewed several other good candidates for this position, and as you're our first choice, we've made you an offer. Can I tell the others the job has been filled?" When lying might affect another person's livelihood, or someone who really wanted the job more than the selected candidate, not many people will lie about their intentions.

It is not unusual to discover that candidates who refuse a job offer did so because they accepted a counteroffer from their current employer. This happens more in a tight market when employers are desperate to hang on to their talent. Turnover in top talent is very costly. If a candidate has not yet signed your offer, don't eliminate your next candidate in the pipeline, if you have one. Even once the offer letter is signed, make sure to let your other viable candidates know if anything changes, you will call them immediately.

As I mentioned early on, this section is the largest of the three, precisely because when you do all you need to do to hire right, the rest is a lot easier, not less important, but easier. You now are likely to have the right person on board whom you wish to retain for a good long time. Your job as the hiring leader is to make darn sure you develop your newest "tribe" member, manage this person's performance, and encourage growth.

Here we are at the end of section A, "Acquisition = Hiring Right." The time has finally arrived. You have done a superb job in finding, wooing, and hiring your best candidate, and the start date is just around the corner. It's time to move on to section R, "Retention = Nurture Right" and explore one of your most important roles as a leader—to retain and develop the great talent you've just hired.

Section R

RETENTION =
NURTURE RIGHT

Chapter Six

Welcome Aboard!

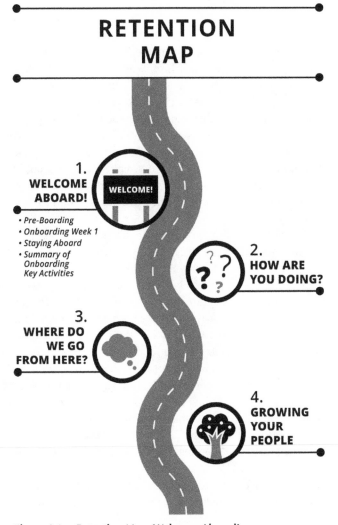

Figure 6.1. Retention Map: Welcome Aboard!

We want to focus on creating a memorable experience for the new hire in the first year rather than processing them in the first few weeks.

—Cheryl Hughey, Southwest Airlines

Great companies don't hire skilled people and motivate them; they hire already motivated people and inspire them.

—Simon Sinek

If I offered you a low to no-cost method to materially increase your odds of retaining your great new hire, would you jump at the chance? Step 1 on our Retention Map (figure 6.1) is the foundation for increasing those odds. When we don't count postage stamps, software you already have or need, lunches, and a company coffee cup or T-shirt, onboarding adds little direct expense to your business; it costs you time and effort, but the payoff is *huge!* Who doesn't want a lot of something for almost nothing? It's not a scam; it's reality, and you could be the winner. *Onboarding successfully is a critical bottom-line business strategy and must not be left to chance. It is as essential as recruiting and hiring right.*

Today formal onboarding programs are a true differentiator between great and not-so-great organizations, and yet, few do it well, and far too many don't do it at all. The range of onboarding efforts and programs different organizations offer can be as little as a single day (which is not onboarding at all), or a program lasting as long as two years. The latter often includes a professional development plan as well. Somewhere between nearly nothing and two years is likely your sweet spot.

My recommendation is to create a focused, well-considered onboarding plan for most positions to roll out for *at least six months*; an entire year is even better. Those months will tick away fast anyway; so it's in *your best interests* to make the new employee's time on the job work for you versus against you. Companies that excel at onboarding and employee retention experienced 2.5 times the revenue growth and 1.9 times the profit margin of companies who struggle with these two critical skills.[1]

There is a direct correlation between onboarding well, getting new employees up to speed quickly, and retaining top talent. The Aberdeen

Group, experts in human capital management, researched and benchmarked the performance of more than 644,000 companies. Their research relied on more than 2.5 million people in over 40 countries, 90 percent of the Fortune 1,000, and 93 percent of the Technology 500. The Aberdeen Group found that best-in-class companies had 62 percent of their new hires meet their first performance milestone on time, and 91 percent of those employees were still part of the company after their first year. In contrast, the worst-performing companies only had 17 percent of their employees meet their first milestone on time, and only 30 percent of them remained at the end of the first year.[2]

Here are two more statistics that may shock you. A recent study by Leadership IQ says that 46 percent of new hires fail within eighteen months! Perhaps more surprising is that 81 percent of those fail due to a *cultural bad fit*.[3] Broadcasting your culture in multiple ways during recruitment, hiring, and onboarding will ensure your new hire has a very clear picture of who you are and how you operate day to day.

Some companies are really serious about making sure there is "culture fit" with their candidates. They only want people to work for them who will flourish within the company's culture. Zappos, for example, offers a five-week course focused on the culture and values of the company. At the end of the five weeks, they *offer employees several thousand dollars to quit* if the company culture is not the right fit for them. Zappos clearly believes if it's not a good fit, it will impact engagement and ultimately performance.[4] This also means they believe their hires are mostly successful, but just in case, here's a "get out of jail free card." If an employee doesn't want them, they don't want that employee.

Having a formal onboarding process that reinforces your company culture can result in

- 60 percent greater annual improvement in revenue per full-time employee and
- 63 percent greater annual improvement in customer satisfaction than those with an informal onboarding process.[5]

I hope you will agree that these are compelling statistics that make a strong case for taking onboarding seriously and making it a core part of your staffing and talent management strategy.

There is a relatively new term out there in the workplace. It's called a "ghost hire." These are people who have accepted your job offer but fail to show up on the first day. They may or may not tell you why, and sometimes they don't even let you know they are not coming. In a tight job market, the job abandonment phenomenon increases. Anything you can do to ensure your top pick doesn't change her mind, and/or get lured away by someone else, is absolutely worth the effort.[6] Beyond being somewhat embarrassing, wasting many hours for many people, and up-ending your business plans, ghost hires are expensive. I'm certain you would want to do anything you can to prevent this happening to you.

A close cousin to a ghost hire is the person who shows up for work feeling excited about the new job and then, without warning, fails to return on day two. I call those people the "show-and-go" folks. There could be several reasons for this; and one of them is about the way they were treated on that first day. I know of even more "show-and-go" people who left their job within the first ninety days. While onboarding well cannot prevent all "ghosts" or "show-and-go" situations, you'll know you did all you could to keep them.

As we delve into the meat and potatoes of your onboarding program, you will find many suggestions intended to provide employees access to and understanding of your people, culture, and position in a variety of ways.

Let's reverse roles for a moment. Imagine *you* have been heavily recruited, have been offered a fair salary and maybe some perks, are looking forward to the challenges of this new position, and arrive on the job site to find that you have no place to sit, or worse, no one in the office is expecting you. Yup, that happened to me, not once but twice! I had to find, furnish, and/or build my own office to make sure I had a space to work—*after I arrived*. This happened for the simple reason that no one was in charge of preparing for my arrival and making sure I felt welcome during my first day or first week, for that matter. You can do better, I'm sure!

Giving candidates a warm welcome should be included in all steps of the search process, beginning with recruitment. Once you have se-lected your top candidate, create a plan for *pre-boarding* this person, *the first weeks*, plus *ongoing, memorable and welcoming opportuni-ties* that integrate the new person into your culture quickly and with success.

The first day *is a big moment* for you and your new employee, and it's important to get it right. It's not just the extensive research that informs us about the need to onboard well; it's about being human. Believing we belong is a primal human motivator. For instance, the need to belong can and does drive people to do both positive and negative things they would not do on their own, in the absence of social or peer pressure. Gangs, social justice movements, rallies and marches, cults, and go-fund-me drives, for example, all get people, often strangers, acting together for a shared purpose.

Humans instinctively know we cannot make it far or live long in complete isolation from others. That understanding creates a powerful incentive to fit in, be part of a "tribe," and join with other humans to support and belong to something bigger than oneself. This invisible, magnetic pull is a clarion call for survival of the species, and *nothing beats survival as a motivator.* So let's begin the process of integrating the newest member of your "tribe."

You may have an onboarding process in place that works for you. The first question you might ask yourself is this: "How do I know it's working well for our new staff members and us?" You can discover a lot by asking new hires, at various intervals, to share their onboarding experiences and ask for ideas about what they would do differently if *they were designing* onboarding for new hires. You might consider asking people within their first year to be part of a standing team for the onboarding program. Fresh eyes and recent experiences within your workplace are likely to be timely and helpful, often even more than suggestions from someone who has been on the inside for a long time. A new hire who leaves within the first eighteen months can provide more and different insights, particularly if you offer a confidential exit interview.

If you decide your onboarding isn't robust enough, or if you're not sure, I'll provide you with checklists for onboarding best practices to which you can compare, contrast, and adapt as you see fit. Assuming you're interested and ready, you can begin your crash course in onboarding now.

Let's begin with goals and *the four C's of onboarding new staff*:

1. *Culture*: provide new employees with information about "how we do things here," both informal and formal.

2. *Connection*: establish interpersonal relationship opportunities and information protocols through experiences and relevant processes.
3. *Clarification*: provide clear expectations for the first week, month, six months, and year that are related to the position and provide the necessary tools and support to ensure success.
4. *Compliance*: educate new employees on regulations, legalities, ethics, values, and both procedures and policies that impact the work and them personally.

This is a broad brush as goals should be. The rest of the story fills in the blanks with details.

> **Pitfall:** Don't fall into the trap of thinking that onboarding begins when the employee arrives to work the first day. Most employees are anxious to learn as much as they can about their new organization and the people they will work with *before* they arrive.
>
> **Solution:** Use virtual technology and other means of communication to connect and engage your new hire with you and other employees from the moment your offer is formally accepted.

Welcoming new employees to your workplace begins long *before* the first day on the job. There are a number of actions that can and should be done well in advance of arrival, all of which will make the transition smoother and, at the same time, send a strong "we're glad you're joining us" message. This is the objective of the "Pre-boarding" process. Following pre-boarding is "Week 1," which focuses on a positive arrival and settling in. An ongoing program for onboarding—I'm calling it "Staying Aboard"—is intended to help you fully achieve the four "C" goals.

PRE-BOARDING

Planning for your new arrival should be intentional versus ad hoc. Pre-boarding procedures need to be put in place well ahead of time. Much like you did with your Search Team, choose the right people to be your Onboarding Team, people who are willing and able to make that first day, and beyond, both helpful and meaningful for this brand-new person. Consider incorporating cross-functional and cross-departmental members onto your team to help new hires get exposure to a broader swath of your organization. If you already have software in a human resource information system (HRIS) or an in-house talent management system (TMS), put either or both to good use in setting up your new staff member in your systems before they arrive.

As soon as you have a signed offer letter or contract, and before your new employee arrives, pre-boarding begins. The Pre-boarding Checklist will help you get going in the right direction.

Pre-boarding Checklist

✓ Send a copy of the offer letter or contract signed by you *and* the candidate.

✓ Send a *handwritten welcome note* from the hiring leader and/or new supervisor that arrives in the mail—with a stamp on it. This is unusual today and a very meaningful gesture that takes under two minutes to do.

✓ Send a welcome packet that includes information on the organization's history, values, culture, and an agenda for the first day (or more) with connections you've scheduled, including names, contact numbers, e-mail addresses, and locations with explanations. Send any additional materials that you know will help new people navigate your organization.

✓ Provide an explanation of what the employee should expect on the first day, first week, and first month of work.

✓ Provide any organizational videos that would be helpful to understand your culture.

✓ Include logistics for the first day such as where to park (provide a parking permit if needed), where to arrive, dress code, lunch plans, and such.

✓ Provide access to a portal or link, if available, to complete necessary documentation and forms prior to arrival.

✓ Send a fun questionnaire to help the rest of the team get to know this new person a little better before they come onboard.

✓ Provide access to appropriate intranet portals for internal events or announcements.

✓ Ensure access details are finalized, and add the new employee to any automated systems you use for things like payroll, benefits, parking, onboarding, security, signature authority, and IT setup that will go into effect *on the day they begin* working for you.

✓ Announce the new employee's arrival in meetings and e-mail as appropriate.

✓ Make sure the new employee's workspace is known, prepared, and set up properly.

✓ Set up a plan for a "culture welcome" and tour of your worksite, interesting things to know, and things to be aware of.

✓ Set up a series of introductions to people who will help your new hire feel welcome and get a good overview of how this job connects to others' roles in the organization.

✓ Provide all necessary materials specific to legal, regulatory, company rules, policies, and procedures in writing; offer to answer any questions prior to coming on board.

ONBOARDING: WEEK 1

Make the first day memorable! While this isn't your first "date," it is the first time you've brought your new employee into your "tribe." It is your job to make sure that first day and the weeks to follow are memorable and welcoming in every way; it makes a huge difference in shortening the time it takes to integrate a new person into your team and increase your retention success rate.

The first day and into the first week of anything worth doing is worth doing well! Onboarding your new staff member is no exception. Regardless of the role—from front line to senior management, take a moment to imagine what it must feel like to be in this new person's shoes, particularly for an external hire.

She is wondering how to fit in and eager to learn what is expected and what success looks like to her new boss. In those first days, she is figuring out "how they do things here." Your culture will be new and most likely different from her previous one. While she may have met a number of people in the interview process, that experience is nothing like integrating into the actual group dynamics of an intact team and working with them. On top of this, she may have just moved her whole life to a new town or city with all that entails.

As she comes on board, consider any upcoming events or activities that are at the core of living your culture and what roles your new employee could play. If you've hired her into a leadership position, a frontline experience might be useful to encourage "managing by walking around," for example, being taught how to do the job of a key hourly employee position or answering customer concerns in a call center. Perhaps she could help a team set up for a holiday party, or be asked to recognize employees at a celebration for years of service. If she isn't in a leadership role, consider giving her smart "shadowing" opportunities with other leaders to experience how they carry out their roles.

That first week is full of information and experiences; it's a lot for anyone to take in, so let's make her transition as seamless and positive as possible. You've invested time, money, and effort into this hire, and I know for sure you want and need to make it stick. The "Week 1 Checklist" will help get you on your way.

Week 1 Checklist

✓ On day 1, have someone meet and greet your new employee. Consider a welcome basket with snacks or a gift like a coffee mug, company T-shirt, or other meaningful cultural gestures. Take care to communicate and answer questions about housekeeping items, like location of the restroom, break room, copy machine, and the workspace; ensure all necessary equipment is reviewed and working properly.

✓ On day 1, make sure your new employee will know where to eat lunch and make sure someone goes along—eating alone isn't welcoming. This is a positive and informal social engagement opportunity, and it's one you should take seriously.

✓ On day 1 or day 2, the hiring leader should have the job expectations conversation. Make it clear how the role fits into the overall goals of the organization and why it is important. Provide any necessary hands-on training with coaching and support.

✓ Plan at least one memorable event that is welcoming and speaks to your unique culture. Ideas for this might range from a weeklong "boot camp," to a formal mentoring partnership dinner, to an afternoon with your CEO.

✓ Pair your new employee with someone, or even better, more than one person who may or may not be on your Onboarding Team. This person (or group) should be positive, knowledgeable, and willing to make the effort to be available. Whomever you choose will be available to be a guide, answer questions, advise them, and help them get to know others in an informal way.

✓ If you have pre-boarded well, you can focus on what the employee needs on the first day and in the first week versus getting bogged down in paperwork. Still there may be some necessary details, so ensure you have anything that needs doing on the first day and in the first week lined up and organized.

✓ Create FAQ sheets regarding the general office and culture (i.e., whether there is a "dress-down Friday," whether pets are allowed, etc.), how to log on to systems, and the person to contact for different functional areas. If available, share access to online training videos and apps.

✓ Schedule tours of your facilities and/or virtual offices. This must happen the first week or within the first two weeks, or it might not happen at all. People get busy! Floor plans or maps and phone lists with pictures of employees are helpful so new hires can match faces to names and see where people are located.

✓ If there are other new employees joining at a similar time, gather them together so they can share stories and questions and have a sense of camaraderie.

✓ Provide your new hire with a "map" of your full onboarding process with timelines, milestones, and other relevant information.

✓ Within the first few weeks, involve senior leaders. Set up one-on-one interactions with leaders your new hire needs to know. This is an onboarding step employees really appreciate.

STAYING ABOARD

At this point in your new employee's tenure, a lot has happened to help them feel welcomed into your culture, and she is settling into her new job. If you look over the Pre-boarding and Week 1 checklists to find outlays of cash, you won't find much. Outlays of time, attention, and effort are what this costs you.

Onboarding does not stop here. Remember the four "C" goals: culture, connection, clarification, and compliance. By now you have touched on all four and done a great job with compliance and clarification. It's important to remember that culture and connection are the two goals that, when achieved, will be more likely to keep your great new hire engaged, believing they belong, and producing in the months and years ahead.

To help you plan your "Staying Aboard" milestones, let's look at month 1, months 3–6, and the first year.

Month 1: It is important to formally check in. Assuming you have an Onboarding Team, it's their job to ensure regular follow-ups and check-ins with the new employee, the work team, perhaps Human Resources (HR), and you. Having more than one work buddy gives new hires a breadth of perspectives as well as depth of support. The check-in should assess engagement and satisfaction, allow for back-and-forth feedback, and answer questions that have arisen. Early on, provide any training your new hire needs to be successful and productive.

Months 3–6: Check in again, show you care, get feedback, and address any pain points that arise. Continue to provide accessibility to a work buddy (or buddies) or a mentor, keep the dialogue going, and really listen and adapt as much as you can to what the new hire is telling you.

The first year: It takes a full year for a new hire to "learn the ropes" of their new role, assimilate into your culture, and experience various business cycles that impact their job. After a year, they are shifting from learning the job to ongoing development. It is also the time for a discussion about next steps for their career growth. And finally, it is essential to have the conversation about everything during this year that has gone well for them and your organization and what goals and challenges lie ahead.

You will need to apply rigor when creating plans to keep your onboarding momentum positive and productive. If you have the means, integrate an employee portal with workforce management software to help you and your employees keep track of onboarding progress; this portal could also serve as a central repository for common questions about your policies, procedures, templates, and such.

In my book, *Lead Like It Matters . . . Because It Does*,[7] there is an entire section devoted to building the skills and using tools to achieve "team mastery" as a leader. I share this now because building a strong team is every leader's responsibility and reward, and because a great onboarding program that includes team building will quickly increase employee engagement and productivity. And that, of course, will increase employee retention.

When a new person joins your team, the entire dynamic shifts. Any change in the makeup of your team has the same effect, coming or going. Each new personality, set of skills, and individual motivations create a ripple effect within your team. You will want those ripples to work for you. This is why I recommend including regular team-building sessions as an essential part of your formal onboarding process. It helps everyone get to know each other, create shared ground rules or rules of engagement, and work together on common goals for a shared purpose.

If you are a leader of leaders, your new team member, as a leader, will experience you modeling team-building activities. With encouragement from you, this will create an incentive for your newly hired leader to do the same with their new team of direct reports and get started on the right foot.

Building social connections at work has a strong impact on employee engagement, which is an important measure of a successful onboarding program. There is no better way to integrate a new employee than to involve the entire Onboarding Team in activities that result in that person feeling welcomed, included, and valued. After all, you hired this person for a good reason!

So, is it working? Is all this effort paying off? To know, you have to ask. It's that simple. It is important to get feedback from your new hires, as well as your Onboarding Team. According to the Society for Human Resource Management, nearly 90 percent of new hires make up their minds about whether they want to stay with the company within the *first six months*.[8] This is why I recommend your onboarding program spans at least six months, and preferably the first full year, during the period your new employee will experience a twelve-month business cycle.

That means engaging them proactively to understand what's working or not for each of your new hires. You want to learn early enough in the process and continue to check in so you can address any issues that arise. Many people are reluctant to give their boss feedback even about their own onboarding experience. The Motley Fool, a financial and investing advice company, tackled this problem by creating "feedback coaches" who are trained to listen, coach, and truly understand the issue at hand and, additionally, to remove fear from the conversation.[9]

You need regular, honest, constructive feedback from your employees. Here are a few ways to reach out without scaring them:

- Ask open-ended questions, such as, "If you were in charge of onboarding what would you do differently for new employees that would make it better?"
- Ask multiple people to request feedback from your new employees. This might be a trusted HR manager, one or more of your Onboarding Team members, or a formal "feedback coach." These folks regularly check in with your new employee to learn what is and is not working well for them and where support or change would be helpful.
- If you have an online employee intranet or portal, use it to create a space for 100 percent anonymous feedback and surveys.

Pitfall: Asking new employees for feedback, including satisfaction or culture surveys, and then doing nothing about the good or bad news people share is dangerous. If your employees believe giving you feedback is pointless, they will be frustrated, share less with you in the future, and probably have a lower opinion of you as a leader.

Solution: Only ask for feedback if you are prepared to acknowledge the feedback, at the very least, and take action wherever possible, all the while being transparent in your communications and actions.

To prevent the loss of your best new employees, make sure your onboarding program will help them become quickly engaged, acclimated to your culture, the new job, and your team. Get creative! With your Onboarding Team, look for fresh ideas to go above and beyond the traditional so you will have a positive and measurable impact on your new staff member's sense of well-being. Check out your competition to learn what they are doing with onboarding, and then figure out how to do it better. It doesn't have to be splashy or huge. It needs to be consistent and authentic, and it should include many small things that add up to a positive experience within and about your workplace, an experience you can be sure your employees will share with others.

The days of "plenty of people would love to have your job" and taking employees for granted are long gone. Great hires simply don't have to and won't work for an organization that doesn't do a good job with recruiting and onboarding. If they don't "ghost" you, you still risk losing great hires—the "show and go" people—who won't stay long when they don't feel welcome.

As we have discovered, onboarding is an ongoing process, not a one-time event. During this time, key milestones should be identified along the way. It isn't just about the new hire feeling great about you, the team, and the workplace; it's about his being productive and delivering the results you need and expect. Pay particular attention to tasks that happen in various cycles throughout the year and make sure someone knowledgeable is available to train, support, and even partner to help with new projects or tasks. Focused training and shadowing also can be useful when the work assigned is completely unfamiliar to your new hire.

You will need to adjust your program for each new employee based on the position, and all onboarding applies to both external and internal hires. For an internal hire, you'll need to adjust based on how familiar the person is with your people, culture, and the job at hand. Still, a new job with a new boss and new team is a big deal, particularly for internal transitions. Here are some examples:

- New leaders experiencing their first management position
- Promotions to roles with greater responsibility
- Leaders moving from a role with limited authority to one of broader influence
- Leaders managing employees who were formerly their peers
- People moving to a new division, a new location, and especially those making global moves

Your onboarding program must be designed to be inclusive of individuals in all kinds of transitions. While the design may vary, and should vary, your onboarding four "C" goals remain the same: culture, connection, clarification, and compliance.

You might find it useful to have a bulleted summary list of key activities for each phase of onboarding: Pre-boarding, Week 1, and Staying Aboard.

SUMMARY OF ONBOARDING KEY ACTIVITIES

Pre-boarding

- Onboarding team
- Set up in HRIS or TMS systems
- Paperwork completed
- Welcome packet
  - Business and culture information
  - Logistics for day 1
  - Expectations of role
  - Compliance information
- Announcements to organization
- Meetings and tour setup
- Workspace identification and setup
- Memorable events plan

Week 1

- Meet and greet
- Welcome gift
- Onboarding guides
- Lunch plan
- Tours and logistics
- Expectations clarified
- Building social connection
- Opportunities to be seen and heard
- Memorable events
- Senior leader involvement

Staying Aboard

- Getting feedback and taking action
- Check-ins
- Team building
- Training
- Projects with appropriate support
- Shadowing
- Building social connection

- Senior leader involvement
- Opportunities to learn about other areas

Now that you have onboarding down to a science and in alignment with your culture, it's time to make sure you and your new staff member are on the same page with job expectations, how you will measure this person's success, and how job performance will be acknowledged. Let's explore these questions by heading over to chapter 7, "How Are You Doing?"

Chapter Seven

How Are You Doing?

Figure 7.1. Retention Map: How Are You Doing?

Leadership is not being in charge, it is about taking care of people in your charge.

—Simon Sinek

This quote from Simon Sinek is an important shift in mind-set for some leaders and moves us into step 2 on our Retention Map (see figure 7.1). Making that shift, though, is a key factor in retaining your best people and a bottom line issue. Keeping that great new hire engaged, productive, and wanting to continue being a member of your "tribe" is the goal. Once you've made the hire and rolled out a successful onboarding program, it can be tempting to slip into a comfort zone and stop paying enough focused attention to retention. Let's make sure that doesn't happen.

When you nurture your culture and your employees, you get the same results as when you nurture your garden—*your people will grow and put down firm roots.*

Working with all types of organizations over the last twenty-five years or so, I have concluded that employee engagement has been one of the most sought-after results senior executives want to increase in their companies, agencies, schools, and such. My clients know that *engaged employees are more productive and successful than disengaged employees,* which in turn *results in higher retention* rates and a *better bottom line.*

While turnover is a fact of life, and some turnover is healthy, losing your best employees is a crushing blow to any enterprise. Preventable reasons people leave play a big part in unwanted turnover of your best people. In an extensive and powerful employee study published in 2019 by Work Institute, they provide the top ten reasons people are leaving their jobs. You can familiarize yourself with a treasure trove of workplace realities in their free downloadable report. One of the many findings is that a whopping 77 percent of the top ten reasons are *voluntary and preventable turnover* factors, as noted by a checkmark in the following list.[1]

1. Career development ✓
2. Work environment ✓
3. Management behavior ✓
4. Job characteristics ✓

5. Compensation and benefits ✓
6. Work-life balance ✓
7. Well-being ✓
8. Relocation
9. Retirement
10. Involuntary

I believe every one of these seven voluntary and preventable turnover factors has a strong connection to employee engagement in the workplace. Five of the seven factors checked are obvious, but even discussions about someone's compensation and benefits require positive and productive employee and leader engagement. Every workplace needs some kind of an employee development system to make sure everything that can be done to retain top talent is being done. If you have a system in place that is working for you, great! You might want to compare and contrast yours with the system I'm providing here. If you have little or nothing in place, you'll soon have what you need to get you well on your way.

EMPLOYEE DEVELOPMENT SYSTEM (EDS)

It turns out that employee engagement isn't all that complicated, nor is it more time consuming if you are already an attentive leader, but it does require each leader's direct and focused attention. Employee engagement can be boiled down to these four essentials:

- An organization people are proud to work for
- Trustworthy leadership
- Positive and supportive work environment
- Job and career satisfaction

An engaged workforce routinely produces these four results:

- Productive and financially healthy organizations
- High-performance teams and workforce
- Committed employees
- Satisfied and loyal stakeholders

Who wouldn't want all that? This chapter will introduce you to my Employee Development System (EDS), one I am certain you will readily understand and can adapt as needed to suit your culture. It is laser focused on three of the employee engagement factors: *trustworthy leadership, creating a positive and supportive work environment, and job and career satisfaction.* Since I have no way of knowing whether your enterprise is one in which people feel proud to be working, we will focus on the other three employee engagement factors.

Let's take a look at your new hire. This is a person you spent a lot of time, money, and effort acquiring and now spent even more time onboarding. A little later in this chapter, the focus will be on you, the leader.

Your workplace may have a talent management system (TMS), human resource information system (HRIS), or other similar technology to keep track of employee demographics, skill sets, onboarding, training and development, milestones, productivity, and performance, among other things. These tools can be very useful in helping you manage a lot of information in one place. Everything we're going to explore fits into *any technology* you may have *and no technology* if you don't.

EDS addresses engagement by creating a strong, open communication connection and relationship between the employee and the leader immediately, and by setting up each employee to succeed at the new job within a supportive work environment.

There are three things everyone, everywhere, needs to know about their job:

1. Expectations: What exactly is expected of me to be successful here, and what learning is expected and necessary to ensure success?
2. Measurement: What metrics are being used to measure my success, and how will I get feedback on my performance based on those metrics?
3. Acknowledgment of Performance: How will my performance be acknowledged—whether positive or negative?

For example, if you have a TMS or HRIS of some kind in your workplace, *expectations* will slide neatly into a number of buckets: training and development, deadlines, and milestones, and such. *Measurement* matches up with things like goals setting, productivity metrics, and actual results. A*cknowledgment of performance* would be part of your scheduled performance and compensation conversations, including achievements and milestones met or missed.

IMPLEMENTING EDS

The good news is this: you do not need specialized technology to implement my system for engaging and retaining great staff; you do need *personal commitment, consistency, and rigor.* Success for any EDS depends on the leader having the discipline to be laser focused on each part of the system at the right times. My EDS is simple, clear, and comprehensive, all of which you will now have at your fingertips.

An overview graphic of the Employee Development System begins our journey (see figure 7.2). You'll notice the arrows are moving clockwise around the circle. This is a dynamic versus linear process. At any

Figure 7.2.   Employee Development System

point in time, you may decide to revisit original expectations, or the metrics for success, or how best to acknowledge performance based on any changes in expectations and/or measurements. More good news: everything about EDS can, and I hope will, be applied *to everyone on your staff*, not just your new hire.

Arguably, all of this is common sense. The fact that it makes sense, however, does not mean it is common practice. Engaging employees in the right ways can more readily become common practice when leaders have a blueprint to follow. Many of us know what works and doesn't from our own experiences. My hope is that you will be able to close the cover of this book and feel confident that you have everything you need to institute an EDS in your own workplace that will increase retention and results for you and your staff.

Let's look at the EDS framework. We will begin at the beginning and roll it out one arrow at a time (see figures 7.3, 7.4, and 7.5).

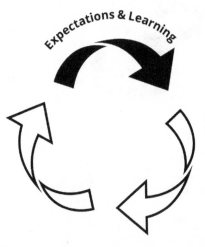

Figure 7.3. Employee Development System: Expectations and Learning

Step 1: Define—Expectations and Learning

Staff member: Make sure you know what is expected of you to achieve success.

- Understand organizational and departmental mission, vision, and values.
- Fully understand your position description.

- Ask for explicit expectations of you in this role, including cultural expectations.
- Request educational opportunities to develop needed skills as appropriate.
- Understand all the competencies you are expected to demonstrate.
- Ask for training and development you believe you need to be successful.
- If in doubt, ask!

Leader: Ensure your staff members know exactly what is expected of them and create opportunities for them to develop themselves and their skills.

- Share your mission, vision, and values.
- Create a comprehensive position description.
- Clarify expectations and goals including cultural expectations.
- Create an Individual Development Plan (IDP).
- Work the Individual Development Plan (IDP) with your staff member.

Figure 7.4. Employee Development System: Measurement and Feedback

Step 2: Deliver—How Performance Will Be Measured and Shared

Staff Member: Make sure you know how you are doing. Ask for specific success metrics over which you have control. Keep your leader informed about progress on specific goals and ask for feedback.

Leader: Make sure your staff members consistently know *exactly* how they are doing.

- Provide access to awareness and assessment tools used for developmental purposes only—*never for performance management.*
- Provide clear department- and job-specific metrics the employee can control.
- Provide clear behavioral metrics the employee can control.
- Ask for customer, peer, team, direct report, and supervisor feedback as appropriate.
- Give your staff member ongoing constructive feedback about both positive and negative behaviors and actions.
- Ask for constructive feedback about your supervision of your staff member.
- Ask your staff member how you can best support individual development and success.
- Monitor progress on measurable goals within an IDP.

Figure 7.5. Employee Development System: Acknowledging Performance

Step 3: Debrief—Acknowledge the Impact of Performance

Staff member: Accept personal responsibility for meeting or exceeding expectations and make sure you understand the consequences of exceeding, meeting, or not meeting the expectations for your position.

Leader: Acknowledge the performance of your staff member, document success and concerns, and follow thorough appropriately.

- Catch people doing things right!
- Provide at least an annual Personal Dialogue (PD) based on agreed upon clear expectations and metrics, with at least quarterly feedback discussions.
- Recognize and reward accomplishments.
- Follow through in a timely manner with the appropriate acknowledgment.
- Engage with the staff member regularly and monitor progress.
- Discuss and document performance highlights and/or concerns.
- Communicate with clarity the positive and/or negative consequences of performance.

For each of these steps, there are some helpful questions you can answer to get to ensure the EDS process is clear for you and your direct report.

Define—What Are the Expectations and Learning for Success?

Questions:

- Why is this work important?
- Who is accountable for what and to whom?
- What are the expected results?
- When are results expected?
- What other information or additional resources or learning are required to be successful?

Assigning Work

- Set clear expectations and goals.
- Assign roles and provide appropriate resources and access.
- Reconcile priorities and priority conflicts.

Accepting Work

- Ask questions to ensure clarity.
- Commit to shared goals.

*Deliver — How Will Performance Be Measured and
Feedback Shared?*

Questions:

* How is success going to be measured?
* What are the checkpoints or milestones for progress?
* What are the quantitative measurements/metrics?
* What are the qualitative measurements/metrics?
* Are these metrics within the employee's control?

Assigning Work

* Measure progress and results consistently.
* Provide support and maintain *appropriate* oversight.
* Expect and then recognize execution.

Accepting Work

* Care about results.
* Take ownership for behavior and results.
* Ask for help and/or resources when needed.
* Ask questions to get clarity.

Debrief — What Is the Impact of This Person's/Team's Performance?

Questions:

* What is the actual impact, and what are the results?
* What are the consequences + or − to the individual or team?
* What are the results?
* What is the appropriate constructive feedback?
* How are the results tied to performance metrics and success?

Assigning Work

* Review results and provide constructive feedback.
* Tie results to performance.

Accepting Work

- Take personal responsibility for behaviors, actions, and results within your control.
- Ask for feedback.
- Clarify any questions that arise.

EDS Implementation Actions

Depending on your internal structure, a Human Resources (HR) professional or someone from your Organizational Development Department may be able to help you work with leaders and departments to implement EDS in a customized way. There are some natural steps that, while fluid, should be internally consistent throughout departments and with leaders as they move through their own implementation process. You can use these action steps as a guide:

1. *Define purpose and roles:* for the senior leader, director, leadership group, implementation group, for example, and communicate these roles and the EDS process to all staff.
2. *Assess:* scope, barriers, definition of desired norms and gaps, opportunities, and possibilities of increased capacity. This is ongoing and not linear.
3. *Readiness:* of the leadership and all staff; create EDS learning sessions and reality checks.
4. *Customize:* blend values—department and division (if needed), department-specific and job-specific competencies
5. *Educate staff on EDS tools*: provide ongoing constructive feedback, Personal Dialogue (PD) training, Individual Development Plans (IDPs), 360s, customer surveys, stakeholder metrics, and such.
6. *Implement*: pilot the EDS implementation, review the process, evaluate, and make necessary changes.
7. *Ongoing integration:* hire the right staff; acknowledge performance; recognize and reward; conduct appropriate and timely discipline; plan for succession; introduce institutionalized communication structures; provide feedback, periodic measurements, reviews, and improvements; and look for continuous improvement in the process and outcomes.

Once you have EDS in place, every participating department will have an EDS process appropriate for their employees. The outcome should be, at a minimum, that every employee will have a properly conducted annual (minimum) Personal Dialogue—a two-way conversation focused on results, new and/or continued expectations, goals, career development, and values-based actions and behaviors that will lead to professional success.

Here's an example of a company integrating organizational values as part of the performance process. Do you remember our Widget Company? We used the example of integrity as one of the core values this company wanted to instill and measure to ensure success. In customizing the Widget Company's EDS, organizational values are defined and behaviors that demonstrate the company's values are assessed as part of the Personal Dialogue process.

Example: Integrity: do the right thing, every single time, whether or not it is popular, profitable, convenient, comfortable, or known.

All Staff

- Listens to and acts upon constructive feedback about her/himself without trying to justify her/his behavior.
- Takes personal responsibility for her/his actions.
- Admits her/his own mistakes.
- Personal feelings and/or relationships do not interfere with doing the right thing.

For All Staff and Especially for Supervisors

- Follows through on commitments—can be depended upon.
- Effectively uses legitimate power/authority.
- Demonstrates professional attitudes and behaviors at work and with all staff.
- Regularly asks for constructive feedback.
- Holds self and all staff accountable for her/his performance.
- Is trusted to do the right thing.

You now have a framework to guide you as you implement EDS in your workplace and with each of your staff members. In the Resources section for this chapter, there is a sample of an Individual Development Plan (IDP). The Personal Dialogue questions are also available in the Resources section for chapter 8. Once implemented and tested, you will have an honest, transparent, and well-understood process upon which you can objectively acknowledge performance. This results in a high level of engagement and accountability on your and your staff members' parts. It may help to ask yourself the following questions to ensure all the bases have been covered:

1. Have my direct report and I had an *explicit* conversation about expectations?
2. Did my direct report and I establish qualitative and quantitative measurements/metrics to which we have mutually agreed and for which he/she is prepared to be accountable?
3. How do I, as the leader, acknowledge the performance of this individual?
4. Have I and other leaders kept our promises to this individual?

Of course, you can, and I hope you will, ask the very same questions about your teams. It is consistent, easily understood, and reaps great benefits for your organization to use the same EDS process with all of your teams—what is expected of our team, how will we measure team success, and how will we acknowledge team performance?

To increase your chances of retaining great staff, use the Leader's Retention Checklist.

Leader's Retention Checklist

✓ Effectively utilize the *hiring right* process to recruit and hire only those people who share your organizational values and demonstrate the A–H factors.

✓ Mindfully onboard new staff over many months and continuously engage current staff.

✓ Explicitly establish job expectations with specific measurements/metrics for each staff member's performance and reward and hold people accountable by acknowledging performance.

✓ Ensure each staff member fully participates in the EDS.

✓ Conduct annual Personal Dialogues and provide regular ongoing feedback.

✓ Create a transparent and trusting atmosphere, free of fear.

✓ Own the culture and morale of your group.

✓ Share your vision.

✓ Pull rather than push change by fostering engagement; encourage an agile response to change and utilize a transparent change process.

✓ Empower staff to take well-reasoned risks and create opportunities to learn and grow.

✓ Communicate decision-making protocols for each decision affecting staff.

✓ The buck stops with you; take responsibility for your group's outcomes.

✓ Build, model, encourage, and reward teamwork and collaboration.

✓ Reward what you want; do not reward or ignore what you do not want.

✓ Design every meeting for maximum staff engagement and effectiveness.

✓ Model an integrated work and personal life.

If you would like to measure your employees' engagement levels, I have provided a sample survey in the Resources section for this chapter that you may use as is or modify to suit your culture and circumstances. Another option is to purchase one from the marketplace such as the Gallup Q[12] Employee Engagement Survey.[2] Thoughtfully create employee engagement questions that matter to you and your organization using examples I've provided to get you started. Again, when you ask people what they think and feel, you must respond in some way. *If you are not prepared to act, don't ask until you are.*

When a rigorous EDS is embedded in your culture, and when individual and team accountability is the norm, you will see trust grow exponentially, people will be highly engaged, great morale will be evident, and finally, high-performing individuals and teams will be the result. It makes perfect sense, doesn't it?

I know you are busy and have a lot on your plate, so let me reassure you, embedding EDS in your culture is not hard nor is it more time consuming than what you are doing already. I am positive you are having conversations, and you are checking on the progress of your staff members' work. This is time you currently allocate to one degree or another. If you are not having those conversations or checking on progress, this will be more work, but it is important work that will save you a huge amount of time and pain in replacing employees whom you can ill afford to lose.

It's *how* you choose to have those conversations and check on your employees' progress that matters most. EDS is simply a framework to help you have those highly productive conversations that will get you the results you want and get them *faster, better, and cheaper.* If I could, I'd stand atop the highest mountain in the land with a huge megaphone and I'd be saying, "Success is *all* about the quality of our relationships."

You may remember I'm a big proponent of *prevention.* Creating great outcomes and preventing bad ones is what EDS is all about. I really cannot stress this enough. Having an EDS helps you build strong relationships with your staff members in clear, honest, transparent, engaging, and productive ways. It sure beats having to devote your precious time to the pain and cost of dismissing someone because you didn't see or acknowledge soon enough that they didn't know or understand, weren't able, or didn't want to get it right, for way too long. On the flip side, when someone is getting it right and you miss it or do not acknowledge it enough, you may lose that high-performing employee due to neglect and suffer a different, but still painful, costly, and time-consuming outcome.

This is a good time to transition into our last topic of this chapter, recognition, something that everyone needs to feel good about work and life, and something *too few* people receive often enough.

RECOGNITION

One of the most powerful retention tools you can have in your toolbox is to have a culture that proactively values recognition. Here I am defining recognition as *the simple act of acknowledging, approving, or appreciating a behavior, action, service, or attitude. Anytime you treat someone like a worthwhile human being can be considered recognition.*

You can give recognition to anyone, anytime—a staff member, leader, colleague, customer, family member, or friend. To raise our awareness, we'll begin with these questions:

- *About you:* When was the last time you felt appreciated at work or at home the way you wanted to be recognized? What happened? How was the recognition and appreciation demonstrated to you? How did it make you feel—about work or your life? How did you feel about the person giving you the recognition?
- *About others:* When was the last time you recognized someone at work or at home the way *they wanted* to be recognized? What happened? How did you show your appreciation and give the recognition? How did the person react? How did it make you feel?

There are some *facts, barriers, and principles* that we can take into account. I invite you to look at six of each from my experience in giving and receiving recognition.

Six Recognition Facts

1. Recognition builds trust and morale.
2. Recognition is an investment in your most valuable resource and improves engagement, performance, and retention.
3. People need to be appreciated to feel positive about their jobs.
4. It is everyone's responsibility (especially the leader's) to recognize good things in coworkers.
5. One size does not fit all; people are motivated differently at different times.
6. Managers think they give it 90 percent of the time, but employees think they get it 10 percent of the time.

Six Barriers to Giving Recognition

People may think the following:

1. It takes too much time, so during an annual review is enough.
2. It costs money.

3. It will make staff "soft."
4. It is only appropriate for superstars and highly extraordinary results.
5. It is understood and doesn't need to be openly stated or demonstrated.
6. I've not received it much myself so I don't know how to give it.

Six Principles for Giving Recognition Well

1. *Be specific:* what did they do exactly?
2. *Be timely:* recognize good performance soon after they did it.
3. *Be sincere:* give recognition from the heart and use "I statements."
4. *Be personal:* recognition should meet the needs of the receiver not the giver.
5. *Be proportional:* recognition should match what they did.
6. *Be regular:* recognition should be often enough that it is not a foreign concept.

The manner of giving is worth as much or more than the gift. All it takes is your heart being open and your attention. Know your people as you decide how best to recognize them and their work. Here are some low- and no-cost ways for you to express recognition and appreciation.

Recognition and Appreciation Options That Cost Little or Nothing

- Always say hello and goodbye.
- Let people know why what they are doing is important and meaningful to you and others.
- Offer a simple and heartfelt thank-you and be specific about what that means.
- Go to the staff member's workspace with only one objective: to thank them personally.
- Have coffee/lunch with people you don't always see to ask them about their work and ideas.
- Give credit where credit is due to the right person/s.
- Send personal, handwritten notes expressing appreciation for a job well done.
- Delegate things you like to do.

- Ask staff what recognition they appreciate; don't assume.
- Offer workshops for growth and development in an area that interests the employee.
- Mention achievements in in-house newsletters.
- Call them on their birthday and/or work anniversary.
- Create symbols of teamwork like T-shirts, mugs, pins, and posters.
- Welcome people back from happy and sad events, vacation, illness, and such.
- Include celebrations and appreciation in meeting agendas.

When thinking about giving and receiving recognition, I hope it is easy to see how simple it can be and how good it feels to both give and to receive. You might ask yourself, "What can I do right now, or tomorrow, to improve the recognition and appreciation seen, heard, and felt by people close to me at work and at home?"

Here's a handy little way to jump-start your thinking: Take a few minutes to think of at least one person whom you want to recognize.

- Who is this *person* (at work or at home)?
- What is this person's *professional or personal contribution*? What *specifically* did they do/say that you want to recognize?
- What is the *performance* result or the positive impact of what they did or said?
- What *kind of recognition* would this person appreciate?

It's so easy, and you will be rewarded for your efforts by the loyalty of your staff as long as you pay attention to the *six principles of giving recognition well*. This can also result in making any staff member feel better about themselves and their work; your recognition alone could lead to your staff's increased productivity. After all, anyone who is still working for you must be doing something right, right? Find out what that right thing is and delight them with your praise.

This is why I believe "nurture right" is your ticket to high retention. It isn't "coddle right" or "hope right" or anything else. If you recall my garden metaphor, it's about planting the right plant in the right soil, with the right amount of sunshine and nourishment, and then checking in regularly to make sure it's doing what it's meant to do and getting what it needs to flourish. It's simple, really. People need nourishment, too.

Chapter 8, "Where Do We Go from Here?" takes us deeper into developing your high-potential employees and preparing them for the future. We'll take a close look into those important performance conversations and explore succession planning because . . . the relationship matters *and* no one stays forever!

Chapter Eight

Where Do We Go from Here?

Figure 8.1.   Retention Map: Where Do We Go from Here?

Good is the enemy of Great.

—Voltaire

At most companies, average performers get an average pay rise. At Netflix, they get a generous severance package.

—Reed Hastings, Netflix CEO

We've arrived at step 3 on our Retention Map (see figure 8.1). In step 2, I mentioned the Personal Dialogue (PD) in rolling out your Employee Development System (EDS). Now it's time to get more familiar with this tool and increase the chances your best people will want to stay.

If you want to be the best, you have to hire the best, reward the best, and either grow or remove the rest. That just about sums up the quote for this chapter. Netflix's Chief Talent Officer, Patty McCord, said, "The best thing you can do for employees—a perk better than foosball or free sushi—is hire only A players to work alongside them. Excellent colleagues trump everything else."[1]

We covered hiring A players in the first section of this book. Now it's time to take a deeper dive with the goal of retaining your A players and having them continue to be A players. While everyone is not and cannot be a superstar who discovers a brilliant new product, process, or service, I am sure you want people on your team who are giving it their all, believe in the work they are doing, and want to increase their knowledge and skills. It really doesn't matter if those employees are working the counter at a fast food franchise, inventing a new device, or looking for a cure for cancer. *Your success depends on their success—*it's that simple.

The question for you to consider is this: "Am I willing to settle for an 'average' level of performance on my team, or do I want more?" You need to know exactly what success means to you and then set yourself and your people up to achieve it.

Shawn Murphy, CEO of WorqIQ, wrote an unflattering article about the traditional way so many organizations deal with performance called, "The Annual Performance Review Is Insulting, Ineffective, and Out-dated. Let It Die." He says, "According to Society for Human Resource Management, 95% of employees are dissatisfied with their company's appraisal process. What's more, 90% don't believe the process provides accurate information."[2]

In a Forbes article headlined "Let's Kill Performance Reviews in 2015," former Fortune 500 Senior Vice President of Human Resources Liz Ryan said, "Performance reviews are the second-worst process in organizations. They are not quite as destructive, expensive and talent repelling as our broken recruiting systems are, but they come close. Every year we shut down our businesses for a month to fill out performance review forms. What a tragic waste! Managers hate them, and so do employees. If we want to save millions of dollars in expensive staff time and focus, we can do away with individual performance reviews altogether."[3]

If you think a traditional performance evaluation or review is needed, you are not alone, and you may be suffering from years of bad advice, training, and entrenched organizational habit. Leaders have had it hammered into them that these annual evaluations are needed to document problems with performance, particularly if someday you have to fire someone. The problem with that logic is it can be too late for an employee to make corrections, and it's very unfair and ineffective for the employee to wait until a performance review to know how they are doing. I've had leaders come to my office and say they need my support to fire someone for cause, but nothing in that person's "personnel file" indicates a problem at all, often quite the opposite is true. It's a chronic problem when supervisors don't like to and/or don't know how to deliver bad news. They'll eventually have no choice, and things can go downhill fast. This is the stuff grievances, arbitrations, and lawsuits are made of and, all too often, lost by management. So, having a performance evaluation isn't a panacea at all. In fact, I'll go so far as to say it's like using a broken crutch for a broken leg.

We're all very familiar with this old way of doing things both on the receiving and giving end of things; I did it, you did it, we all did it. Today, many Human Resources (HR) professionals agree the typical annual performance evaluation is a badly flawed and antiquated system that may or may not have been useful for a different time and a different workforce. We need something far more effective because the old way is not going to help you retain your best talent, and therefore it is a waste of your time and money. There's a better way to lead your talent.

Consider this scenario: you hired the very best candidate in your search and told her how excited you were to have her join your team. Then, a year later, you tell her that as much as you appreciate her work, relative to her peers, she is now only average on the company's rating scale of 1 to 4 simply because that's the only metric you have to work with. You've now pitted her against other members of her team and put her right back in high school and given her a mediocre grade. If that doesn't crush motivation and create dysfunctional behavior, what would?

Rankings are often over focused on looking backward. Ranking encourages employees to try to look good for their boss, especially in the weeks prior to the evaluation, instead of moving forward and asking how they can get even better. It can also lower risk taking, truth telling, and discourage "stretch goals" when employees are concerned about reaching "too high" and landing less than an A grade from the boss.

It is the conversation between the leader and direct reports that matters, not a policy, process, or ranking system. When that conversation feels like a once-a-year visit to the principal's office, it ceases to be effective or meaningful. In fact, it is often antithetical to your goals. This is a big clash between your intent and your impact.

We all know, through experience, that no matter how many good things are said in a traditional performance evaluation, it often feels like a report card, and just like a report card, it's the less-than-good news people remember, no matter what else is said. It's the big "but" that employees hear, and little else. The impact is worse when the employee is surprised by bad or even less-than-great news. In fact, it's not unusual to see voluntary turnover rise after annual review time.

Remember, we are talking about retention of our best people, so let's not shove them out the door as a result of hanging on to a bad system or trying to make a bad process less bad. Let's, instead, manage our talent with care. Let's *nurture* them so they grow into what we believe they can become.

One of my former clients is an employee-owned, successful, midsized private company. They do two things to acknowledge performance—they reward people on their personal performance *and* on the company's overall annual performance. Everyone wins when the company wins because they all own a part of the pie. But still, they use a ranking system that has too much riding on an annual review, and those rankings are at the mercy of each leader's ranking philosophy: some are high graders, and some are not. They do ask for multiple feedback data points and pay attention to performance against expected competencies, business results, and behavioral results. In the world of traditional performance evaluations, they cover a lot of bases, even using a robust talent management system to keep track of employee progress and potential. As innovative and creative as they are in many other ways, in today's world, they are still lagging behind when it comes to talent management because too much of their reward system is dependent on the supervisor's subjective and potentially biased annual ranking.

If we go back to our Netflix example for a moment, they say they don't measure performance, but of course they do, just not in the traditional way. They don't have individual performance reviews or performance improvement plans. Netflix calls itself a high-performance culture because, as you can tell by Reed Hastings's quote, everyone is expected to be a great performer, period. There are metrics, and overall performance is evaluated, but it is tied to market value and company performance rather than individual performance. They have a relatively flat hierarchy and don't believe in promotions that are based on individual employee performance. More recently, they limit their conversations to focus on just "start, stop, continue" feedback. Since they also need to fire people, Netflix is, of course, having conversations with people about their individual performance. Yes, it is radical in the world of HR, and it's been working for them for a long time.[4]

I offer this example to help us shake off some of the old beliefs of, and chronic resistance to, changing the way we have operated for so long. I *do* believe in having one-on-one conversations with individuals, and I'm going to invite you to try my system for creating highly productive and important conversations.

The idea of throwing out your old performance evaluation process and replacing it with something that isn't as formalized, restricted, or rank based can be scary and a big mind-set shift. That is why we need to have something to replace those traditional and tired processes with something you can feel good about. Before we go there, I'd like to tell you a story.

When I was teaching in the Industrial and Labor Relations School at Cornell University, I needed to give students a letter grade for my four-credit course. Grades are a *really* big deal for these highly competitive students. It's a deeply embedded ranking system in most colleges and universities, and, good or bad, it is the system that got them into college in the first place. And finally, it is what will afford them a degree if they succeed within that ranking system.

My way of turning the system on its head was to give every student an A at the start of the semester. I said I was certain they were all perfectly capable of being A students in my class. There were no exams. Their challenge, I said, was to *keep their As* by doing excellent work in the four areas that would be graded: team effectiveness, an individual journal, a team project with a paper, and a team presentation. Notice, only one of the areas is an individual effort. I did this on purpose because the course was all about leadership, teams, and organizational culture. My students were randomly assigned to teams of five to six students for the entire semester—just like it happens in the real world. They were fully aware that they would have to swim or sink together. After learning about my expectations and reviewing our full curriculum, students had the option of dropping the class within two weeks with no penalty.

As I was giving out big blue A stickers, many of the students thought it was a hokey joke. A month into the semester, students began taking their big blue As seriously. If anyone on the team wasn't pulling their weight, they asked to have a team coaching session with me to help get them back on track. Most of the time, team coaching worked out well. It wasn't successful when one individual was not willing to collaborate and only wanted to be graded on personal results. That, of course, wasn't the student's job in this class, and it wasn't possible; there were too many moving parts, and there was far too much work for anyone to do everything on their own. I had performance conversations with recalcitrant students, and their grade reflected how well, or not, they met our agreed upon expectations.

My point in telling you this story is: *Reward what you want; stop rewarding what you do not want.* I wanted the students to keep their As, learn about creating a healthy team culture, learn how to recognize their own stages of team development, and learn how to identify the work culture they were creating inside and outside of class. I rewarded them when they did great work, and while I encouraged, coached, and advised, I did not reward them when they didn't do great work.

During the entire course, each student received feedback from the class, their team, and me, so there really could not be any surprises. I was fully accessible to them by phone and e-mail, as well as after class and during office hours. Every student had all the resources needed to keep or, through extra credit work, increase that highly coveted A grade. It was up to each student to choose how to utilize the available resources and deliver A-level results.

The best students really got it and told me it was one of the most powerful life and work lessons they had ever experienced. The poorest students complained that they would rather have had an exam, shouldn't be expected to depend on others for their grade, blah, blah, blah. My answer to that was simple: "You knew the job description for this class; together we created and you signed on to clear expectations; you accepted by staying in the class when you could have dropped it; you knew the metrics for success and had all the same resources as every other student. Now you must own the choices you made." I also reminded them that this class was simply a microcosm of real life and real work.

Every semester a handful of students were upset by the results of their choices; they had fooled themselves into believing my course was going to be an easy four-credit A. The rest of the class, year after year, walked away with a deep appreciation for the lessons they learned about themselves and about how a high-functioning team and culture can create outstanding work.

IT'S ABOUT THE CONVERSATION

In chapter 7, I introduced the Employee Development System (EDS) framework. Within EDS, we explored setting clear expectations, then using measurement and feedback, and acknowledging performance. People want and need to know if they are meeting or exceeding those expectations, and one way or another, they need to know what will happen based on their performance results. In my experience, powerful dialogues and conversations about EDS are not viewed as *a performance review or an evaluation*. They are viewed as a way to build relationships, clarify ongoing expectations, consider appropriate metrics, and acknowledge the work the employee has achieved and, if appropriate, the work that was not achieved, while fully exploring current reality and looking to a future that both parties want to create together.

Let's begin by *trusting* those terrific people we've so thoughtfully chosen and who agreed to come onboard to work with us. They are adults and should be treated as such. Instead of dreading the "annual review" conversation, imagine how it might feel to have a conversation you both are looking forward to. Think about how much stress could be removed from you and your employees' lives with your combined energies focused in engaging and positive ways that add real value. Nice thought, isn't it?

We want to keep our A employees in high-performance mode, and we want to move our B and C players up to As if we and they can. If not, we have tougher decisions to make; we'll talk about that in section C, "Closure = Fire Right."

Routine check-ins and candid conversations with employees are essential. Waiting until there is a problem or hoping a problem will go away by itself, or fixed by a performance improvement plan is a near guarantee you will lose money and people. The real question is not *if* you have ongoing conversations, but *how* and *when* you will have them.

The system I am inviting you to try has been a welcome change and worked well for thousands of employees in both for-profit businesses and nonprofit organizations. I recommend you give it at least two annual cycles to normalize within your culture before passing judgment. For instance, when we began using the Personal Dialogue (PD) at Cornell University with bargaining unit employees, there was a lot of pushback from the supervisors—but interestingly, *not* the union. Union wages are determined by contract, so our busy supervisors saw these conversations as a pointless waste of time. In fact, they didn't want to do any kind of performance conversation unless, of course, there were problems! We made it happen anyway.

THE PERSONAL DIALOGUE (PD)

After two years of enforcing our requirement to have Personal Dialogues, our employees began looking forward to them, even asking when they were going to happen. Our supervisors, who had, at first, been highly resistant, had a change of heart. Once they were all trained in how to have these conversations, they could see the great value in it for them. *The main reason behind this attitude shift was the measurable increase in trust these conversations generated between the supervisor and the union member.* We also enforced our policy after supervisors were trained at year 2. Any supervisor who did not complete this process would not receive a pay raise until it was complete. We followed up with employee climate checks to evaluate the quality of the conversations they were having and the impact on productivity and morale. The Personal Dialogue became a solid cornerstone of the cultural sea change within our division!

Let's cut to the chase. A Personal Dialogue *is not* a Performance Evaluation. It is a powerful conversation between the supervisor and the employee that happens *at least once a year* and is followed up by *at least quarterly check-ins*. It uses the EDS as its foundation and looks at both the past year and forward to the next. When you see the ten questions, I think you will be able to identify the clear connection to EDS's expectations, measurement, and acknowledgment of performance and I'd like you to notice the shift in emphasis that takes place.

It's important to have a methodology in place that everyone understands and agrees to follow. Both givers and receivers need to learn how the Personal Dialogue works and understand each person's role and responsibility.

Personal Dialogues should be scheduled at a mutually convenient time for both parties with plenty of time—at least a week—for employees and their supervisors to have enough time to review and consider the questions thoroughly.

A place should be designated that is agreeable to both parties. My first preference was to leave the location decision up to the employee if at all possible. It might be their workspace, if private, or out of the office entirely, such as over an extended lunch. I've had these conversations in my office, in their office, in a park, on a boat, at a restaurant, and even in a botanical garden.

We both brought our answers to the ten questions to the session and take as long as we need to have our conversation. I often spent more than an hour preparing my answers because I had two years at least to consider—one past and one ahead. This may shock you . . . all my Personal Dialogue took at least two hours and often as many as four hours. I blocked off a half day just in case we needed it.

"That's crazy!" you might throw up your arms and say. "Why would I do that?" you might ask. "I don't have time to spend up to a half day with every one of my direct reports," might be your response. How about we look at this from another perspective—*what if you don't spend that time with your employees*?

I'm going to assume you are having some kind of performance conversation anyway, and that's likely to mean at least a couple hours of preparation and meeting time. The Personal Dialogue process may require more face-to-face time, but it isn't intended to make more work for you; *it's intended to make the work you already do far more productive and help you retain your best employees.*

Let's say you have ten direct reports, my recommended maximum per leader. If you take the maximum of four hours for each person, that equates to five days, or one week, out of your year. Sounds like a lot, doesn't it? Well, consider this—how much time and money did you spend recruiting these ten people and onboarding them? Or if they've been there awhile, how much time and money will it cost you to replace even one of them if they leave because they aren't happy in the job, aren't feeling valued or recognized, aren't challenged or engaged, or are underperforming?

The statistics about today's employees are *beyond alarming*. In one Forbes article, David Sturt and Todd Nordstrom compiled a list of ten workplace statistics that will likely blow your mind. Here are some of them: The Gallup organization tells us that nearly 70 percent of employees are disengaged. A recent Career Builder study shows that 58 percent of managers have received no management training, instead being promoted because they were good at what they did as individual contributors. Only 12 percent of employees leave for better pay versus the 89 percent of managers who think that's why employees leave. And how about this—a *Harvard Business Review* survey said that 58 percent of people trust strangers more than their own boss! And finally, *recognition was the one thing* employees say would inspire them to produce great work.[5]

Your time invested in high-quality Personal Dialogues is like *buying retention insurance*. It can and should build trust and help employees feel valued by you. There are no guarantees it will keep your best people working for you, but without investing in those relationships, your retention odds are going to be much worse—and that *is* guaranteed! The high-quality time you spend building relationships in these conversations with your direct reports provides the space to go beyond checking off boxes and having a superficial, "have to do" meeting. Your staff will treasure this time with you long after the conversation has concluded.

Stephen Covey famously said, "The main thing is to keep the main thing the main thing."[6] To up our game with retention, *the main thing is the relationship.* The relationships you pay the most attention to in your life and in your work are the ones that will be the most satisfying and successful. Being an effective leader means you must want to invest in your people and to spend quality time coaching and developing them. That means having important conversations.

I agree that *traditional performance evaluations are a huge waste of time and resources* and often have counterproductive and costly results.

The Personal Dialogue is not that!

There are three perspectives—not just one or two: (1) the employee's perspective; (2) the employee's *beliefs* about the supervisor's perspective; and (3) the supervisor's perspective. The second perspective can be a game changer in a Personal Dialogue. It's insightful to see how accurate or inaccurate the employee's "reading" is of their supervisor. Individually, the supervisor and the direct report write down the answers to the questions *prior to meeting* where they will discuss their respective answers. They both get valuable information about how much they are or are not on the same page and can course correct on the spot. Once you've checked in with each other, ordered lunch or whatever, the Personal Dialogue can get under way.

The process for *each question* goes like this:

a. The supervisor asks for the employee's thoughts and listens carefully to the answers without interruption and asks for clarification where needed.
b. The supervisor asks how the employee thinks he/she will answer, again, without interruption, and asks for clarification where needed.
c. The two parties discuss *a* and *b*.
d. The supervisor then shares her/his thoughts without interruption, and the employee asks for clarification where needed.
e. The two parties discuss where they are the same and where they differ. It is not unusual for an employee to have a different view from the supervisor about strengths and areas for improvement. Employees can underestimate their accomplishments and be overly self-critical—and vice versa.

f. Post meeting, the supervisor and the employee share their final notes with each other, or combine them, so they have the *same record* of their conversation—including where they agreed and disagreed.
g. If required, both sign a form for the official "personnel file" that simply says they had the conversation and when, but notes of their meeting do not get filed centrally.

The PD has a big payoff for both parties. It creates the opportunity for the employee to be heard first and for the employee to share perceptions about the supervisor's views. When the supervisor shares his/her views, they can then compare similarities and/or differences of their perceptions for each question and of each other. This prevents a one-sided monologue and employees trying to say what they think the supervisor wants to hear; instead, it opens up new topics to explore and keeps assumptions in check. Applying rigor to this conversation creates greater trust and understanding, which is a *key ingredient* to greater retention.

THE PERSONAL DIALOGUE: THE TEN QUESTIONS

Part 1

1. Please note three to five things you have done especially well in your job in the past year.
2. How did you measure your own performance this year, and what were the results?
3. Please note three to five things you would like to have accomplished but didn't. Why? Are any of these a priority for the coming year?
4. What have you *liked most* about working here this year?
5. What have you *liked least* about working here this year?

Part 2

6. What goals and projects are most important to you in the year ahead? How will you know you've been successful? Are there any factors— personal, supervisory, or organizational—that might block you from accomplishing your goals?

7. What skills, education, experiences, or assistance (including from your supervisor) do you think would help you accomplish your goals and increase your job satisfaction?
8. What behaviors of yours *help you* in your interactions with others? What behaviors of yours *get in your way* in your interactions with others? Please give specific examples of each.
9. Who are you developing to succeed you in your position, and what is your succession plan?
10. What has gone well, and what needs to be improved in your relationship with your supervisor? Please be as specific as you can.

At the close of the ten questions, I like to ask my direct reports if there is *a question or a topic we have not covered that they would like to discuss*. Usually, the ten questions produce lots of content and cover most, if not all, of what is on the employee's mind. There have been times, though, when one of my staff has said they didn't really tell me the whole story about something and want to do that, or one of the questions made them think of something they hadn't considered before. The point is, be ready to offer, "Is there more?" to the conversation. More often, staff members have told me that they couldn't imagine a more in-depth conversation and felt it was a perfect time to bring it to closure. In every case, we thank each other for the time and thought we've both put into our relationship and the PD.

Pitfall: It is tempting to rush through this process, particularly in places where you agree with each other. In doing so, you can miss the opportunity to be specific and dive deeper into the topic whether it is about what's working well or not working well.

Solution: Use excellent and deep listening skills. Get clarification, summarize what you've heard, and ask if there is more. Expand and deepen your responses wherever you can to provide great examples of this person's impact, behaviors that matter, and nuances about your relationship. Take your time and be mindful that everything you say and do will be absorbed by your staff member.

When preparing for the PD, I make sure that everything I want to discuss falls within one of the ten questions. Of course, you can adapt these to suit your culture and needs, but I caution you *not to stray too far* from this format if your goal is to have a dialogue instead of an evaluation. The opportunity for a rich and meaningful discussion comes from years of experimenting to arrive at the ten questions I'm inviting you to use. You'll notice that while performance is discussed, it is in the context of the employee's overall experience in the job. It provides a way for the supervisor to demonstrate respect, honors the employee's dignity, and recognizes the employee's shared professional partnership by delving into their job, achievements, hopes, disappointments, goals, and needs. Together they create ongoing expectations and metrics for the future. It also gives the supervisor ample opportunity to recognize the employee.

This process can be used with any employee, unionized or not, non-exempt or exempt, frontline staff, managers, or senior staff—everyone. The wording may be adjusted where appropriate for the employees, but the intent of each question is kept true. We want to know what the employee thinks about their performance, what's working and not working for them, what goals they have, and what they need from their supervisor.

It is true that not all employees want to grow into something else or learn new skills. Some folks are really happy being excellent at what they do and want to keep doing it. If so, it is important for a leader to know and understand and continue to support high-performance employees where they are as long as the job doesn't outgrow them.

For instance, let's look at two outstanding finance managers: one who loves the details, balancing books, and keeping everything running smoothly, and another who is fascinated by the bigger picture, trends, and strategies. The first manager may be content with continuing to be an excellent gatekeeper in her area of expertise. The second manager may long for more development and influence over decisions that impact the entire organization. The leader of these two people needs to understand each employee and recognize them for what they each do well. However, if the first manager's job needs to get bigger or more complex, requiring significant skill upgrades, she may or may not still be suited for or want the job of the future. The PD, when done well, unearths these truths so both parties can move forward with a full understanding of what's important and possible for both the employee and the organization.

Pitfall: There should be no nasty surprises in the Personal Dialogue (PD).

Solution: Performance issues that have arisen over the past year should have been dealt with in *other conversations* and either a plan is in place or the issue has been resolved. While some reference to a past performance issue is bound to arise, the PD is not the place to belabor them.

We'll cover how to manage performance issues in real time and in much more detail when we get to section C, "Closure = Fire Right." What is inexcusable is to have that information conveyed to an employee for the *first time as a "gotcha"* in the Personal Dialogue.

We've onboarded your great hire; we've put the Employee Development System into place; and now we've had some time to see your great hire in action and experienced a powerful Personal Dialogue. In chapter 9, "Growing Your People," we will complete our Retention Map by exploring the benefits of coaching, mentoring, and succession planning. So let's get going!

Chapter Nine

Growing Your People

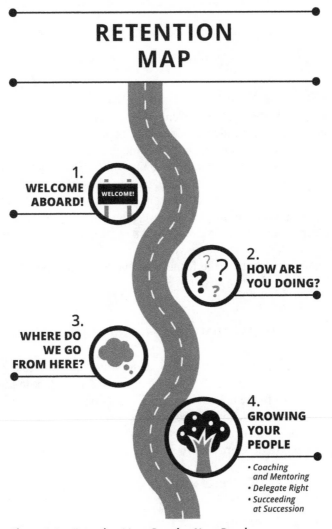

Figure 9.1. Retention Map: Growing Your People

If there is anything I would like to be remembered for it is that I helped people understand that leadership is helping other people grow and succeed. To repeat myself, leadership is not just about you. It's about them.

—Jack Welch

A mentor is someone who allows you to see the hope inside yourself.

—Oprah Winfrey

A leader's lasting value is measured by succession.

—John Maxwell

In step 4, the final step of our Retention Map (see figure 9.1), we will be focused on *you*. As a leader, you have the opportunity and, arguably, the responsibility to provide coaching and mentoring to help your people grow into roles they and your organization value. You may take on one of those roles, or you may offer to engage a professional coach, or help your direct report find a mentor to help guide that individual. You also have the responsibility of preventing gaping holes in your talent pool that adversely affect your business; and that means acknowledging that no one stays forever, including you.

First, let's look at the generic meaning and function of both the coach and the mentor.

COACHING AND MENTORING

Coaching and *mentoring* are terms that are often used interchangeably even though there are significant differences. It's important to identify which role will fit the need at hand. There is no point in providing your employee with a coach when they need a mentor or vice versa. In the workplace, the term *coach* has a vastly different meaning than what we see in the world of sports where most of us first heard the term *coach* at school.

Definition of a Coach: *A coach offers a partnering relationship to the coachee to help the individual become who they want to become* *and achieve a desired outcome. It is a creative process that empowers and inspires the coachee to make choices and take action that will serve the coachee's goal. The coach does not give advice but, instead, asks powerful questions, makes observations, and offers assessments to help unlock and amplify the coachee's awareness and commitment.*

The word *mentor* is derived from the proper name Mentor, a character found in Homer's epic poem, *The Odyssey*, and has come to mean someone who teaches or gives help and advice to a less experienced and often younger person. Mentor was a trusted friend of Odysseus and advised his son with the objective of preparing him to take on important responsibilities during his father's absence.

Definition of a Mentor: *A mentor is an experienced and trusted advisor whose only goal in the mentoring relationship is to support the professional and personal development of their mentee. The mentor is usually more senior and/or more experienced than the mentee and serves as an advisor, model, counselor, and guide to someone with less experience. The mentor is responsible for sharing knowledge and providing advice and counsel to the mentee.*

I have had the good fortune of having informal mentors for over the past twenty years by simply asking that person to mentor/advise me, when there was no structured program in my workplace. Mentoring is a long-term relationship based on mutual trust, respect, and commitment. The relationship should have clear, mutual expectations, but it is generally less structured and has less frequent interactions than coaching. While some organizations offer in-house mentoring programs, sometimes as a follow-on to a leadership program, it is just as common for mentees to have mentors outside their organization. When it is a part of an internal development program, I recommend creating a clear process that spells out the expectations and responsibilities of both parties. I've included a list of considerations and benefits in the Resources section for this chapter.

Coaching also requires mutual trust, respect, commitment, and clear expectations, but it often spans a shorter period of time, typically lasting from three to twelve months. Coaching follows a more regular and structured approach. When I have a coaching client, my only objective is to help each client reach his or her goals. I have no attachment to a specific outcome; that must come from the client's own motivations, or it is a pointless from the start. I often describe my role as the "tour guide" and the client as the "driver'" on this journey we're undertaking together. I listen deeply and ask powerful questions, noticing what comes up when the client considers those questions. Clients consistently do a superb job in identifying what is *really* going on, and they figure out what must happen to achieve their goals. Within the safety of a successful coaching relationship, people evolve, make significant discoveries, and shift mind-sets as they are invited to tap into their own well of wisdom.

Both coaching and mentoring are relationships that require complete *confidentiality and unconditional positive regard for the individual.* This means that the coach or mentor is a confidant who is unfailingly supportive and nonjudgmental. We must remember that there is an adult on the other side of the relationship. The coach or mentor's job is *not* to "fix" anything or anyone; it is *not* to parent, enable, judge, or insist on a particular path forward. It is about helping that adult understand their choices and how those choices relate to their goals.

Coaches and mentors *are not therapists, trainers, or consultants.* Coaches and mentors provide a safe space and opportunity for individuals to discover what they need to know in order to reach the outcomes they desire. Mentors have the additional role of providing advice and guidance requested by the mentee.

Let's make another distinction here. Training is not coaching. Training is focused on *transferring specific knowledge or skills*, like what is or is not a legal question to ask when interviewing a candidate, or how to fix the Widget Company's widget-making machine. Coaching and mentoring are about *enhancing and building upon an individual's knowledge or skills* for developmental purposes by asking powerful questions and making observations that can lead to greater awareness, learning, and change.

In chapter 8, we talked about the Personal Dialogue. That conversation, and regular check-ins, may find the leader and the direct report discussing the possibility of coaching, mentoring, or specific training opportunities.

A side-by-side comparison of *coaching* and *mentoring* is listed in table 9.1. Coaching or mentoring are not the same activities as day-to-day performance management and supervision. Employee supervision *is not formal coaching*, although supervisors may see better results

Table 9.1. Coaching versus Mentoring

	Coaching	Mentoring
Timeline	Engagement is likely to be *short term* (up to six months or one year) with a specific outcome in mind. However, some coaching relationships can last longer, depending on goals.	Engagement tends to be *long term*, lasting at least a year or two, and often much longer.
Intent	Coaching is intended to enhance or improve the coachee's engagement and job satisfaction; it may be focused on specific performance areas.	Mentoring is *development driven*, looking holistically at the person and their long-term career goals.
Format	These are *structured*, with regularly scheduled meetings, such as weekly, biweekly, or monthly.	These tend to be more *informal* and often on an as-needed basis requested by the mentee. Expectations and responsibilities of both the mentor and the mentee must be determined and mutually agreed to.
Who	Coaches are either the supervisor or someone who is internally or externally assigned or hired for the benefit of the coachee. The coach may or may not be a subject matter expert. This is *not advising or training*.	Within organizational mentoring programs, mentors generally have more *seniority and always more expertise* than mentees where the mentee wishes to learn and grow. The mentee can learn from and be inspired by the mentor's experience and modeling.
Content	The coaching agenda is *cocreated by the coach and the coachee* in order to meet the specific needs of the coachee.	The mentoring agenda is usually *determined by the mentee*. The mentor supports and offers stretch opportunities beyond the mentee's comfort zone.

(continued)

Table 9.1. (*continued*)

	Coaching	Mentoring
The Conversation	The coach should ask thought-provoking questions to help the coachee come to their own insights and make real commitments when they recognize the challenges that require action.	In the mentoring relationship, the mentee is more likely to ask probing questions, tapping into the mentor's expertise. The mentor also has the job of making sure those questions are digging into growth areas for the mentee.
Expected Results	The results expected from a coaching relationship and agreement are *specific and measurable*, with the coachee demonstrating positive change in the chosen focus areas.	The results expected from a mentoring relationship can shift and change over time. There is less focus on specific, measurable results and *more focus on the overall development of the mentee's goals*.

when using a coaching approach and techniques. Specific performance issues that arise, and the best way to address them, need to be identified, explored, and put into action. Managing performance in real time, with clear expectations, clear measures, and clear consequences is part of every leader's normal job.

When considering whether to provide a coach or a mentor, identify the goal you and your direct report wish to achieve. If you are wondering whether a coach or a mentor is the best fit for your need, here are some guidelines.

Choose a coach when you want to

1. prepare a high-potential employee for advancement in the organization;
2. address a behavioral habit that is blocking or slowing professional progress;
3. encourage someone to take on new responsibilities quickly;
4. support leaders in addition to, or in place of, formal training or development programs; or
5. inspire high-potential employees to maximize their talents.

Choose a mentor when you want to

1. provide a role model for highly effective leadership or other important roles;
2. transfer knowledge from more senior and/or departing staff to more junior staff;
3. increase cross-functional interactions and collaboration;
4. broaden diversity of ideas, people, and perspectives within the organization; or
5. inspire high-potential employees to imagine what is possible in their career and life.

Here is an example of each:

Coach: Kevin is an energetic, skilled, effective facilitator who has been identified as a high-potential employee. While he is highly successful in front of the groups he leads, he is nervous and awkward in front of senior leaders. He is unable to put together coherent presentations that report results or advocate for change. He trips over his words and misses key points, and his leader has had to interject on several occasions. His leader believes that working with a coach could help Kevin increase his confidence. He wants Kevin to build upon his natural abilities so he can demonstrate his positive energy and share his wisdom with anyone, regardless of their ranking in the hierarchy.

Mentor: Jennifer is new to the IT department, and she immediately demonstrated her outstanding interpersonal skills with the company's internal customers as well as her coworkers. Her leader sees huge potential in her. He offers to groom Jennifer for a leadership position within the next two years, and she welcomes the opportunity. He decides to coach her himself on some of the technical aspects of her job and send her to leadership development training, but he wants to find a different senior-level leader to mentor her. He speaks with Jennifer and offers her one internal and one external leader—both of whom he respects. Jennifer chooses the internal mentor because of the added value of knowing the organization's culture. The mentor and Jennifer agree to begin with a one-year commitment and create clear expectations of each other and the process.

Being involved in a coaching or mentoring relationship can enhance one's professional and personal life in ways a person could not achieve

Pitfall: When leaders and/or organizations (e.g., Human Resources [HR]) hire or retain an internal or external coach, there can be a risk of pressure being applied to the coach or the coachee to share what should remain within the confidential coaching relationship (e.g., conversations).

Solution: *Prior to having an introductory coaching conversation,* the coach and the hiring leader or HR must discuss *coaching ethics* and agree to an explicit agreement about confidentiality. The rules and expectations of the coaching relationship must be discussed and agreed upon, and then a written record must be created for all parties to have *prior to commencing with the coaching agreement or contract.* No coach worth hiring or assigning will share the content, tone, or outcome of private coaching conversations without receiving explicit permission from the coachee.

on their own. If you have ever been coached or mentored, you know what I mean. Whether you are the coach or mentor, or you find a different coach or mentor for your employees, paying it forward is not only the right thing to do, *it is the smart thing to do* in your quest to retain top talent. People put a lot more energy into things they *want to do* than things they *have to do.* That means, as leaders we need to take the time to be present, observe, and ask staff members about their motivations. We then need to provide productive and appropriate opportunities to keep them engaged and wanting to continue to work for us.

If you would like more insight and guidelines into how to coach an employee, and/or what to consider in setting up an internal mentoring program, I've provided more detail in the Resources section for this chapter.

DELEGATE RIGHT

One of the most effective methods to prepare your talented people for future roles, and thereby increase the likelihood of retention, is to delegate new and interesting work to them. When you think of delegation, what comes to mind? Is it assigning tasks, off-loading work from one person to another, or maybe getting rid of work you don't like to do? I hope not. While leaders, of course, have every right to assign work, delegation is something else; in fact, it has a purpose way beyond assigning work.

Definition of Delegation: *Delegation is a planned and well-managed new learning opportunity for another person that transfers duties and/or responsibilities and authority to that person for a mutually beneficial purpose.*

The vast majority of an employee's learning happens on the job, so if you are coaching and developing the talent in front of you right now, decide what you can delegate next, and next and next, without overwhelming your employees, but instead, to challenge them and increase their knowledge and skills. This might even mean shifting something you love to do off your plate to your staff member's plate.

There is no question in my mind that you are where you are today, at least in part, because someone trusted you enough to delegate new work to you. We all learn and stretch by trying new things, and maybe stumbling, but then getting back up and working at it until we get it right. Many leaders I have worked with and observed admit to having a tough time delegating both responsibility and authority. Since developing your people is a key part of any leader's job, and delegation is about development, it's important to delegate well. Let's take a look at ten solid principles to delegating right.

Ten Principles of Delegation

1. Select the right person. Choose someone who is capable of doing the task and give that person the accountability and equal measures of responsibility and authority to do it.
2. Delegate interesting, rewarding, and challenging projects.
3. Take your time. Your delegate will need time, maybe up to a year, to acquire the training, practice, and expertise to handle a complex new task or role.
4. Delegate gradually and with the person and situation in mind. If you have been under-delegating, don't transfer all that responsibility overnight.
5. Delegate proactively. Don't wait for a problem to develop before delegating a task.
6. Delegate the whole. Whenever possible, delegate a complete project or action to one person rather than giving away just one piece. This

will give your delegate the full picture, provide control and coordination, and reduce confusion and errors.

7. Delegate for specific results. Instead of describing just the general scope of the job, describe the specific results you expect.
8. Avoid gaps and overlaps. A gap is a job for which no one has been assigned responsibility. An overlap is when two or more people have responsibility for the same job.
9. Delegation flows both ways. Let your delegates participate in determining what is being offered to them.
10. Leave the delegate alone. Once the decision has been made, let him/her do it. From now on, he/she makes the day-to-day decisions, gets the headaches, and has the free rein to use his/her own resourcefulness with you as expert support for questions and concerns.

To apply the principles of delegation, use a good process. There are four steps that will answer the core questions of scope, results expected, and timeline. Let's take a closer look at the delegation process.

The Delegation Process

Step 1

- Define the assignment.
- What is to be done?
- Why is it important?
- What end result do you expect?
- When is it to be done?

Step 2

- Determine who is to do it.
- Consider availability and suitability.
- Distribute responsibilities fairly.

Step 3

- Communicate the assignment to all relevant parties.
- Convey the purpose and expected results.
- Encourage input and participation.

- Provide direction and support.
- Agree on a time frame and target date.

Step 4

- Establish controls and checkpoints.
- Promote open communication on problems and progress.
- Determine checkpoints to evaluate progress (meetings, verbal or written reports, direct observation).
- Provide constructive feedback and positive reinforcement. When the leader demonstrates interest in following through, the staff member will too.

In the Resources section for this chapter, I've provided sample templates of a Personal Delegation Profile and a Delegation Agreement. These can help clarify *exactly* what is happening, with whom, and by when.

SUCCEEDING AT SUCCESSION

You have coached, mentored, delegated to, and developed your employees. And while they remain with you, they are adding tremendous value. Still, all organizations lose good people for various personal or professional reasons. Planned or unplanned, losing talented employees can leave large skill and knowledge gaps. We also know that filling critical vacancies can prove to be challenging, expensive, and time consuming.

Right now, everyone is or will be massively impacted by the rapidly aging workforce. It's a big, big deal! Filling key roles with the right people is a bottom-line business imperative. It's no longer a nice idea to have a well-run succession program in place; it's a critical strategic imperative to gain or keep your competitive advantage and, frankly, to even stay in business.

Definition of Succession Planning: *Succession planning identifies and tracks the progress of high-potential employees to ensure you have the right people in the right jobs now and in the future who are in alignment with the organization's long-term goals. Succession planning* *is a key part of any successful talent management and development program.*

The goal of succession planning is to build a strong "bench" for an organization to ensure its health, growth, and stability over the long term. We need to prevent doing too little too late and find ourselves losing the talented people who will help us grow and succeed. Whatever you and your business make, do, serve, produce, or fix, *you can't do it without the right people.*

We've explored hiring and developing your people from multiple perspectives and strategies. *Successful succession planning is a significant business strategy to meet an organization's retention goals, and yet too often, it is an afterthought.*

As a critical part of your retention strategy, successful succession planning needs top management's focused attention. Teala Wilson, a senior consultant for Saba's Strategic Services, shares with us a free download of the report *The 2015 State of Succession Planning* in her blog post "8 Steps for Effective Succession Planning." It looked at six hundred organizations worldwide. The report told us that 21 percent of those organizations had no succession program or process in place, and nearly 50 percent are failing in one or more ways to institute best practices for succession. And yet, every year at the top of the list of concerns by senior management are grave concerns about their talent pipeline.[1]

Before we go any further, I'd like to make sure we draw the comparison between the terms *replacement* and *succession*. These are two different efforts and require different approaches. In her book titled *The Recruiter's Handbook*, Sharlyn Lauby reminds us that *replacement planning is focused on short-term results, while succession is focused on long-term talent strategy.* Some positions may only need a replacement process because the talent pool makes it easy and fast to fill, or perhaps the position isn't as critical to your business as others. The two processes can dovetail when tracking your talent, gaps, risks, and opportunities, but a replacement plan identifies backups for positions that are generally less critical to fill versus planning for purposeful and long-term succession.[2]

If you have talent management system (TMS) software, there is likely a component for succession planning, and/or it holds most of the information you need to create a succession-planning process. If you do not have TMS software, you can do this with a spreadsheet and keep track of changes as they occur. Let's take a look at an example of a succession-planning overview. There are only three key components: *identify*, *assess*, and *capture*.

Succession-Planning Overview

Identify:

- Business challenges and goals for the next one to five years
- Mission-critical positions that may, or are known to be, vacated in the next one to five years
- Competencies, skills, and knowledge needed over the next one to five years
- Current gaps in competencies, skills, and knowledge

Assess:

- Current high-potential talent
- The competencies, skills, and knowledge needed versus what currently exists in those high-potential employees
- The gaps (categorize them and give weight to each gap's importance)
- The interest of high-potential employees in gaining the competencies, skills, and knowledge needed
- The ability to attract new talent with the competencies, skills, and knowledge needed for the future
- The strength or weakness in your "bench" of high-potential employees

Capture:

- Wisdom, skills, and knowledge from individuals *before* they leave the organization
- The opportunity for seasoned and successful employees to serve as role models and to mentor and/or coach more junior, high-potential employees

There are five steps with simple worksheets that line up with the overview to help you create a successful succession-planning process. All these worksheets are also provided in the Resources section for this chapter.

Step 1: Identify Business Challenges and Goals for the Next One to Five Years.

This can start with your strategic plan, if you have one. If you don't, you can do an "environmental scan," which is the process of gathering information about trends, relationships, events, and/or competitors within an organization's internal and external environments. The goal is to prepare for things that are or are expected to happen and then inform your succession-planning process and actions. An *environmental scan* usually includes the key players in determining the direction of your business. It can be as simple as regularly asking the following questions and filling in these worksheet answers.

Plan Worksheet

What do you know is happening inside and outside your organization that impacts your business?

Right Now?   The Distant Future (1–5 years)?   The Near Future?

Step 2: Identify the Mission-Critical Positions That Impact the Success of Your Business, Using the Wisdom of Key Leaders and HR Professionals

Review both leadership and key individual contributor positions that are hard to or take a long time to fill. Evaluate the positions against strategic business goals and assign a vacancy risk factor to the current incumbent.

Position Worksheet

Position title: _____

Position incumbent: _____ or Vacant (how long?) _____

Position impact on key business operations: _____

_____

Risks: Vacancy _____

If not filled _____

Estimated time to fill a vacancy: _____

Step 3: Identify Competencies, Skills, and Knowledge That Are Critical to Business Success

Once you have identified the mission-critical positions, particularly those that have a high vacancy risk or are vacant, identify what is needed in the successor to that position that you will either groom internally or hire externally.

Competency Worksheet

Position title: _____

Core leadership and/or interpersonal competencies:

_____   _____   _____
_____   _____   _____
_____   _____   _____

Essential skills competencies:

_____   _____   _____
_____   _____   _____
_____   _____   _____

Unique or preferred but not essential competencies:

_____   _____   _____
_____   _____   _____

Education: _____

Experience: _____

What is unique about this position (institutional knowledge, relationships, skill sets, etc.)? _____

Who working here now could do this job? _____
Where and by whom is critical information and knowledge held currently?

_____

What is the plan for sharing documentation and knowledge? (e.g., mentoring, job rotation, job shadowing, documentation on secure server, training, etc.) _____

_____

Step 4: Identify High-Potential Employees for Key Positions Over the Next One to Five Years

Who are current staff members or known external individuals who have the competencies required to assume the role and/or who have high potential and the motivation to grow into the role over a period of time?

High-Potential Worksheet

Name: _____

Current position title: _____

Division/Department/Unit: _____

Years in current position: _____

Current leader: _____

Target position: _____

Core leadership and/or skill competencies needed for this position: (take list from step 3)

What competencies/skills does this person need to develop to be ready for this position?

_____   _____   _____

Readiness: Current___ Within 6–12 months___ Within 1–2 years___ Within 3–5 years___

Action plan for this high-potential employee:

_____

_____

Step 5: Create a Targeted Individual Development Plan (IDP) With and for Each High-Potential Employee Who Wants to Grow into a Mission-Critical Position and Whom You Believe Can Do So

Individual Development Planning Worksheet

Name: _____

Current position title: _____

Division/Department/Unit: _____

Current supervisor: _____

Succession position(s): _____

Current incumbent and incumbent's supervisor: _____

Division/Department/Unit: _____

Short-term goals: _____

Long-term goals: _____

Core competency, knowledge, and skill development plan:

Competency/Skill   Learning Plan   Dates   Costs   Outcome

Pitfall: Conscious or unconscious bias will kill the quality and results of your succession-planning efforts short and long term. Managers tend to hire people who are like themselves, creating homogeneity and a lack of diversity and therefore lack of trust by employees in the process.

Solution: Your succession team should be made up of a wide variety of leaders. Be open and collaborative and be transparent about your process while keeping individual assessments confidential. Don't play favorites. Be objective and fair. Also keep in mind that high-potential employees may not be distributed evenly throughout the organization; you may discover more people ready for succession opportunities in one unit than another. Keep the greater good for the business in mind.

Every employee should be having Individual Development Plan (IDP) discussions with their supervisor and have access to appropriate professional development opportunities. Everyone who is motivated to do so should be encouraged to grow and develop his or her competencies and skills to the fullest. Employees who want to aim for a specific role or roles in the future need to have an IDP that is laser focused on the competencies and skills for that type of position, especially if a future position is a mission-critical role within the organization.

There are a few questions that, when answered, will help everyone see where there is or is not good alignment between the employee's career goals and the business's future needs.

- What are the employee's career goals?
- How aligned are the employee's needs with those of the organization?

- What development has occurred so far, and how was success measured?
- What competencies or skills does the employee need to develop to achieve career goals?
- What support are you willing and able to provide to help this employee reach his/her career goals (training, mentoring, coaching, certifications, education, workload accommodations, flextime, etc.)?

I cannot emphasize this enough: *your succession strategy requires top management's focused and continuous attention.* It is so closely tied to increased retention of your best talent that it should be right up there next to hiring right as a top priority! Succeeding at succession means identifying your organization's future needs, finding the people who may be able to fill those needs, and having a plan to get them from here to there.

Most of us like happy endings to stories, so I'll share a true story of an example of a purposeful succession.

My last leader at Cornell was the Vice President for Administration and CFO, Dr. Harold D. Craft Jr. Hal and I shared an executive assistant, and we needed to find a confidential, professional associate for this key position. We hired Kathy. She wasn't a typical hire because she had dual bachelor's degrees and was only available because her previous department had lost its funding. We couldn't believe our good fortune in being able to attract her to our much different and lower-paying role.

Fast forward to 2020. Dr. Kathryn Burkgren is the Associate Vice President for Organizational Development and Effectiveness for Cornell University. While working for Hal and me, we invited Kathy to attend our leadership development courses, and she found that organizational and leadership development were her true calling. She was accepted as a student at Cornell and, over several years, received both a master's degree and a PhD while working full time for us and raising a young family. We saw the immense potential in Kathy and supported her every step of the way, through coaching, mentoring, and exposure to new experiences. She never once missed a beat.

You might say this is simply an example of a smart and motivated employee who had supportive supervisors. It was much more than that. We each expected that we would be leaving Cornell in a few years, and we didn't want all our success in building a values-based leadership culture to diminish or disappear; we needed a strong champion. Preparing Kathy to be that champion was all part of the plan. Today, beyond our wildest dreams, the program has spread from our division to all of Cornell's multiple campuses.

It happened because of Kathy's hard work and determination and because of Hal's and my strong belief in supporting high-potential talent to fill a future need. That, in a nutshell, is what successful succession planning looks like. Success requires both strong, intrinsic motivation from the individual *and* focused senior leadership support for growing the talent to meet current and future organizational needs.

We've come a long way from pre-boarding, onboarding, the Employee Development System (EDS), the Personal Dialogue (PD), the Individual Development Plan (IDP), coaching and mentoring, delegation, and finally, to succeeding at succession.

Here's a list of a few reminders and tips to help you keep your great people.

- **Measure** your retention reality regularly. You need to know rather than guess what's happening within your organization. Look for "hot spots" and find out why turnover may be higher in one area than another. Is it the leader (start there first), the work, coworkers, pay, workspace issues, hours . . . ? Find out why good people are leaving or transferring out.
- **Develop** and grow that important relationship with your staff member—continuously.
- **Delegate**, with appropriate support, as much as the employee agrees to and can handle.
- **Provide coaching, mentoring, training**, and other experiences that demonstrate you value the employee as much as they add value to the organization.
- **Be accessible and approachable**. This does not mean anytime, anywhere. It means creating known and sufficient time for anyone on your staff to have your full attention.
- **Listen carefully**. Everyone needs to *know* their voice is being heard by their leaders.
- **Pay attention** to personal occasions and events (birthdays, work anniversaries, educational achievements, illnesses, weddings, deaths in the family, births, etc.).

- **Send handwritten notes** of thanks, appreciation, and recognition.
- **Send a copy** of your positive e-mails about an employee to the next level of management.
- **Be present** and vigilant about the employee's expectations, development opportunities, and performance. That means utilizing the Employee Development System, the Personal Dialogue, and Individual Development Plan with ongoing follow-up conversations.

One last word about retention: In a 2019 Retention Report conducted by the Work Institute, among many other statistics this one stands out. A whopping 27 percent of US workers voluntarily left their jobs in 2018, and they predict that if this trend continues it will be 35 percent by 2023, creating enormous risk and major gaps for businesses nationwide.[3]

It's abundantly clear that retention starts with hiring right in the first place, but that process only gets good people in the door. To keep them on the job and productive, you have to invest time, effort, and attention in your employees—every day, month, and year—to ensure your investment pays off for you, for them, and for your organization.

This brings us to the end of the "Retention = Nurture Right" section. The final section of this book—titled "Closure = Fire Right" (how appropriate!)—is up next. While it is the shortest section, it has *at least* as significant an impact on your bottom line as anything else you do. All you have to do is look at one lost labor lawsuit to know how painful and expensive it can be when an employee termination is carried out poorly.

As we all know from experience, closure is not *just* about firing right; it is about saying "goodbye" to any employee for any reason when their employment ends. It could be a voluntary resignation, or a retirement, a layoff, a serious illness or death, a family crisis, going to jail, or getting promoted or transferred. *Each ending of a current employment relationship requires graceful closure.*

The toughest employment ending for most people is firing someone, so that's where we'll begin with chapter 10, "When It's Really Over: Part 1—Involuntary Closure." Perhaps this topic is one of the main reasons you picked up the book! So take a deep breath and turn the page. I guarantee you'll be better prepared for all your "goodbyes" at work when we're finished!

Section C

CLOSURE = FIRE RIGHT

Chapter Ten

When It's Really Over

Part 1—Involuntary Closure

I don't even like firing people. I don't think I've ever said "You're fired" to anybody.

—Martha Stewart

I agree with Martha. I don't like firing people either, and I have also never said those exact two words—"You're fired!"—to someone whose employment I've terminated. During the conversation, I have said things like, "This is not working because of XYZ and that means we must end our work relationship," or "Unfortunately, because of XYZ, we can no longer employ you here." The situation dictates the context, of course. Yes, it is a firing, but you don't have to use those two words, and I recommend against it. There is no question that firing or laying off someone is an onerous leadership task. Still, there are going to be times when we have to end someone's employment, so the question is not if, but *how and when*, we will bring that relationship to closure.

Aside from death or disability, there are only two ways an individual's employment is brought to closure by the employer or the individual—it is either *involuntary or voluntary*. Involuntary terminations of employment fall into two categories: getting fired or being laid off. We will focus first on involuntary terminations in this chapter. In chapter 11, we'll turn our attention to voluntary separations. However, in all employment separations, voluntary or involuntary, you will want to have a clean and graceful closure.

For an involuntary termination, clean closure means this: dot your i's and cross your t's with every aspect of the decision, the process, and the conversation. Graceful closure means treating the individual with dignity and kindness. After all, they're losing their livelihood, status, and security, not you, so graciousness is both the *right* thing to do and the *smart* thing to do.

Clean closure was not what happened when I was fired the first and only time. I was working for a national retail record chain as a regional director on the east coast, covering four states. I was promoted into this position by the previous leadership (all men). When the company changed ownership a couple years later, the new leaders (all men) decided to fire nearly all the women who had regional and other management roles. My new boss called one morning and told me to hand over my company car and building keys to my assistant and leave the premises immediately. When I asked the reason for this hasty termination, he stammered and coughed and finally told me that I just wasn't aggressive enough. I asked what that meant because I'd never heard this feedback before, and he had no answer. "I said you're fired, so just go," he said. Such a reason made no sense because the sales in my region had increased more than 30 percent that year. Hmmm.

It was also an interesting coincidence that I was fired only two weeks after the new head of the company told me, in person, that if I liked my job I should meet him to discuss my employment in his private bedroom. Fortunately, two leaders who cared about integrity witnessed the conversation. They told me they would testify for me and tell the truth, so I sued the company. This was not my first choice, mind you, but it was a matter of principle for me, and for you now, a case study in *how not to fire someone.*

As it turns out, I must have been aggressive enough after all because I won an out-of-court settlement and was granted unemployment insurance as well!

My goal in this chapter is to help you do what you need to do in a firing situation, do it for the right reasons, and do it in the right way. We've journeyed through the first two sections of this book together focused on hiring and retaining the best people for your organization. When you do that well, you won't need to turn to this chapter very often. And yet, there will be occasions when things go wrong no matter how well you've hired, onboarded, developed, or coached someone.

The toughest job for most leaders and Human Resources (HR) professionals is *terminating an individual's employment*. Firing someone is a decision few leaders, including CEOs, want to make and leaders tend to put off far too long, even when doing so prolongs the inevitable ending and causes more damage to both the business and the individual.

When you're a leader, *firing right* is just as important a part of your job as is *hiring right*. Yes, it's emotionally loaded, complicated, and just plain uncomfortable to fire anyone, no matter the circumstances. I remember a client's reaction after he had been struggling with this decision for months. He's a CEO of a mid-sized company and called me bursting with relief, "OMG, I'm finally going to get some sleep tonight! He just told me he wants to resign! Can you believe it? Now I don't have to fire him."

There are times when no matter how diligent we are, people can fool us, or perhaps an employee's life implodes for unpredictable non-work reasons, or the job outgrows them. And then there are those moments when one incident makes the decision to terminate someone's employment imperative. Sometimes, no matter how valuable an employee has been, you are forced into a layoff situation through no fault of the employee. When you have no other choice but to fire or lay off, it's important to do your utmost to help the employee retain his dignity and ensure the organization's reputation (and yours) is not irreparably damaged.

It is essential to give people an opportunity to make course corrections whenever you can. With the exception of dangerous and/or egregious behavior, employees must receive constructive feedback and be given a reasonable amount of time (dependent on the issue) to turn things around. *No firing should be a surprise!* So, what is a reasonable amount of time? Each situation and each person will be different, but a good rule of thumb is this: *address concerns quickly, provide immediate constructive feedback, and/or undertake an intervention—then be clear about the specific measurable results you expect to see within a specific time frame.*

I'd like to add a cautionary note about bias as you're contemplating firing someone. If personal bias seeps into your decision about an employee, it erodes productivity and engagement with that employee and with others. People will notice, and others may not feel safe.

When people experience and even witness biased treatment, from their leader or coworkers, it has a profoundly negative and far-reaching effect on morale, motivation, commitment, and the desire to stay with the organization. Even subtle bias is exhausting and can be both illegal and soul destroying to both the individual and the organization. Just as we discussed conscious and unconscious bias in evaluating candidates, the same holds true for discipline and termination of employment.

It's important to have frank and respectful dialogue about the issue at hand and eliminate any assumptions by checking your own biases at the door. The antidote, to bias-laden decisions, is to stick to the facts and stay laser focused on the behaviors and/or actions at issue. (See the Resources section for chapter 3.)

You will learn a lot during a constructive feedback session. I've known employees who genuinely had no idea something was amiss and/ or did not understand the leader's perspective or expectations. Once they did understand, they were more likely to succeed. If, on the other hand, you find the employee to be dismissive, blaming others, acting like a victim, making excuses, or constantly justifying their behaviors and not hearing you, it's time to get serious about ending the relationship.

Employees should be able to question your information or opinion to get clarity; if they believe the facts are incorrect, they should be able to tell you why. How they question or push back says a lot about who they are. For instance, if you tell someone that their tardiness in submitting their work every week is unacceptable and the employee says they never saw or heard a deadline for that work, check the facts. If you realize that you were indeed vague about deadlines (e.g., "soon, please") and realize that "soon" can mean different things to different people, it's not time to fire or even discipline someone; it is time to sort out expectations and communication. If the response is more like, "What's the big deal, I got it done didn't I?" you have a much bigger problem than missed deadlines.

There's an old saying, "the wife/husband/partner always finds out last." Problem behaviors or actions are often observed by other people long before you, the leader, know what's going on. Employees, new or not, who are wrong for your team and organization often have the ability to appear to be exactly the person you need when they are with and around *you* and exhibit very different behaviors with peers and direct reports. I call this *termite behavior*.

Termite behavior in employees does the same damage to your business as those creepy crawly termites do to your house foundation—they hide from sight while wreaking havoc, one bite at a time! There's also a Scottish term I equate with particularly snarly behavior—*a smiling knife*. This is a person who says all the right things to the boss and then sabotages others, including the boss, behind their backs. You'll know a "termite" or a "smiling knife" when you see one, *if* you are paying attention. The trick is having your eyes, ears, and instincts wide open.

A "Termite" Story

Joanne was in a leadership role and a brilliant subject matter expert, but she wanted her leader's (Andy's) job badly. She decided to begin to undermine Andy with her own direct reports, their leadership team, and then his boss. She told her staff that Andy only wanted *her* to bring their concerns or problems to him, telling them (while she rolled her eyes) that he said he was too busy to be bothered. Joanne made unpopular decisions but said Andy approved them, or that they were his decisions, not hers. She'd claim that no matter how hard she tried to convince him otherwise, he wouldn't budge. She made "under her breath" negative or dismissive comments about Andy to her peers. Then she began "triangulating" by going around Andy to his leader with her ideas, claiming Andy was not interested or too busy. All the while, when meeting with Andy, she was upbeat and complimentary about everything he said or did. The "smiling knife" indeed!

Andy started noticing people avoiding him when he came in the room. His own leader was questioning why Joanne was stopping by so often—asking why Andy wasn't paying attention to Joanne and her interesting ideas. Finally, Andy got it. "I think I might have a termite in Joanne," Andy said, and he was right!

To uncover the truth, Andy made it a priority to set up individual meetings with his peers and all of Joanne's direct reports telling everyone he was beginning quarterly "checking in" sessions with staff and colleagues with the goal of having candid conversations and an exchange of ideas. Joanne's meeting was set up last. Andy asked open-ended questions and promised confidentiality. He got an earful that painted a clear and very consistent picture of lies and deceit. Once he had fully verified his "termite" theory with facts and evidence, completed his due diligence and exit plan, and received the support he needed from his boss and HR, he was able to confront Joanne about her deceitful behaviors and actions.

She got caught, and she knew it. He told Joanne she needed to find the job she wanted outside their organization. Because of his concerns about her poisoning the workplace even more, he allowed her to resign, handed her a modest severance check, and said goodbye.

Andy's public communication was short and sweet. His formal announcement said that Joanne was moving on to other opportunities outside their organization and had resigned as of that day. He appreciated the success she and her team had in X, Y, and Z and wished her the best for the future. Privately, he told her staff and peers that her values and theirs were not well aligned, so they had agreed she needed to find somewhere where her goals and values were a better fit. Both statements were true. Start to finish was just short of thirty days, and Andy decided to continue his quarterly check-in meetings.

If firing were easy for leaders, it would happen faster and more often because there are some consistent underperformers and bad behaviors in every organization. Because it isn't easy, there are a host of reasons that can cause a leader to hesitate at best and, at worst, fail to fire a person who needs to be fired. Here are *six common blocks to firing*, each with an *antidote*. If you can name some others, make a note to yourself and look for ways to unblock yourself.

BLOCKS TO FIRING

1. Arrogance: "I hired you, so I couldn't be, or don't want to be wrong." Another word for this is *ego*. No one is perfect, and hiring anyone is always going to be a measured risk. You have no control over the choices that lead to the behaviors and actions of another person. You can only do your best to set them up to succeed; you cannot make them succeed. If you've hired, onboarded, and developed right, you've given it your best shot. *The antidote to arrogance and ego is stepping back, applying objectivity, having the ability to admit mistakes, being open minded, and paying close attention to both the data and your instincts instead of your ego.*

2. Conflict or Pain Avoidance: This is about your pain or the employee's pain or both. It could be a reluctance to, or even fear of, engaging in a potentially tough conversation or conflict. Or, you might be feeling guilty that you hired someone into a job where they cannot succeed, forgetting for a moment that they applied for and accepted that job. There may be an organizational culture, *based entirely in myth*, that by dealing directly and appropriately with bad behavior and/ or poor performance you're not being inclusive of diverse people or ideas. You might think you didn't do enough to support this employee; you could be worried about doing damage to that person's future career or emotional state. Feeling guilty or letting conflicts escalate helps no one, including the employee. *The antidote (situation dependent) is to summon the courage to have a very candid conversation about the situation. This will either transform the conflict into positive action by the employee, or it will move your closer to an exit process.*

3. Fix-It Syndrome: Most leaders know that providing appreciation, constructive feedback, and development opportunities are all parts of the leader's job. However, when all the evidence tells us that an employee's ability to thrive in the job is just not there, prolonging the agony amplifies the employee's failure. No one can turn a pine tree into an oak tree, and taking too long to recognize and address a mismatch is unfair to both the employee and the organization. *Employee development does not replace employee responsibility, fitness, or performance.* It's good to offer development, but don't keep trying when it's getting you and the employee nowhere fast. There can be a misconception that more and more development is the answer to everything. It is not. No business can afford, or should "carry," marginal or underperforming staff. Trying to "save" an employee for too long, when it's clear they are a mismatch for the job, is a mistake that can carry far-reaching consequences. *The antidote to the fix-it syndrome is to perform due diligence, have direct and candid conversations, and if possible, support the employee in finding other employment options.*

4. Image and Perception: There may be a fear of having your organization, team, or even you perceived as being out of control or bad decision makers, or that rumors will fly if you fire someone, particularly a highly visible, well-known employee. If you are concerned, keep in mind that it's far worse to ignore poor performance than it is to deal with it. You can't control rumors and gossip, but you can control communications and your own behavior and actions. *The antidote to image and perception concerns is to be as transparent as possible in your communications without violating an employee's privacy.*

5. Fear of Loss: Leaders can get stuck, frozen even, with the fear of imagined or even real upsets and disruptions to operations if an employee who has a key role or is deeply imbedded in positive relationships with external stakeholders (clients, customers, alumni, vendors, etc.) is fired. Other losses can drive a failure to act—loss of time, resources, and the support of one or more of your stakeholders. There is a lingering myth we carry around about thinking some employees are indispensable. No one is, no matter how hard he or she may try to convince you they are. If they left of their own accord you'd have to figure out how to replace them. While some of what that employee is doing could be mission critical, if they are doing real damage at the same time, you have a big problem. Justifying keeping someone because they are "so smart" or "know more than anyone about ABC" or are "loved by everyone" is not going to serve you or the organization in the long run. Customers, employees, and other stakeholders care more about getting the support or results they need than who, specifically, is providing for their needs. Stakeholders tend to have fairly short memories when they are satisfied. *The antidote to fear of loss is having well-considered transition and communication plans that you can snap into place immediately without leaving gaping holes in your operations.*

6. Fear of Litigation: Leaders, HR professionals, and even legal counsel may avoid a firing, no matter how egregious the employee's behavior or actions have been, for fear of being sued, or in the case of a union, going to arbitration. This is particularly true when an employee is in a protected class (e.g., gender, age, race, ethnicity, religion, or disability). Tiptoeing around someone whose performance is problematic sends a message of weakness and uncertainty both to the employee and everyone else involved. While a full review of the facts and thoughtful consideration must be given, and while ensuring bias isn't operating in your decision, *fear of litigation must not stop a firing that needs to happen.*

When you are confident that due diligence fairness, and objectivity (including documentation and discipline), have been addressed, and you are certain that a firing is justified, the fact that someone *can* sue you or grieve a firing need not scare you. You don't know whether they will or not. Even if they do, they will rarely, if ever, win when you've executed your due diligence properly. There are two options frequently used by organizations when threatened by litigation or arbitration—pay the employee enough to entice them to go away, or let the suit or arbitration proceed. You'd be surprised how many people back down when the employer lets the litigation or arbitration threat stand. Employees who sue generally have to pay an attorney, and unions who expect they are going to lose will often try to negotiate a settlement rather than spend resources on arbitration. *The antidote to fear of litigation is firing right in the first place, including completing your due diligence and being 100 percent aligned with your values.*

REASONS TO FIRE

People ask me time and again, "Do I need to put up with this or am I justified in firing for it?" Within these five reasons to fire, I am confident that you will see at least one that fits most, if not all, *firing for cause* terminations of employment you may encounter.

1. Does Not "Play" Well with Others: More people are fired for this reason than any other no matter what the public cover story is. Using a schoolyard metaphor is appropriate here because it is an experience all of us have witnessed at some time in our lives. We know what it means, we know it when we see it, and we know how to describe what we see. When an employee, for whatever reason, demonstrates a pattern of being hard to work with, high maintenance, unwilling to collaborate, unwilling to share information, arrogant, a bully, or a loner, for example, a bright red light is flashing. It's telling us this person has few, if any, emotional intelligence competencies. In *The No Asshole Rule*, author Robert Sutton tells us why banning jerks from the workplace matters because of the devastation they inflict on coworkers' emotional well-being and work quality. This, of course, ends up as a negative hit to your bottom line.[1]

The inability to work well with others has been, and will continue to be, the Achilles' heel of too many very bright people who fail because of a serious deficit of emotional intelligence competencies. Self-awareness, self-management, social awareness, and relationship management *are not being demonstrated* when an employee has a pattern of not "playing" well with others.

How much you invest in supporting someone in increasing emotional intelligence competencies is up to you. For instance, if the employee adds great value to your organization in other areas with brains, character, and drive, then explicit feedback, consistent performance management, training, and/or coaching may be worth it. If the employee doesn't respond to that kind of support, or is not deserving of the investment, it's time to fire—and fire fast—before more damage is done.

2. Loss of Trust: Loss of trust is a root cause behind many terminations. Behaviors that lead to loss of trust include such things as consistent poor performance, broken promises, ethical breaches, sabotage, policy violations, lying, a disruptive/unacceptable pattern of behaviors, disloyalty, and stealing. Trust is created or broken based on our collection of experiences with another person. When there is history of solid trust between two people, one incident *may or may not* destroy the relationship. When there is little history, one incident could end it. Only you can determine the degree of significance of the breakage.

We know in our gut when we do and don't trust someone and often why we feel that way. Loss of trust is a first, and very important, signal that something is wrong. *Don't ignore it.* Human beings all have built-in radar systems; our "BS" meters are operating 24/7. Sometimes we pay attention to the warning signs being broadcast by our "BS" meters, and sometimes we ignore them. *Never, ever ignore the warnings!* You may know why your meter is flashing, or you may need to take the time to figure it out. If need be, test your assumptions and verify or disprove what your instincts are telling you. Bottom line, you'll need to find a way to rebuild trust together or that person needs to leave your organization. *No trust, no job.*

3. Blame Shifting and Avoidance: When an employee avoids meetings or conversations about performance, and/or shifts the blame for something they were supposed to be doing to another person to avoid being held accountable, there are a number of problems going on. The first problem is avoidance. They suspect they will be held accountable and don't want to have that conversation. When they try to make their poor performance someone else's fault, you're witnessing blame shifting and the failure to take responsibility for their choices, decisions, and behaviors. Even worse, they are trying to throw someone else under the bus. When it's a leader doing this, it's magnified exponentially. The leader who shifts the blame for poor performance onto their employees is admitting they aren't leading well and is taking no responsibility for the outcomes of their team. If this behavior does not change with feedback and coaching, it's time to fire.

4. **Insubordination:** This is a subcategory of both trust and not "playing well with others," but it's egregious enough to stand on its own. Insubordination is a direct or indirect refusal by an employee to perform a legal, ethical, and reasonable directive from a manager or supervisor when the directive has been clearly understood.[2] When an employee blatantly refuses to honor the request, or simply ignores it, it is insubordination. For instance, perhaps you told an employee to cease and desist using foul language in meetings. If the employee says, "That's just who I am and I'm exercising my first amendment rights!" that's blatant insubordination. If the employee apologizes after using foul language but keeps doing it, that's a bit more passive but still insubordinate. Insubordination can be grounds for immediate dismissal, depending on the seriousness and/or the pattern of the incident(s).

If you believe there is reason to be optimistic the person can change behavior, follow the Employee Development System (EDS) process of clarifying expectations, providing metrics for success, and acknowledging performance. Assuming you have remained calm and been explicitly clear about the behavior that is unacceptable and why, you may want to involve a neutral third party to mediate and try to understand the source of the problem so you can work toward a resolution. However, if an employee is threatening, harassing, or exhibits abusive behavior with you and/or others, it's time to fire, particularly if there's a documented pattern of these behaviors.

5. **Lack of Engagement:** All the A–H factors in the "Acquisition = Hire Right" section apply here. You hired for attitude, brains, character, drive, emotional intelligence, fit, gut, and heart, and you needed all those things to show up in that person at work. Lack of engagement can be an outcome of someone who has "retired in the job" or a newer employee who came in sprinting but couldn't go the distance. If you see low or no drive, a lack of a can-do attitude, and it's clear their heart isn't in it, then at least four of the eight A–H factors you need for success are missing. If those were once there and now they are not, you need to find out what created the shift. The employee may have believed the job was one thing, and it has turned out to be something else. A change in the team dynamic may have caused disengagement. There are lots of reasons that may or may not be the employee's doing. Before lack of

engagement becomes a cause for firing, do your best to get to the root cause and help the employee course correct. However, if you believed you hired one kind of person and discover it's not the case, you probably were fooled in the first place, and it's time to either find a better fit for that employee or time to fire.

Some organizations have a culture of almost never firing anyone. Others have a culture where firing is a handy go-to option at any moment. There are times and situations when firing fast is absolutely the right thing to do, and the same is true with firing slowly. *Too fast and too slow are both bad for business.* Since *firing right* is the goal, it's worth taking the time here to explore the pros and cons of each.

FIRE FAST

When even national recruiters tell us consistently that roughly 50 percent of new hires fail within the first eighteen months on the job, identifying and dealing with bad hires quickly makes a lot of sense.[3] It makes more sense, of course, to hire right in the first place, and we've already talked a lot about that. You need to get bad hires out of your organization. If you don't move them out, poor performers can have a detrimental influence and drag down other employees as well as your business.

When you are paying close attention to your new hire, it shouldn't take long to get a good read on them. The employee will either exhibit behaviors and performance you expected, or they won't. Some employees can fool you for a few weeks, even a month or two, but if there's going to be a problem, it's likely to show up sooner than later. Don't dismiss or brush off yours or others' concerns—deal with them immediately.

Employees, new or long serving, who don't "play well with others," aren't collaborative, can't be trusted, or don't respond well to your feedback may need to go—and go quickly. This is a bottom-line issue for you because *the longer you put off a necessary firing the more quickly you lose the value proposition of that employee.* Long delays prevent you from moving ahead with your team and business, and worse, the problem often becomes more complex and can begin to spread, thereby impacting more people and your business results. For those of you running startups or small, growing companies, firing quickly may save your business, particularly when poorly performing employees sit on your executive team.

Jeff Hyman, author of the book *Recruit Rockstars*, is the Chief Talent Officer at Chicago-based Strong Suit Executive Search and a professor at Northwestern University's Kellogg School of Management. He wrote a provocative article for Forbes titled "You Need to Fire More People."[4] Although this may be a somewhat shocking opinion for a lot of leaders, he's right. Too many organizations tolerate mediocre and poor performance for too long. He and I also agree that, in most cases, people need to be given consistent feedback and a fair opportunity to change course. If all that fails, we then need to make a firm firing decision and do so as humanely as possible. We'll take a good look at *how to fire right* later on in this chapter.

A lot has been written in favor of "hire slow, fire fast," and it all boils down to one big thing. When the largest percentage of your budget is paying for people, as it is in most organizations, you need those resources to be working for you, not against you. We all benefit from healthy, growing, high-performing organizations, and we suffer when they are bogged down in mediocrity. One person should not be allowed to make an entire team struggle or fail. Weigh the realities for the greater good in every firing decision, and it might help you get to your decision a lot faster.

I love this quote from Greg McKeown from an article in the *Harvard Business Review*: "lacking courage is not the same as having compassion."[5] It's important to take into consideration how unfair it is for a failing employee to receive negative performance feedback over and over again rather than helping her get a new start, hopefully in a role somewhere else in which she has a better chance of success. Playing games with people's lives is just plain wrong. Moving them around your organization like chess pieces is a big mistake when you know they are not a good fit for your culture, and frankly, it's cruel. I've witnessed leaders telling their direct reports they have to hire a known poor performer for any number of upside-down reasons that may sound righteous and compassionate, but it isn't. Instead, it is lacking the courage to do what must be done and makes everything worse for both the employee and the organization. The reasons may be based on real problems, but keeping a poor performer isn't the solution to excuses like "we're losing too many women"; "no one else will take him, and we need his wife to stay here"; or "maybe she'll be better on your team than mine." It's time to step up and deal with the problem of the poor performer.

I once, only once, allowed myself to be cajoled into taking on a transfer of an employee from a colleague who wanted to be rid of her. He said, "Roxi, I just don't trust her, and I'm not sure why." He genuinely believed I would be a better leader for her. He also thought her skill set would be useful on my team. He was right; her skills were very useful . . . for a while. And he was right; she was untrustworthy. No surprise there. I had to fire her.

A picture *is* worth a thousand words, and a picture that sticks with me is a cracked egg with a Band-Aid on it. When an employee is truly failing at the job, sometimes there is no putting Humpty Dumpty back together again no matter how many patches you attempt. All eyes are on you, their leader, to see how you're going to handle the situation, particularly when it's a senior leader, or a person in a protected class, or a well-liked employee who is in the hot seat. You can almost hear the whispers—"He'll never be fired because . . ." Your best employees will be aware of the problem and will be troubled. Some may leave if they see or believe you are doing nothing, true or not.

As we discussed in chapter 7, two of the four key employee engagement factors are *trusting in the leadership* and *having a positive and supportive work environment*. In all my years working with thousands of employees and leaders, it is clear that far more people leave because of the eroding of trust in management than because they want another job. Your staff will trust you more when you deal fairly and quickly with problem behaviors and performance; they will stay with you longer when their work environment is positive and not being contaminated by a rotten egg player.

FIRE SLOWLY

The other side of the coin can be just as troubling for organizations, leaders, and teams for several reasons. When leaders say "goodbye" by firing because they believe it to be the *only* option, special care must be taken to do it right. That means *slowing down long enough to make sure you are proceeding in the right ways.*

You know the human and financial costs of hiring a new staff member, particularly when you have to recruit externally versus hiring from within. No doubt you have, during your career, observed or experienced the ripple effect, or sometimes tsunami effect, of firing someone. That is why, if you have not already done so, I'm inviting you to *press pause before you fire someone too quickly.* Take some time to explore anything you may have overlooked and consider what prevention efforts might be possible *before* there is no chance of turning back the tide. I suggest this because acting *too fast can be even worse than acting too slowly* and because I have observed a troubling mind-set in some leaders that I wouldn't want you to fall prey to.

"We can always fire him if it doesn't work out, right?" This thought can play out in the back of some leaders' minds, even if it is never said out loud. When a firing goes badly, which unfortunately occurs with alarming frequency, the human, organizational, and financial costs are staggering and often long lasting. When this mind-set is ever present in the culture, it is like the sword of Damocles dangling over employees' heads, and it contaminates the entire workplace and culture.

You may have heard a leader say something like this to an employee, "You know your job is up to me, so you better do it my way" or, perhaps, "If you're not happy here, there are plenty of people who would love to have your job, so . . ." I have heard statements like these and much worse. Unfortunately, these are not uncommon attitudes, and their very existence creates a toxic culture of fear, low risk, and high turnover.

Being allowed to fire someone at the drop of a hat may also encourage some leaders to take shortcuts in problem prevention—hiring right and retaining right, for example—especially if they believe they have a "get out of jail free card" in their back pocket. In these cases, leaders are ignoring, or don't realize, the potential of the massive financial, operational, and human costs that may come rushing in—until *it's too late.* Klara's story is a perfect example of this attitude in action and what not to do.

Klara's Story

Klara, a highly visible vice president, decided she wanted to redesign her division quickly by getting rid of about twenty of her lowest performing staff, but she couldn't be bothered having conversations, or ask her supervisors to have conversations, with the people she'd targeted. Instead, Klara fired, except for her cabinet, the entire staff of more than two hundred people on what some still call their own personal "Black Friday."

Klara told the employees they could apply for whatever jobs they were interested in from the new list she created, but she had the final decision about who got what job. When the massive amount of dust settled, many of the finest employees had jumped ship. Word spread fast in the industry, and competing organizations snatched up as many of the best and the brightest as they could.

It's now more than twenty-five years later; several vice presidents have come and gone in Klara's role, but anyone who still works for the organization carries that painful story in their cultural DNA and passes it on to new generations of employees.

If you have seen or heard the news over the last few years, even on occasion, you and the entire world have witnessed a national case study of this mind-set in action. The forty-fifth president of the United States routinely and publicly fires people whom he has hired with and without vetting. He has lauded every one of them as the best, brightest, and most respected . . . anywhere on earth. Then, without warning in many cases, these supposedly fabulous people are fired unceremoniously by text, by proxy, with no notice, with public demonization, and labels like "lazy, stupid, and nut cases." Regardless of your political views or what you may think about any single individual on the long, long, long list of people *fired* from many of the highest-ranking positions in the land, this behavior sends a devastating message about working for the Office of the President, and most likely gives pause to anyone considering a career in the federal government.

Firing slowly enough to complete your thorough due diligence increases the likelihood you won't have missed something important that will come back to haunt you. You'll know it's too fast when one day, for whatever reason(s), you say, "She's got to go," and the next day she's gone. Now it may be more than a day, and still be too fast, if you haven't explored your options, had several direct conversations with the employee, and documented your concerns.

It's not too fast if you hired someone with a ninety-day probationary period and at thirty and sixty days, or more often, you've been clear and explicit about performance shortcomings. It is not too fast if you've offered training, coaching, and supervision to help the employee be successful over a reasonable period of time. It *is* too fast if you have done little or none of those things.

Before deciding to fire someone, explore alternatives that could save you much of what you've already invested in that employee. If the job is a bad fit and a different job within the organization has a high probability of being more successful, then by all means explore that option. This isn't passing the buck, it is creating possibilities that your due diligence has unearthed. For instance, if you have an employee who is brilliant at working as an individual contributor but horrible at leading people and doesn't really want to be a supervisor after all, then if possible, it may be worth it to find a way to apply those skills where they can add the most value.

For others, perhaps adjusting the job responsibilities would get better results. Extending the probationary period could have a positive effect. Would providing a coach or a mentor make a difference? If you make a bad hire for this position and that's why it's not working, ask yourself what attracted you to this employee and if there is a way to leverage those qualities in some way that makes good business sense. The point is to ask a lot of tough questions before making a too-hasty decision that will more than likely impact you, the employee, and everyone connected to that employee, in one way or another. Matt is a good example of firing slowly for the right reasons.

Matt's Story

Matt was a smart, talented, and all around terrific guy. He was doing half his job well and the other half horribly. Sylvia, Matt's boss, had spoken with him regularly for three months providing clear expectations and sharing the metrics he was missing consistently. Each time, Matt promised to do better and didn't ask for any help. Then he dropped the ball once again, and it caused several serious problems for the team.

As much as she hated to do it, Sylvia was ready to fire Matt or reduce him to half time. Before she did, Sylvia had one last conversation with him where she asked him to describe his dream job. Matt first said he didn't know. Sylvia insisted. Finally, he shared that letting go of all the detail work and being allowed to just facilitate groups full time was his passion. He'd assumed that wasn't an option and therefore shouldn't even ask.

Sylvia was taken aback to hear this for the first time and decided rather than fire Matt, they would look for ways to get him fully engaged in the work he loved. Sylvia had been ready to say "goodbye" to Matt. Because she asked him a key question, and they were able to find a win/win solution, Matt succeeded in his redesigned job for many years.

HOW TO FIRE RIGHT

OK, you've pressed pause long enough to reach a "Goldilocks" pace of not too fast and not to slow. You are certain there is no better option than to fire this employee. You and I know it's not going to be fun or easy. The good news is that it will be much easier on your nerves when you follow my process. It has helped me, and other leaders, feel a lot better knowing they fired someone the right way—with accuracy, fairness, and grace. Since, even in our highly litigious society, no one I have fired has won a lawsuit, arbitration, or even a level-three grievance, I am confident that my process works. It works because of the attention to having *a human relational approach and employing rigorous due diligence.*

There are *five principles* that must be included when you are delivering your decision to involuntarily terminate someone's employment. These principles will give you a higher rate of success as you say "goodbye"; I call them the five "BE" principles: BE truthful, BE fair, BE clear, BE respectful, and BE smart.

1. BE Truthful

Employees should know *exactly why* they are being released from their job. Tell them the truth. While this may be an "employee at-will" position, and is an employer right for nonunion staff in most states (be sure to check your state), most employers also have some kind of due process written in their HR procedures and policies. Those need to be honored and clearly communicated to all employees.

People fill in blanks with inaccurate and bad news most of the time, so don't leave room for doubt. You do not need to create gaps that may cause more resentment or bad will. Gross misconduct is gross misconduct, and poor performance is poor performance. Sometimes it's a matter of a bad hire or a bad fit and it's simply time to part ways. Don't embellish and don't minimize; tell the truth with accuracy, sincerity, and kindness.

There's nothing wrong with feeling badly for the employee and expressing your genuine sadness. Even when I've been mad as hell at someone for what they've done or not done to get him or her fired, I know losing a job is a traumatic event and I always feel some sadness that it's come to this. *Showing sincere compassion is not a weakness* in a leader, and it often helps the firing conversation go much more smoothly. I've actually had some employees thank me for firing them (after a few months, mind you); this happened because each one knew they were being told the whole truth, and they knew the truth was squarely on their shoulders. They were not right for the job, and the reasons were clear. These folks went on to do something that suited them better and were much happier.

The same truth telling applies to your remaining team members. It's not uncommon for other employees to be irrationally fearful that the same will happen to them. Sometimes, there is "survivor guilt" even when people are relieved to see someone go. It's important to be timely and honest in accordance with your organization's policies while being respectful of the employee who's leaving. For instance, if I fired someone because they violated our organization's values, I was clear about that. I would say something like, "Sam is no longer going to be working with us as of . . . I am truly sorry this is the case, and I believe it's the right decision for Sam and for our team because our values were not compatible." Of course, if someone steals something, or is involved in workplace violence or sexual harassment, or any single incident that requires instant termination, you need to be particularly cautious about what you say to others. In cases like that, my response to the team might go something like this: "Sam is no longer going to be working with us as of . . . I am truly sorry this is the case, but our policies are clear about acceptable workplace behaviors and actions and the consequences of not adhering to them." Say no more and be clear that you will not being saying more—and then don't.

I think you'll find that referring to your organizational values works for most situations. For instance, if someone won't or can't work well with others, and you have a value of teamwork, it fits. If someone purposefully cheats on a time card and you have a value of integrity, it fits. Take a look at your organizational values (assuming they are widely known) and see if you agree that most employee terminations result from a violation of your core values.

2. BE Fair

Fairness is a fundamental human need and expectation that we all have, at least in the United States. It is also a major factor in how the employee and others on your team feel when he or she exits the organization. Whether the employee is perceived to have been treated fairly *is the question* upon which everyone makes judgments.

The way I look at fairness is simple. What would feel fair to me on the other side of the table? What would make me feel like I'm not a bad person, and that this was just not a right fit? Even if I know I've done a wrong thing as an employee, do I believe the punishment fits the crime? If I've worked here successfully for ten years, is any of that taken into account as I'm going out the door? Am I the only one being punished this way? You know this person pretty well by now, so consider how this employee needs to hear the news. Put yourself into their shoes and imagine what they might be feeling and thinking before you cut the cord.

Before deciding to fire, you must have a heart-to-heart talk with yourself. Did you really do your part as their leader? Did you hire well, onboard well, offer to help this person develop, provide clear expectations and success metrics, and provide constructive feedback? Do you own any part of this unfortunate situation? If you've done everything you should have and could have done to help this person be successful, and they still didn't cut it, then sleep easy. If not, you have more work to do before you go to sleep and before you fire that person.

Let's say you are sleeping well and you are thinking of ways to make the firing to go as smoothly as possible. Fairness matters in your offer if you are providing one. For instance, if it's reasonable, I offer the employee the opportunity to resign versus being fired. I have a resignation letter prepared and waiting for their signature. This isn't about your being right and the employee being wrong. At the end of the day, it is about doing what you have to do to remove a person from your workplace with as little trouble, drama, and blowback as possible. It is in your best interests for that person to leave your employ with their dignity reasonably intact. It's also about doing everything you can, within reason, to lower the risk of that person taking you to court or showing up with a weapon to air their grievances.

While you and that fired employee may disagree about what is or is not fair, I recommend that you to do more than you have to, be kinder than you have to, and be more gracious than you have to because, in the end, that employee will still go away. The only question that remains is whether or not they'll go quietly.

3. BE Clear

Whenever possible, you should have had at least one, and preferably several, discussions with your employee where you've made it crystal clear that their job was on the line and exactly why. If the termination is due to an incident of gross misconduct like lying on a resume or stealing or sexual harassment, then say that right up front. Of course you need indisputable proof of your assertions before saying any of this.

If the person is let go after a lengthy process of attempted improvement, remind them what was discussed and when (and what needed to happen by when) and spell out how they didn't succeed in making the changes necessary to continue in their position. *Document all of these conversations carefully.*

Do not get into a lengthy dialogue with the employee about why, who else, or what could have been done differently. Do not put yourself in a position to have to defend this decision with the employee; *it is not a negotiation, it's a final decision.* The decision to terminate employment should have been made with excellent due diligence and should not be a surprise. In this conversation, you're following through with what you said would happen. There's no more "if only" or "what if" to be discussed.

The blame game is a tactic some employees use. "Mary did/didn't do exactly the same as me, and she's not being fired." That's when you say, "This conversation and decision isn't about Mary today—it's about you." That kind of response puts the conversation right back where it belongs without having to speak about Mary at all. You're being firm and clear without being cruel.

Cut to the chase, make whatever offer you have decided upon (resignation option, money, severance, reference responses, timing, etc.), then stand up, put out your hand, wish the employee well, and, when they are ready, walk them to the door. If the employee becomes despondent, is crying, or angry, give him or her some time and space to get their emotions together. Do not fill the time with chitchat or more conversation about the decision. *Be quiet.* Crying is a normal human reaction to strong emotions, so have a box of tissues on the table and take a deep breath while you let your employee cry as long as they need to. This will likely be embarrassing to him or her, so just be kind, understanding, and human. It isn't a weakness to show another human being your compassion for them.

4. BE Respectful

Always take the high road. Believe it or not, you could be fair with the process and not respectful to the person. Being respectful to the employee is not only the right thing to do but also is the smart thing to do. It's a well-known fact that people rarely sue people, including their doctors, when they like them and *feel* they've been treated respectfully, even when there is ample cause to sue. The opposite is true. People, including doctors, are sued without ample cause, far more often when the relationships are cold or nonexistent, or when a person feels disrespected. Regardless of the circumstances leading to the termination, keep in mind that *this is a relationship* between you and the employee, *not just a job.* This should not feel or be transactional any more than hiring should be transactional; it's about the relationship as much as it's about the job. You are ending it, and you need to acknowledge the pain in doing so. It's in your best interests to keep that relationship respectful and professional every step of the way. In other words, never, ever "lose it" with an employee or treat a firing like just another transactional task. Doing so will come back to haunt you.

This is definitely not the time to say, "I told you so," or list off all the things they could have done differently, or to lecture them about this or that. This is also not the time to make yourself feel better about your decision by belittling the employee or minimizing their contributions to help you feel justified in firing them. It's not about you; it's about them.

Keep in mind that this person is an adult, and the conversation needs to treat them that way.

Have your meeting at a time during the day in which the employee will have little exposure to colleagues. You can't predict what a person will do, but you can manage the situation to a large degree. My normal practice is to have this conversation at the end of the day to give the employee enough time to gather their thoughts and feelings and then privately exit the building. There were times when someone just wanted to leave immediately and pick up their personal belongings later or have them delivered to their home. Some people want to say goodbye to colleagues; you need to orchestrate the time and place of that interaction on terms you feel good about, particularly if you have not yet been able to talk to your team and others who are impacted.

5. BE Smart

There are emotional aspects of the termination discussion, and there are other factors to consider. Might the employee become volatile? Do you need security precautions? Should someone from HR or others be present in the room? You'll also need to ensure your exit checklist is complete—keys, access, passwords, equipment, credit cards, and such must be retrieved or cut off. Your organization should have a solid termination process to follow to keep you out of legal and any other kind of jeopardy. If you haven't already, make sure to review the Termination Checklist in the Resources section for this chapter *long before* you begin a termination meeting with an employee.

I once terminated a 350-pound, six-foot-four man whom we observed carrying guns in the trunk of his car. We discovered that he also lied about a felony record when he applied for the job. That allowed us to fire him without having to make a case for the other problems like his intimidation of coworkers. His male supervisor, a female HR professional, and I, the senior director, were all in the room, and we arranged for our well-trained and armed security staff to be in plain clothes right outside the door.

It was my job to deliver the news. I could have just fired him for lying because we had proof and he had no recourse. Instead, I told him we were sorry and disappointed that we could no longer employ him due to his false statements on his application and that was why we were terminating his employment. I offered him a check for a month's pay to help him in this transition. We collected his keys and told him his supervisor would help him gather up his belongings and he could take the rest of the day off with pay. He had already earned two weeks' vacation pay, so it wasn't a lot of extra money we were offering.

At the close of the meeting, he thanked all of us for being so fair because we gave him a month's pay to "get him on his feet." He shook my hand and left immediately without incident. That result was worth every penny!

This was not the first or last time a decision to be responsibly generous with money paid off for me in a firing situation. While you may say, "hell no, they don't deserve a dime," consider the rest of your team, everyone's time and trouble, and the disruption an employee can and often will cause if they feel they've been treated badly.

Unless your organization specifically forbids it, don't let money be a barrier to removing a troublesome employee. You don't have to go crazy, but don't be so cheap that you end up spending many times that money in lost time, productivity, and morale. Err on the side of being generous with severance or "administrative work-from-home" assignments when it's reasonable and smart to do so. It is *almost never worth it to be stingy* when offering some money (or other transition options) could go a long way to making a bad situation turn out a lot better. Having said that, when the firing offense is so egregious that you'd rather risk a lawsuit, then, by all means, offer nothing of value.

It is the smart thing to take all the time you need to be prepared, to know what you're going to say and do, and to stick to that plan unless something truly extraordinary changes your mind. In my experience, serious and proper preparation significantly reduces the odds you'll have to change your decision.

Being fired is a terrible experience for the employee and for you, even when it is fair, done respectfully, and with grace and integrity. Everyone acts differently when they are fired. People cry, they laugh, say nothing, go quietly, storm out, threaten this or that, and so on; it just depends on what's going on for them at that moment. Once all is said and done, it is the emotions that often wear you down from the start of this process through to the finish. It's important to remember that it's both OK and important for you and the employee to *feel what you feel* and acknowledge that. We're all human. Just don't let your feelings about one person, and the pain of that sad conversation, get in the way of doing what has to be done and doing it right.

LAYOFFS

The layoff conversation is nearly as tough as a firing one. In most layoff situations, the leaders know well ahead of time what's coming and when. It's nearly always based on a business reason that someone in management has decided must happen. It requires a plan to be put into place and implemented, and it signals the closure of an employment relationship with one or more employees. It is beyond the employee's control and may even be beyond the direct leader's control.

The five "BEs" are as relevant in a layoff as in a firing, although they may be rolled out differently. For instance, if jobs are being eliminated, you should be able to give employees a heads up to give them time to look for another position. In the best-case scenario, your valued employees will be assisted in finding another position within or outside your organization. I always advise to provide as much time and financial support as possible in a layoff situation. It can buy you goodwill with employees and other stakeholders.

Layoff talk spreads like wildfire in any organization. To prevent misinformation, rumors, and gossip from getting a firm grip on your highly efficient grapevine, head them off fast. I was once required to implement a top-down "workforce planning" process with no input from those of us affected. I didn't like it one bit, as you can imagine. I used what authority I had to calm the waters with our staff. Instead of letting rumors and fear spread, I met with everyone involved immediately and told them we were required to reduce by two full-time equivalents. I also said that I didn't believe either of those needed to happen through layoffs.

We created a diverse task force to produce a plan that would meet the requirement through vacancies, reassignments, job sharing, reduced work week, and such—anything but layoffs. I knew we could get creative and find solutions. And we did. The task force included people who were most likely affected. They got deep into the weeds and figured out how to absorb one vacant position and reassign the second one to another part of the organization. This was a major change effort that worked because we did it together, with full transparency, and by telling the whole truth to everyone involved.

If you have no choice but to lay people off, tell them the truth as early as possible and be fair, clear, respectful, and smart. In being smart, also consider that you may want to rehire a valued laid-off employee down the road. Keep the door open by conducting a respectful closure process and staying in communication from time to time. Being able to rehire someone you already know and trust will save you a ton of time and money, so do everything you can to help the laid-off employee land in a good place, including being as generous with severance as you can.

When a fired or laid-off employee applies for another job, it's important to know what your organization's policies say about providing references to another employer. Most businesses have their own layoff policies and procedures, so I will not attempt to guess yours. Take a look at those policies before you need to put them into action and be well prepared for the conversation with your employee. Consult with an HR professional if you are not sure. You and the employee may be able to agree about what you'll say; if not, be clear with the employee about what you're able and willing to say and do.

In most cases, employers are not legally prohibited from telling another employer the truth about a firing or layoff. You can share the reasons you let someone go. Many employers are cautious about sharing information that might be harmful to a former worker for fear of legal repercussions. That can lead to HR policies that limit what is shared to dates of employment and job titles. You cannot make false statements or exaggerate the reasons for termination and thereby damage someone's reputation with inaccurate information. Do that and you could have a defamation lawsuit on your hands, particularly with high-profile positions in large, wealthy organizations. While this type of lawsuit is fairly rare, the best solution is to simply tell the truth without any fanfare.

There are also federal and state laws about layoffs that you must obey. The federal government has a notice requirement law that requires an employer to provide its employees with adequate notice when it plans to go out of business or lay off a large number of people. The law is called the Worker Adjustment and Retraining Notification Act (WARN Act).[6]

And finally, regardless of the reason someone is leaving, make sure you do not neglect the rest of your employees. They will undoubtedly have questions, even if they don't express them to you directly. They will want to know how this change affects their jobs, workload, and the team dynamic. Create a plan, include them as much as possible, and keep the lines of communication open.

As I mentioned earlier, there is a more detailed Termination and Resignation Checklist in the Resources section for this chapter. I hope you'll find it useful as a guide to save you time and effort, as well as prevent mistakes. It's a valuable tool to use for any employee departure, involuntary or voluntary. In the meantime, as closure to this chapter, here's a quick termination checklist of things to be certain that you consider.

Quick Termination Checklist

- Predetermine the content and the appropriate time, place, and person (or people) who will be involved.
- Be prepared for the face-to-face conversation with a formal letter of resignation, firing, or layoff.
- Decide who should be in the meeting and if there are any security risks.
- Collect company property (keys, car, cell phone, computer, credit cards, etc.).
- Sever IT access.
- Complete paperwork (payroll, address, benefits, immigration, any contracts or legal documents required, etc.).
- Provide a reference check approval letter for signature (what you will or won't say).
- Ensure rigorous record keeping (for all relevant reports, e-mails, letters, documentation, etc.).
- Determine any impact on facilities and workspaces.

As we turn to chapter 11, we'll find that a voluntary "goodbye" is a much happier one in most cases. This kind of goodbye is also important to do right. You'll want anyone leaving your organization to exit on as high a note as possible, to choose to speak in positive terms about you and your business to others inside and outside your walls, and maybe even to return one day to another position. It seems fitting to end the "Closure = Fire Right" section on a happy note!

Chapter Eleven

When It's Really Over

Part 2—Voluntary Closure

If you're brave enough to say goodbye, life will reward you with another hello.

—Paulo Coehlo

CONGRATULATIONS ON YOUR NEW JOB!

Voluntary departures can happen for a host of reasons, such as joining another employer, staying home to care for children or elder family members, moving elsewhere with a partner or spouse, becoming an entrepreneur, or even getting promoted in the same or another part of the organization. Departures can also be a result of employees being unhappy about their leader, their coworkers, the culture, the pay, the working conditions, the lack of challenge, and the lack of development or opportunity for promotion, among other things. When you're vigilant with all the material we covered in the section "Retention = Nurture Right," the latter are all issues you will likely discover *before* it's too late and someone decides to leave. When you're relational versus transactional with your employees, they'll often tell you far more about what they're thinking and feeling. If you're having regular conversations with your staff, and you've developed a trusting relationship, you'll be able to detect the things that are and aren't working for them. Pay attention.

When an employee you value surprises you with this news, it can feel like a painful gut punch. Knowing what to say in that moment can be a challenge. With any luck, you'll have had some prior indication this might happen, but sometimes you don't. It's fine to ask questions about why the employee is leaving and where they are going, but don't interrogate them. Most people leave to move on to another job. No matter whether you were surprised or not, it's important to offer your congratulations and to stay calm and professional.

That's not quite what happened early in my career at Cornell. After four years on the job, I told my boss I had been offered another position at the university. He did *not* congratulate me. Instead, he was sarcastic and condescending and said I would regret it. He tried to talk me out of leaving because, according to him, the new job would be hell and no fun at all. The truth was that he didn't want me to leave because he knew I was doing half his job as well as my own. He was furious at me for leaving, and I was positive I'd never consider working anywhere near him again.

While you may wonder what you could have done to keep your employee, don't get stuck there. You can, of course, ask if there is anything you can do to change their mind, but don't continue on that course if it's clear they have accepted the new position and moved on mentally and emotionally. What you can do is show them how much they are appreciated, assuming it's true.

After you and your employee have documented the resignation with a signed and dated letter, along with all other due diligence required for a departure, you will need to agree upon the way the two of you will announce it. It might be the employee sharing at a team meeting and then a wider e-mail distribution that you send. If the employee wants to include personal contact information and other details of the move, that is their decision, not yours. Before they go, you'll need to work together to figure out if, how, and when to wrap up projects, any loose ends, and any reasonable transfer of duties to someone else.

Finally, decide together if there is going to be a farewell event to graciously send off your staff member. Not everyone will want an event, preferring perhaps to have an informal gathering or lunch with a few close colleagues. Others will cherish a larger gathering with a wider group, particularly if they have a good amount of organizational tenure.

Personally, I loved all my farewell parties, the laughter, the "roasting" Roxi stories (of which there were many!), and the silly as well as the lovely parting gifts. I still cherish the words and the faces of each group of my colleagues. So ask, don't assume, what a departing employee would like as a farewell gesture, and then plan it with a few people who can make it special. People may leave a job, but that does not mean they've left their relationships behind.

One of my most productive, bright, and valued employees dropped by my office unexpectedly, sat down, and started to cry. In short order, I discovered she was crying because she felt so badly about telling me she was leaving in two weeks. Then I wanted to cry! I hadn't seen it coming at all. It turned out that she had been head hunted by a recruiting firm and was offered a more senior job in another city for much more money than we could pay. It wasn't about lack of support or development or anything we could provide. She loved her job, but she also knew we didn't have a similar job or the money, and she needed to move on for her family's sake and to advance her career. No argument there.

The way we parted had everything to do with the way our relationship continued into the future. We collaborated with a few clients; we presented at a conference together; I helped her with a huge project; she referred me to a big client, and so on.

If you have no idea why someone is leaving, and they won't tell you, you might ask them to help you and your team be more aware and proactive in keeping great people by providing a *confidential exit interview* with someone else in the organization, perhaps someone who works in Human Resources (HR). It's so important to know why someone is leaving and not assume it's just better pay or a better job. There is usually something more to the story and finding out what that is could help prevent more losses.

The moral of the story here is this: *don't burn your bridges*, get resentful, angry, or spiteful when you lose a great employee to another employer. Be happy and even proud of them for their success; after all, you had something to do with it. You never know what might show up down the road, so continue to *build bridges* with former employees when and where you can. Your paths are likely to cross somewhere, sometime, so always take the high road.

CONGRATULATIONS ON YOUR RETIREMENT!

When someone retires, it usually means they have several years of their life invested in your organization. While it's true that someone could retire after working only a short time for you, it's not the norm. Let's assume the retiring person has a history with your organization that could be great, just OK, or mediocre. You may be sad to see them go and concerned about the institutional knowledge that will go with them, or you may be relieved. In any case, you need to honor your retiring employees and be gracious.

Never ask someone, "When do you plan to retire?" This question will likely be interpreted as an attempt to push someone out, which could land you in an age discrimination suit. You can ask any employee the generic question, "What are your plans for the next three to five years?" as part of your ongoing conversations about the future. Then, you'll need to work with whatever answer you receive. You can have early and phased retirement options that are voluntary and generally available to employees who are age fifty-five and over. You can have workforce planning discussions with your team, and you can certainly discuss the subject of proactive succession planning with anyone, all without asking anyone, "So, what are your retirement plans?"

Mandatory retirement is illegal under the Age Discrimination Employment Act[1] unless there is a "Bona Fide Occupational Qualification (BFOQ) or they are age 65 and are a 'Bona Fide Executive' or in a 'High Policymaking Position.'"[2] I recommend doing your research before going down this road. The rules are so specific that there is no value in digging around in the details here. Every case requires a deep review before having this conversation with an employee, so I advise caution. Even if you believe your position is defensible, think some more. No one is going to take kindly to being pushed out of a job they want to keep. Take your time and make sure you are approaching this situation for the right reasons and in the right way.

Demonstrating your appreciation for your retirees is really in your best interests. You may be asking them to partner with you in planning strategies for a graceful exit, and when they are feeling valued and engaged, you and your organization benefit. You may even want to keep them engaged in some way, such as a coach, mentor, or consultant. Everything we covered in voluntary resignations applies to retirees. It is the human element that matters most because this transition is all about a person's livelihood as well as a huge chunk of their professional and personal identity. Showing kindness and respect will go a long way to ensure a positive "goodbye."

By creating a fitting farewell for long-serving employees, you will be sending a message to the entire organization about your traditions, culture, gratitude, and how much you value people for their service. Each retiree should have significant input into how they want the acknowledgment of their retirement to happen. The range of choices goes from one extreme to the other with a lot of options in between. There will be people who are really excited about leaving. Others are retiring before they really want to for one reason or another. Your retiree may want absolutely nothing to happen, or they may want a big bash or something in between. You won't know without asking.

No matter how the goodbye is celebrated, keep in mind that memories are at least as important as parties and gifts for someone who is walking away from a life they've known for decades—a life of work, a community of colleagues, and a sense of purpose and meaning. Whatever you can do to create tangible and intangible positive reflections of this person's contributions to your organization and to other people will be cherished. Options might include a memory book, awards, plaques, songs, poems, posters, videos, photo albums, and speakers who matter to the retiree. The list is as big as your imagination.

Being gracious and thoughtful with your meaningful goodbyes is as important to your organization's culture as providing meaningful "hellos" at the start of someone's relationship with you. It's worth your time and effort to do it right.

SAVING YOUR BRAIN TRUST

There is an *urgent* consideration for employers today when we look squarely in the eye of the country's demographics. *Ten thousand people are turning sixty-five years old every single day!* One-third of today's workforce is made up of baby boomers. HR professionals are scrambling to curb the damage caused by massive employee retirements. The average loss is around forty years of working knowledge and experience per retiree. Think about that; if you have ten people retire from your organization this year, you will lose four hundred years of wisdom unless you capture it!

There are three huge retiree challenges for employers today: *loss of knowledge, skill gaps*, and *the cost of delayed retirements*. The latter may seem contrary to the first two—and it is. Delayed retirement can and often does cost 1–1.5 percent of your entire workforce budget when people delay retirement by only one year.

We are faced with a balancing act between having too many people delay retirement for financial or other reasons and losing too many people without planning for the knowledge and skill gaps that are going to happen without intervention. You could even be experiencing both at the same time with different people! Once those people go out the door, and they all will eventually, organizations that have not addressed the gap problems are at a severe disadvantage.

There are good business reasons to prepare your organization for someone's retirement *and* to consider variations and options to a full retirement that you might want to offer. Knowledge transfer takes time, a conscious process, and effort on everyone's part, so plan accordingly. No matter what methods you use—mentorship, job sharing, job shadowing, cross-training, or other techniques—it is important to engage your upcoming retirees and help them share the what, how, and why of the work they do. Employees with long tenure have many relationships throughout the organization and a treasure trove of knowledge. If you don't already have a robust knowledge-sharing process and a way to document important information across the organization to prevent gaps and silos, at the very least, you'll need to ask your retiring employee to share and document as much knowledge as possible before it's lost.

Once you are having conversations with an employee about their retirement transition, it's important to learn what you can about the retiree's postretirement plans. Some people want to just be done and out, end of story. Others may be interested in staying connected to your organization in some capacity, such as working as a part-time consultant, being a mentor to younger employees, or working on a specific project. Whether the job held by the retiree remains essentially the same, or changed in some way, your retirees may be able to add value.

Being proactive with both sides of this coin will serve you and your organization well. There are at least four solutions I offer my clients that can be mixed and matched depending on what is already in place in the organization versus what is missing and needed. Our goal is to keep the engine humming while the tires are being rotated.

1. *Phased-Retirement Program:* There is a lot to be said for "phased retirement" from both the employee's and employer's perspectives. It's also possible for a retiree to be tapped to fill in as an interim for a vacant position. This happens frequently in government, business, public schools, and higher education posts while a search process is under way, such as a permanent agency head, COO, superintendent, dean, or president. For retirees, alternative work arrangements can keep important *social and professional relationships* alive. These are often the hardest things to lose as one retires. There may also be a renewed sense of purpose for the retiree along with some supplemental income. For the employer, a part-time retiree can help ease the transition, cost less, and continue to add value. The goal is to strategically transition employees from full-time work to full-time retirement from the organization over a mutually agreeable time period by identifying and orchestrating desirable options that are *beneficial to the retiree and the employer.*

2. *Succession Planning:* This systematic process prepares employees for future vacant positions and may include a number of strategies, such as cross-training, job sharing, and job shadowing. Succession planning can apply to nearly everyone and certainly everyone in key roles. There needs to be a plan and method in place so high-potential employees have time to learn from their colleagues and get ready to step into those roles when the time comes. A good succession plan helps prevent vacancies from going unfilled for too long.

3. *Mentoring Program:* This can be a formal or informal program for preretirement and high-potential younger employees to improve multigenerational collaboration and bridge knowledge and skills gaps while developing employees with the help of seasoned staff or external mentors. Experienced employees need to believe that it's an essential, and highly valued, part of their job to help develop and train the younger generation. Younger employees need to know it's their job to learn from their more experienced colleagues. Leaders who create and model a culture that honors experience and knowledge will minimize ageism attitudes in the workplace, particularly during retiree transitions.

4. *The Encore Program®:* This is a proprietary and customized benefit program for preretirement employees to support and encourage successful transition to retirement. Many retirees are lost when they leave their job; they have questions like the following: What's next? How do I stay in control of my life? Who do I want to be after retirement? What gives me a sense of purpose and meaning? My business partners and I surveyed this age group and found three consistent needs across gender, race, and income brackets. Retirees want a *strategy* or road map to help them envision possibilities and take action during this huge transition in their lives, a *community* of people going through similar challenges, and *professional coaching support* to help them create a new life they feel good about. It's not just about financial planning. Life planning is where they need guidance that they are not currently getting. When only 30 percent of retirees are having "what's next?" conversations with family members, and when there is a 40 percent higher risk of depression and a 60 percent increased risk of serious illness when retirees are without a positive life transition plan, there's a ballooning problem for our society that needs to be solved. Employers can support retirees in making this huge life transition a positive one and provide this kind of benefit *before people retire.*

I mentioned cross-training in terms of succession earlier. There are more advantages to cross-training. Having this as a normal part of your business strategy can also help prevent parochialism and silo building. Cross-training is a smart business strategy for ongoing knowledge sharing organization wide; you don't need an upcoming retirement to justify such a program. In an upcoming retiree situation, your most tenured staff can be of great assistance in helping spread knowledge and skills throughout the organization, and they might enjoy being given that opportunity.

Whether you decide to put in place phased retirement, succession planning, mentoring, an Encore Program®, or knowledge sharing and cross-training programs, you should conduct a retirement assessment at least annually so you can estimate and prepare for the staffing and gap challenges that can arise with upcoming retirements. Your assessment should include talking with seasoned employees about what their three- to five-year plans are and to fully understand what they actually do and how they do it rather than depending on what their job description says, especially because it's likely to be way out of date.

SAD FAREWELLS

When an employee leaves a job because of an unfortunate situation, such as a long-term illness, disability, accident, family crisis, it is so very important that the employer, leader, and colleagues demonstrate kindness, compassion, and understanding. Your employee likely had no control over this outcome and, yet, has to leave their job and livelihood because of it. This is the time to *step way up* and offer every method of help you have at your disposal.

One of my clients ordered the company's private jet to fly a long-time staff member across the country when her adult child was suddenly killed and there were no commercial flights that could get her to him that day. She didn't report to my client directly, and she hadn't done anything more remarkable than being an excellent employee. My client simply put himself in her shoes and made the call. This story is still mentioned to new hires by long-time staff, and it is deeply embedded in the culture as part of "who we are."

Visiting hospital beds, organizing food drives, and offering a leave of absence versus a resignation are examples of compassionate responses. My guidepost is to put myself squarely in my employee's shoes and ask, "What would I need and want from my employer that would most help me with this situation?" And then, of course, ask the employee what he or she wants and needs, and then do your best to help.

The Family and Medical Leave Act (FMLA) provides an alternative to resignation for an employee and employer. The FMLA entitles eligible employees of covered employers to take unpaid, job-protected leave for specified family and medical reasons with continuation of group health insurance coverage under the same terms and conditions as if the employee had not taken leave.[3] Some employers allow other employees to donate paid time off (PTO), or equivalent, to a colleague to supplement the employee's disability, sick leave, vacation, or other paid time off to offset unpaid time off the employee would have to bear alone. FMLA-eligible employees are entitled to the following:

Family and Medical Leave Act

Twelve work weeks of leave in a twelve-month period for

1. the birth of a child and to care for the newborn child within one year of birth;
2. the placement with the employee of a child for adoption or foster care and to care for the newly placed child within one year of placement;
3. the care of the employee's spouse, child, or parent who has a serious health condition;
4. a serious health condition that makes the employee unable to perform the essential functions of his or her job;
5. any qualifying exigency arising out of the fact that the employee's spouse, son, daughter, or parent is a covered military member on "covered active duty"; *or*
6. twenty-six work weeks of leave during a single 12-month period to care for a covered service member with a serious injury or illness if the eligible employee is the service member's spouse, son, daughter, parent, or next of kin (military caregiver leave).

Once again, being gracious and thoughtful is what matters the most. Take the time, consider the circumstances, and be as helpful and supportive as possible, both from the organization's perspective and in your own relationship with your suffering staff member. Tomorrow it could be you or someone close to you in a similar situation. It's simple, *just do the right things*—and I'm sure you'll know or can find out exactly what these things are.

We've reached the end of section C, "Closure = Fire Right." What a journey! It's time now to turn the page for a few closing thoughts.

Conclusion

If you think you can do a thing, or think you can't do a thing, you're right.

—Henry Ford

Well, here we are at the end of this journey together. This work can seem, and truly be, daunting at times, but I also know *you can do it*, and I also believe that you will feel better and lead better when you do. We've completed our exploration of ARC (Acquisition, Retention, and Closure), which is every employee's story, including yours and mine. During our careers, all of us have likely experienced being hired or not, nurtured and developed or not, and have left an organization of our own choice, or were fired or laid off. This is what happens in the world of work unless you have, since your first day of work, been without a boss. It is therefore safe to say that all we've talked about within these pages touches nearly everyone's life, one way or another, sooner or later.

As we've explored the ARC of an employee's work life, we've been close to the action and focused on the details that make it all happen. When we look at it from a mile-high view, there are five tenets that form the foundation of the three systems within ARC:

1. Everything in ARC is *relational not transactional.*
2. Success in every part of ARC depends on using proven processes *proactively versus reactively.*

3. What and how you *do* every step of ARC speaks volumes about your style of leadership and the work culture you want demonstrated in your workplace and on your team.
4. You can't afford to ignore or fast-track any part of ARC.
5. Your success is 100 percent dependent on the success of your people during every step of ARC.

WHAT'S IN IT FOR YOU?

Leading people within all aspects of ARC *is your job, and you are already doing it.* The question is this: How are you doing it? When you hire and retain the right people in the right jobs doing the right things, you, your team, and your work will flourish. This is just common sense, and we all know it. And, of course, the reverse is true.

You, like most of us, have plenty of priorities on your plate. And yet, *if everything is a priority, nothing is a priority.* People must be your first priority as a leader, and managing ARC well becomes a *brilliant strategic and competitive advantage* in any enterprise. So few people do it well that you will far outshine those who don't. No matter what your career goals are, as long as you choose to be a leader of people, everything we've covered in these pages will *advance you and your work.* I *can* promise you that.

During the writing of this book (and my first book), I learned a lot, and I deepened my commitment to helping leaders navigate and master those things that matter the most. In *Lead Like It Matters . . . Because It Does*, I delved deeply into Personal Mastery, Interpersonal Mastery, Team Mastery, and Culture and Systems Mastery. In writing this book, I wanted to provide laser-focused tools for your leadership toolbox as you undertake the work you're doing with ARC. When you lead like it matters and when you hire, nurture, and fire right, you've got a winning combination that will serve you well wherever in the world you work.

Most of us would like to leave where we work better than we found it. We want our contributions to be meaningful and hope to leave a positive legacy wherever we have touched the lives and work of others. If you're reading this now, you're one of those people, and it's been my honor to spend this time with you!

Afterword

Dear readers,

Since submitting *Hire Right, Fire Right* to my editor at the close of 2019, our entire world and all the people who live and work in our world have had their lives turned inside out and upside down. Very few of the billions of people living on this planet, if any, have been untouched by the COVID-19 pandemic and the economic and social fallout it has and will continue to cause. I liken this virus to a spark that falls on a tinderbox while no one is looking, creating a disaster that fuels many more. There are big lessons here for all of us to learn and integrate into our future behaviors and decisions, no matter where we live and work. If you are a leader, there are even more lessons to be learned from what has and has not worked around the world.

COVID-19, an invisible enemy, was just the beginning of what has become a series of massive economic, political, and social disruptions. As I write this in June 2020, our country is in the midst of a long over-due reawakening to the racial, social, and economic injustices that are and have been pervasive for hundreds of years—in government, health-care, workplaces, law enforcement, schools, and communities. I do have hope, though, because huge disruptions always offer new incentives to innovate, soul search, discover, and redefine what it means to be human and what kind of world we want to create with the immense talent and creativity humans can muster. It's not for nothing that Plato's quote, "necessity is the mother of invention," has stood the test of time.

The question is not *can we learn?* but *will we learn?* and then act on that learning?

Given our current challenges, I believe this book may matter more, and be even more useful today than ever before. Most of us need to work, and people will always need to work in thousands of jobs doing thousands upon thousands of things for ourselves, our families, and for the stakeholders who depend on us to deliver. Most likely, you are both an employee and an employer. You will continue to be in relationships with those employees you are Acquiring, Retaining, or bringing to Closure. It may be less or more than your old normal, but work will continue to happen and will need people to get the work done.

One thing is for sure—*you really, really, really can't afford to make a bad* hire right now, as human and financial resources are shifting daily. The employment landscape is changing, laws have and will continue to change, expectations and attitudes will change. Nothing will be "business as usual" for a long time, maybe ever, and that reality must inform how you invest in the people who work for and with you.

The people looking for work may be particularly numerous for a time, but it won't last. And beyond that, they will leave you as soon as they can if it's not a right fit, if the culture isn't welcoming, and if you don't treat them well. This truth still holds true—the highest-potential employees, the hardest working, the most determined . . . often get to choose where they work and for whom. So, if you want the best, you and your organization need to be your collective best.

Here are some practical questions for you to consider. Take your time. Some of these questions may be more relevant than others or may stimulate ones of your own. I offer them to help you *to be mindful* as you navigate these uncertain waters and to create a higher likelihood that you will *hire and retain* your most valuable asset—your dedicated, hard-working, talented people.

- What do you expect from *your* leaders? This can inform what others need from you.
- What do your staff members need and expect from you? How do you know?
- How will this pandemic, economic crisis, and social unrest affect your recruitment, hiring, and development of future new hires, promotions, and job assignments?

- In what ways can you tap into the creativity and talent you have available to help reinvent, reimagine, reinvigorate, and redesign how you move forward?
- How *deeply* have you looked within your organization to find high-potential employees, particularly those in protected classes—and have you made proactive efforts to develop, coach, and mentor this talent?
- How transparent have you been in telling employees what you know, and don't know, about what they can expect from you moving forward?
- How will a virtual workplace change your workforce dynamics? Consider what is gained and what is lost.
- What conversations are you having about conscious and unconscious bias in your workplace, community, and home?
- What are you doing to plan for another massive crisis that could arise in the near or not-so-distant future?
- How educated, informed, and aware are you about the history and today's realities of being Black or Hispanic in America's workplaces?
- How are you—or are you—having social unrest conversations in meetings, boardrooms, and on teams? If not, what can you do to learn how to have those often uncomfortable but vitally necessary conversations?
- What written and unwritten cultural messages are ever present in your organization and in your teams? Are they inclusive or exclusive messages? How do you know? If you don't know, safely and confidentially ask people of color, with disabilities, women, older employees, younger employees, etc., what they have seen and heard that makes your culture and workplace either welcoming or not.
- How much heart versus head is showing up in your decisions, in meetings, and in conversations with employees? Are you paying attention? How's your empathy showing up?
- How are you addressing the likelihood of trauma, depression, anxiety, and pain that your employees may be experiencing?
- Are you keeping in touch with employees you've lost to layoffs or furloughs; if so, how and how much?
- How are YOU taking care of YOU so YOU have the bandwidth and clarity to take care of those you lead?

Everything I've written in this book repeatedly highlights the need for all of us to be *relational vs. transactional* in our dealings with other people. It's not only the *right thing* to do; it's the *smart thing* to do.

I close this letter to you, dear readers, with just one more question: *What does it mean to you to be human?* How do you bring your answer into recruiting, hiring, retaining, and bringing closure with staff? Whatever it means to you, I hope you will bring your best human self to work every day in every way. I promise you'll lead a much more productive, fulfilling, and joyful life. As we all know, nobody gets out of here alive, so my wish for you is that your heart and head work together to give you the balance, wisdom, grace, and peace you deserve.

In gratitude and hope,
Roxi

Resources

CHAPTER 2

Internet Resources for Recruiting and Posting Jobs

Most companies are still finding the most qualified candidates through referrals and their own company career sites. In an article in Forbes, Jacquelyn Smith wrote, "It turns out that job applications who come in through internal sources get the same number of interviews as ones from outside. However, internal sources, such as employee referrals, inside hires, walk-ins and a company's career site, produce almost twice the number of hires as external ones, which include job search engines, job boards, print advertising, and job fairs."[1]

Hiring and accepting a job are relational activities, not transactional! Even in our massively connected information age, it is still all about people connecting to people and having relationships. And that means it's always going to matter "who you know" and "who knows you" because that's still what creates the most hires. Internal employee referrals continue to be a big source of new hires particularly because, first, candidates coming through that channel generally have a heads up about the culture and the players and, second, they have done their research about the organization. This means their retention rates are typically higher than average because these folks tend to know more about the job and the business before they even apply.

That isn't a flat-out argument against using the internet's power to connect employers, jobs, and candidates. External recruiters do it all the time and with reasonable success, and you can, too. As of this writing, the following online sites are highly rated for employers and would-be employees. You'll still have to shop around to see if an online aggregator or job board is right for your situation. Some are free, and some are not. Look for sites that post your job openings *and* engage candidates in the content. It's a lot like shopping for anything else—that "job store" has to be appealing and user friendly to get the best candidates' attention.

Top-Rated Aggregators: Aggregators pull together results from employer job boards, newspapers' job sections, company career pages, recruiter sites, and more; they can save a lot of time with one-stop shopping for candidates.

- **Indeed:** Indeed started in 2004 and was the trailblazer for all job search engines and is still the largest. Indeed keeps expanding globally and is now available in 19 different country-specific versions.
- **CareerBuilder:** CareerBuilder has been around for more than 20 years, and it is one of the biggest job boards. Its robust search function allows you to filter by several criteria, including location, job title, and pay range. Job seekers can upload their resumes in any format. CareerBuilder partners with news media around the country and collects job listings from them. The site also provides career advice and resources for job candidates.
- **SimplyHired:** It looks and feels like Indeed, but SimplyHired has more add-on applications that connect you to social media for easy sharing and research on the jobs you find. Available in 17 countries worldwide, SimplyHired is a job search engine that collects job listings from all over the web, including company career pages, job boards, and niche job websites. They claim to list job openings from 700,000 unique employers and operate job search engines in 24 countries and 12 languages.
- **Careerjet:** A similar application to Indeed, Careerjet claims to scan more than 58,000 websites daily, and it's available in more than 50 countries and in 20 languages.
- **LinkedIn/Jobs:** This professional network now hosts a huge job board that scrapes career sites and job postings on the internet.

- **Google for Jobs:** Google for Jobs aggregates job listings from multiple search engines. It's easy to use. Candidates can use key phrases like "teaching jobs" to get a list of available positions and click to go directly to the job listing and apply. One key benefit of using Google for Jobs is that it eliminates redundant results and displays only one listing for an open position.

Job Boards and Other Media: One of the most common ways today's job seekers find employment opportunities is by using online sources. There are hundreds of job boards, both generic and niche, as well as the aggregators, social media channels, networking groups, and staffing company websites to choose from.

- **Monster.com:** Monster.com began in 1994 and was one of the first commercial websites. Today, it offers services in more than 40 countries. Monster.com allows job seekers to upload their resumes to its site. It also provides networking boards, company profiles, a resume review service, and a mobile app.

The rest of these job boards do much the same as Monster.com in their own way and some with their own specific niche.

- Job
- ZipRecruiter
- MightyRecruiter
- Robert Half
- Ladders (jobs with salaries of $100,000 or more)
- Glassdoor (now allows employers to market their companies)
- Dice (tech jobs)
- Facebook Marketplace

Pre-Search Checklist

Position Storybook

- Review the current job/position description in detail and critically answer these questions:
  - Why do you need this position?

- What do you need in this position now that has changed from the past?
- What impact does this position have on others' work?
- What are the absolutes for education, experience, and KSAs (knowledge, skills, and abilities) that you *know* are essential for any candidate to succeed?
- What are the "nice to haves" you would like to see and why?
- How should this position fit within the organization's organizational chart?
- Final check: What, if anything, is still missing or should be removed from the new position description?
- Describe what success looks like.
- Is it welcoming and inclusive or exclusive?
- Is the language clear and explicit enough?
- Are the all the expectations and requirements clear, including values-based expectations?
- Is it interesting to candidates?

Scorecards

- Determine all requirements you have of all your candidates.
- Evaluate assessments to ensure they are instruments authorized for use in hiring and not biased by gender, age, race, religion, or ethnicity.
- Do not use 360 assessments or self-scoring personality or style instruments for the purpose of hiring.

Your Team and Your Strategy

- Establish your Search Team and your search process plan.
- Define your search strategy and identify your most promising means and methods for attracting the candidates.

Recruitment Firm Checklist Questions

- Cost
- Timing
- Quality
- Offer acceptance
- Sustainability

- Pool potential
- Inclusion
- Relationship
- Guarantees

For additional resources on choosing a recruiter, these articles can help:

Insperity Staff. "Recruiters Reveal: Discover the 16 Best Interview Questions to Ask." *Insperity* (blog). https://www.insperity.com/blog/professional-recruiters-reveal-16-of-the-best-interview-questions-to-ask/.
Johnson, Lana. "Important Questions to Ask When Choosing a Staffing Agency." *Wunder Blog*, June 15, 2018. https://blog.wunderlandgroup.com/important-questions-to-ask-when-choosing-a-staffing-agency.
KAS Placement. "20 Questions to Ask a Recruiter." http://www.kasplacement.com/20-questions-to-ask-a-recruiter.php.
Undercover Recruiter Staff. "Important Questions You Should Be Asking Your Recruiter." Undercover Recruiter, May 31, 2018. https://theundercoverrecruiter.com/questions-you-should-ask-you-agency/.

CHAPTER 3

Advertising Checklist

- Know your audience. Explain the job well enough so those reading the ad can decide whether they are interested and qualified.
- List the job title along with a brief description and a few examples of duties.
- List the minimum education, experience, and skill levels that are required and/or acceptable, if applicable. Point out any special criteria such as extensive travel or relocation that will weed out applicants who aren't interested in those requirements.
- Don't use jargon or abbreviations and acronyms that make it difficult to understand. Do use proper grammar and spelling.
- Be specific about any specialized skills or equipment that applicants should know how to use or operate.
- Check with your Human Resources (HR) professional or legal counsel if you have questions about the legality of your ad under federal and state laws, including nondiscrimination laws.

Hiring Leader and Search Team Responsibilities and Process Flow

1. Complete the Pre-search Checklist.
2. Clarify each Search Team member's role and responsibility.
3. Set up meeting times for Search Team members.
4. Create a timeline for the search.
5. Implement the recruitment/posting plan.
6. Create the criteria sheets for evaluating resumes *and* Beyond the Resume submissions.
7. Cut the pool to those who will get a first phone or video interview.
8. Create the phone interview and Beyond the Resume questions.
9. Cut the pool to those who will be asked for an in-person interview (e.g., on-site interview).
10. Create full interview packets for all interviewers, including evaluation sheets.
11. Create and rehearse the scenario interview, including the evaluation sheets.
12. Determine any tours and other logistics.
13. Receive interviewer and Search Team feedback.
14. Choose the top candidate.
15. Make the offer.
16. Plan onboarding.

Legal and Illegal Interview Questions

Topic	Legal	Illegal and/or Inappropriate	Legal after Hiring
	Questions asked in an interview should focus on the candidate's qualifications for the job. They may offer information about many things about themselves, like their marital and parental status, but you must not bring it up or ask.	If it's not job related, don't ask. These questions are illegal and inappropriate to ask under any circumstances. This is a good list, but people can create variations that will also be illegal. If in doubt, leave it out!	These questions are necessary after hiring in most if not all cases. Once someone is officially your employee, you will need certain information in order to comply with the law, process paperwork, and so on.

Topic	Legal	Illegal and/or Inappropriate	Legal after Hiring
Age	Are you over the minimum age for the hours or working conditions?	How old are you? What year were you born? When did you graduate from high school?	Necessary insurance and tax information.
Marital Status	What name(s) are your work records under?	Are you married, divorced, separated, engaged, widowed? Is this your maiden or married name? Does your spouse/ partner work? If so, where? What is the name of your spouse/partner/ children? Do you live with your parents? Any questions concerning spouse/ partner, including employment, salary, arrangements, or dependents. How will your spouse/ partner feel about . . . ? Do you own or rent your home?	Marital status and dependent information on tax and insurance forms.
Parental Status		Do you have children? If so, how many? How old are your children? Are you pregnant? Is your spouse pregnant? What do you have or need/want for care arrangements?	Dependent information on tax and insurance forms.
Criminal Record	Have you ever been convicted of a crime other than a traffic violation?	Have you ever been arrested? Have you ever spent a night in jail?	

Topic	Legal	Illegal and/or Inappropriate	Legal after Hiring
Disability (Title I of the Americans with Disabilities Act [ADA]) and Medical	Can you perform the specific tasks/ duties for this job? Are you willing to take a drug test? Are you able to perform this job with or without reasonable accommodation? Do you have any conditions that would keep you from performing this job? Do you currently use illegal drugs? Have you ever used illegal drugs? What illegal drugs have you used in the last six months? (current illegal drug users are not protected under ADA) For certain positions, employers may require that a job candidate pass a medical exam relevant to the responsibilities of the job, as well as pass a drug test.	How is your health? Do you have any disabilities? What is your medical history? How does your condition affect your abilities? Have you filed a workers' compensation claim? Have you ever been hospitalized? If so, for what condition? Any question that refers to past drug addiction. Do you have any physical, mental, or other disabilities that would prevent you from performing the job? Have you ever been treated by a psychiatrist or psychologist? If so, for what condition? Is there any health-related reason that you may not be able to perform the job? How many days were you absent from work because of illness last year? Are you taking any prescribed drugs? Have you ever been treated for drug addiction or alcoholism? What is your height and weight?	Medical history for insurance forms.

Topic	Legal	Illegal and/or Inappropriate	Legal after Hiring
Citizenship and National Origin	Do you have the legal right to remain permanently in the United States? What is your visa status? Are you able to provide proof of employment eligibility upon hire?	Are you a US citizen? Are your parents/ spouse/partner US citizens? If so, are they natural born or naturalized? If naturalized, what are those dates? What is your nationality? Where were you born? Where are your parents from? What is your heritage? How did you acquire the ability to read or write a foreign language? What language is spoken in your home? Can you vote? If so, what party do you belong to?	Verifying legal US residence or work visa status. What languages do you speak, read, or write fluently?
Race	None	Any question or statement that refers to race in any way. What race are you? Are you a member of a minority group? How do you feel about . . . ?	None
Education and Experience	What education do you have? What experience qualifies you for this job? Do you have licenses and certifications for this job?		
Sexual Orientation	None	Any	None

Topic	Legal	Illegal and/or Inappropriate	Legal after Hiring
Religion and Military	Can you work on weekends? (only if the position requires working on weekends) Have you served in the military? If so, what was the period of your service? If so, what was your rank at time of discharge? If so, what type of training and work experience did you receive while in the service?	What, if any, church/ synagogue/mosque do you attend? What kind of discharge did you receive from the military?	None
Other	Are you willing to travel? Are you available for overtime? Are you willing to relocate? Do you have any concerns about handling the long hours and extensive travel that this job entails? What professional or trade groups do you belong to that you consider relevant to your ability to perform this job?	What clubs or organizations do you belong to?	Insurance forms can inquire about age. A copy of your birth certificate, Social Security card, passport, and identity photographs. Your marital status (married or single only). Proof of citizenship. Physical examination and drug testing.

For Human Screeners and Interviewers: Bias Awareness

Employers rarely set out to discriminate against candidates—but it happens anyway. One way to prevent this is by using software that removes identifying information from resumes. Most employers don't have that option. By talking about the risks of biases openly and candidly, the search process will have a much greater chance of success. We're human, and we have biases, like it or not. Some of them we can readily identify because we are conscious of them. "Bike riders are always . . ." "Only women can understand . . ." Whenever we describe a group of people with the words *always* or *never*, or even *usually*, we're likely in or approaching the zone of conscious bias.

Unconscious biases are just that—they are unknown to our conscious selves. Our brains make shortcuts that subconsciously affect our decision making. It is a prejudice or stereotype for or against something or someone. Unless we pay attention, they will stay deep down inside our brains and nothing will change.

Everyone involved in the search process should become familiar with what is meant by conscious and unconscious bias and work to eliminate it from the workplace and certainly from screening and interviewing candidates. Creating proactive methods and raising awareness will go a long way to ensuring a fair hiring process. Overcoming bias helps diversify your talented workforce and enriches the organization.

With or without software that does unbiased screening, begin by removing identifying factors from resumes (name, age, race, ethnicity, hobbies, and perhaps schools attended, etc.). If you don't start your process with a "blind" resume reading, biases can set in even before your candidates' resumes have a chance to stand on their merits because the people screening the candidates may be applying their own conscious or unconscious biases. For instance, it's important to verify the required education of a candidate in screening, but it's not important to know where the education was received unless it's truly a differentiator for a particular position. When that's the case, it should be noted in the job posting: "Must have attended one of the top three Hotel Schools . . ." To prefer one institution over another, if you didn't advertise that way, would be making a biased assumption that perhaps one candidate is smarter or better educated or better prepared than another. If you have no factual data on which to make that assumption, don't do it.

Implicit hiring bias can occur early on when we make judgments about people based on something other than their ability to perform the job at hand. These *conscious biases* are a problem when they color judgment in resume reviews and interviews.

Examples of Conscious Bias

"We need to hire a person just like . . ." "I don't like people who are
. . ." "I prefer to associate with people who . . ." "Anyone who owns
a trashy car has got to be . . ." "Last time we hired a guy from there
. . ." "You know if she's under 35, she's probably going to . . ." "It's an
engineering job, we really need to find a smart guy . . ."

Unconscious bias is making judgments and having prejudice against
people or ideas that you may not realize. Unconscious bias includes assumptions or things that you might accept as true without realizing that
they are actually stereotypes or generalizations. Having unconscious
bias makes you human, not a bad person. To raise your awareness
and reduce or prevent bias from contaminating the search, make sure
your evaluation about a candidate is based on all relevant measures
of the individual's ability to do the job well and *is not based on any
assumptions*.

Whenever you catch yourself making an assumption about anyone or
anything without checking the facts and going deeper, you are probably
experiencing unconscious bias. These are things you believe as if they
were proven facts. These are all assumptions and prejudices that may
have very little to do with the actual person who is applying for a job.

Examples of Unconscious Bias

"Anyone who is [cultural group] is usually good at math . . ." "Men
are insensitive . . ." "Women are too emotional at work . . ." "If I want
a hard worker, I'd better not hire [cultural group]." "Anybody with a
family won't want to . . ." "You people . . ." or "Those people . . ."

*All of these indicate you are deep into your own bias, whether you
know it or not.*

Common Bias Traps

Interview order: Being first or last can have a positive or negative
impact for candidates, and it should not be a factor.

Halo effect: Focusing on one or more of the candidate's accomplishments versus the whole picture and whether or not that accomplishment
is meaningful or relevant to the position at hand.

Reverse halo effect: Focusing on one or more attributes of the candidate that are not meaningful to the position at hand (e.g., drives a rusty car, has longer hair than most, has a different accent than me, etc.)

Splashy resumes: Resumes that have great summaries at the top of the resume and an impressive skills section at the bottom are often viewed more favorably than those that don't—it's about *form not substance*, and that is not a good basis on which to judge a candidate.

Personal appearance: While it matters that people are dressed appropriately, clean, neat, and presentable, a person's looks should not matter in choosing a candidate. Pretty and handsome does not mean smart, good fit, effective, or anything else. Choosing a person you or your team find more attractive than other candidates results in too many bad hires that turn into terminations that are not at all fun or attractive.

Feelings: How someone left you feeling matters, but it's only one factor to consider. Keep in mind there are eight factors to evaluate: attitude, brains, character, drive, emotional intelligence, fit, gut, and heart. It's risking bias and a bad hire when only one or a few of those are considered important.

Addresses and modes of transport: A person's address does not affect a person's ability to do the work. Where people live and how they get to work does not matter; it matters that they get there. These details are not only unfair but also are none of anyone's business but the candidate's.

Gender, age and race: Pay attention to the way you evaluate the candidate based on what biases you have of their gender, age, or race. For instance, if a man and a woman said the same thing in the same way, would one of them be just fine and the other too aggressive? If a fifty-year-old says the same thing as a thirty-year-old, do you take one more seriously than the other? If three candidates, of three different races, said and did the same exact thing, would you respond differently? If any of these are true or even likely, your bias is showing.

Fashion: When people are *not hired* because of their hair or clothing style, it is a demonstration of flat-out conscious bias. This isn't about professionalism, it's about personal style and preferences. While it is still legal for an employer to enforce a dress code, it is a bias that could lose you a great candidate.

Affinity and likeability: People can be drawn to others who share the same hobbies or pursuits, traits, attitudes, and so on. This is human

nature. It becomes a problem when an affinity bias positively or negatively affects resume screening, interview evaluations, inclusion, and
career advancement. For example, personality biases are hard to ignore.
If you are an extraverted, big idea person, you may prefer candidates
who think and talk just like you, even if that's not relevant or what
would work best for the position at hand. While "natural chemistry" is a
bias, there's no need to ignore it; just pay attention to how much weight
you are giving it. If you are rating all candidates on the same questions
and same qualifications, then likeability can be one of those factors
within the "gut" factor, perhaps, and then it's out in the open and won't
carry undue influence on the hiring decision.

Unemployed candidates: While *s*ome employers refuse to hire unemployed candidates, this is a bias and based on assumptions. Many
unemployed people are talented and qualified. They may have lost their
previous position due to any number of reasons beyond their control,
like downsizing, a new corporate owner, politics, relocation, military
service, injury, family crisis, or a natural disaster, etc.

Names: Another reason to practice blind resume screening is to
prevent conscious or unconscious bias when a screener associates a
name with a race, gender, or ethnicity and ends up eliminating the
candidate without a fair evaluation of qualifications. While this may be
less prevalent than a decade ago, there is still evidence that names are
associated with gender, race, or ethnicity and can influence whether or
not an individual gets past the resume screening. It is wrong, but it still
happens far too often.

If you're curious about your own biases and want to learn more about
how implicit bias works, Harvard created the Implicit Association Test
(IAT) that can provide some powerful insights about your own bias
traps.[2]

Resume Evaluation Sheet for Human Reviewers

On your first review of applicant resumes, do not overemphasize the
format or writing style of the resume; look instead for the quality
of the content and adjust the evaluation sheet as needed for specific
requirements.

Candidate _____ (*Blind review* = Use a number or letter. Avoid the applicant's name, address, gender, or other personal information to limit biases.)

Rate each question 1–6 (1 low and 6 high) for each category.

(Review the position description prior to evaluating resumes and return your ratings by DATE.)

1. The candidate has the *must-have* qualifications/experience ____
2. The candidate has the *preferred* qualifications/experience ____
3. The candidate's employment history has few, if any, gaps, and/or gaps are well explained ___
4. The candidate has been given increased responsibilities over time ____
5. This job looks like a good fit for this candidate's skills/career/history/ growth ____
6. There are no concerns about "job hopping" (an excessive number of jobs in a short time) ____
7. The candidate's resume demonstrates ability to collaborate with others ____
8. The candidate's resume indicates both "hard" and "soft"' skills and abilities ___
9. The candidate's resume indicates both doer (accomplishes requirements), and achiever abilities (is creative, goes beyond requirements) ___
10. The candidate's accomplishments are clear, specific, measurable, and relevant ____

Please comment on these open-ended questions:

1. In considering your rating of the 10 questions above, what additional comments do you have?
2. What is your impression of the candidate's changes in positions over time? For instance, do moves appear to be progressive, lateral, or other?
3. Does this candidate have any special/unique skills, experiences, or knowledge not required for the position but would be beneficial and add value in this position?
4. What other observations do you have about this candidate?
5. What questions does this resume raise for you? (e.g., Is there anything missing that you think should be there? Is there anything that is confusing in the resume? Is there something more you would like to know about this candidate?)

OVERALL RESUME RATING: I believe this candidate is:

YES = very qualified ____ **MAYBE** = qualified second tier ____ **NO** = not qualified ____

Beyond the Resume Questions

The maximum number of written questions should be six, and the minimum three when you include these in your screening process. The questions are the same for all candidates applying for the same position. They should be written with the goal of getting a deeper understanding of each person, how they express themselves in writing, and how they answer the questions you choose to ask. Design your questions to get at important qualities you want to explore for a particular job and the challenges the job entails. All the Search Team members who read and rank them will fill out the evaluation sheet for these questions and their answers. This is a screening step before a phone or video interview, so carefully word your questions to get the most benefit.

Instructions: Complete these questions within _#_ typewritten pages by 5 p.m. on DATE and e-mail your answers to NAME at E-MAIL.

Sample Questions

Position: Administrative Assistant to Vice President of Human Resources

1. In your career, when have you been *most* energized and engaged? Please be specific.
2. In your career, when have you been *least* energized and engaged? Please be specific.
3. Describe a conflict in which you were involved. What was it, and how did you respond to it? (no names, please)
4. Have you ever felt uncomfortable with a request from a peer, supervisor, or another person at work that you deemed illegal or unethical? If yes, please describe how you handled it. If no, describe how you would choose to handle such a situation.
5. Describe a situation when you knew you made a mistake and what you did about it.
6. What do you think would be helpful for us to know about you that is *not* related to work?

Beyond the Resume Evaluation Sheet

(A rating of 1 is low and 6 is high.)

Who: Candidate #1   **Evaluator: Search Team Member's Name**

Position: Administrative Assistant to Vice President of Human Resources

Q1. In your career, when have you been *most* energized and engaged? Please be specific.
- How specific was the candidate? _____
- What is the quality of the answer? (authenticity, depth, meaningful, self-aware, etc.) _____

Comments _____

Q2. In your career, when have you been *least* energized and engaged? Please be specific.
- How specific was the candidate? _____
- What is the quality of the answer? (authenticity, depth, meaningful, self-aware, etc.) _____

Comments _____

Q3. Describe a conflict in which you were involved. What was it, and how did you respond to it? (no names, please)
- How specific was the candidate? _____
- How good was the example of the conflict described? _____
- How do you rate the way they responded to the conflict? _____

Comments _____

Q4. Have you ever felt uncomfortable with a request from a peer, supervisor, or another person at work that you deemed illegal or unethical? If yes, please describe how you handled it. If no, describe how you would choose to handle such a situation.
- How specific was the candidate? _____
- How appropriately did the candidate deal with the questions of risk, confrontation, and personal values? _____

Comments _____

Q5. Describe a situation when you knew you made a mistake and what you did about it.
- How specific was the candidate? _____
- How authentic did you find the answer? _____
- Was the quality of the answer helpful in understanding this candidate's self-awareness, ability to accept responsibility, and attitude toward mistakes in self and others? _____

Comments _____

Q6. What do you think would be helpful for us to know about you that is *not* related to work?

- How well did the candidate follow instructions and truly answer the question?
- How in depth and revealing was the answer? ____
- How helpful was the candidate's answer in getting to know him/her better? ____

Comments _____

After reading this candidate's answers, please give your current opinion of this candidate.

1. Should continue ____ because:
2. Not sure ____ because:
3. Should not continue ____ because:

Sample First Interview Questions

(See also A–H factor questions under chapter 4's resources for more options.)

These are sample questions to choose from during the first phone/video call in which two (recommended) of your Search Team members will participate *and* for your on-site interviews for your top three to four candidates. You may want to select some of these questions for the Beyond the Resume. *This is not a one-size-fits-all process.* You know best whether to choose from these questions or create your own that may be specifically related to the position and your candidates.

When the questions are to screen the candidates and decide who will move on to the next round, keep in mind the first interview is likely to be an hour or less, and even on-site interviews rarely last longer than an hour and a half, so do not over pack it. Leave plenty of time for the candidate to talk and for you to follow up.

If you are using some of these (or other questions) to give to *on-site interviewers who are not on the Search Team*, remind those folks to be consistent in asking all on-site candidates some of the exact same questions so they and you can compare answers.

A good test for any question's value is to answer it yourself and evaluate the depth and breadth you stand to gain from asking that question. If each question takes about three minutes to ask and answer, you might have time for 15 to 20 questions. Plan accordingly so there is time at the end for the candidate to ask you questions.

1. What can you tell us that will help us get to know and understand you better?
2. Walk us through your jobs with ___ and ___ and ___. Why did you leave each one and join the next one?
3. How does this job fit into where you want your career to go next?
4. What's something you love about your current (or previous) job and why?
5. What do you want to do differently in your next role?
6. What about our company/organization/agency grabbed your interest?
7. Why do you want to leave your current position?
8. Of all the people you've worked with, whom do you admire the most and why?
9. If we were to ask your current leader/boss/manager to describe you, what would we hear?
10. If we were to ask your coworkers/colleagues to describe you, what would we hear?
11. If we were to ask your direct reports to describe you, what would we hear?
12. Tell me about a time when you disagreed with your boss.
13. Have you ever had to fire someone? How did you do that?
14. How do you express your anger with colleagues, customers, or your boss?
15. What are you really good at but never want to do anymore?
16. Tell us about how you handled an awkward or difficult situation at work.
17. What is your approach to conflicts with other people? Examples?
18. Tell us about an accomplishment you are most proud of and why.
19. Tell us about one of your biggest mistakes. What was it? What did you do about it? What did you learn?
20. What are your strengths?
21. What are challenges for you?
22. What do you want to learn?
23. What do you think we can we offer you that someone else cannot?

24. What do you think you can you offer us that someone else cannot?
25. What motivates you to bring your best self to work?
26. Where do you see yourself in a year, and in three to five years?
27. What questions haven't I/we asked you?
28. What questions do you have for me/us?
29. Tell us about the gap in your employment between [*insert date*] and [*insert date*]?
30. Do you have a mentor or a coach? What has that experience been like for you?
31. How do you know you are stressed, and what do you do about it?
32. What are your bosses' strengths/weaknesses?
33. What makes you uncomfortable?
34. Looking back on the last three to five years of your career, what are your top three highlights?
35. What do you like the most and least about working in this industry?

Sample Phone and On-Site Interview Evaluation Sheet

The Search Team has screened this person's resume. The candidate appears to have the education, experience, knowledge, skills, and abilities required for an interview. This evaluation is asking for your *overall live interview experience* with the candidate.

Please include as much information that would be helpful in making a good decision about this candidate for this job.

Who: Candidate   **Evaluator: Interviewer's Name**

Position

1. What, if anything, impressed you about this candidate and why?
2. What, if anything, concerned you about this candidate and why?
3. What, if anything, stood out as the interview evolved (good or bad)?
4. Was the candidate able to answer the questions you asked to your satisfaction?
5. What questions did you want to ask but didn't?
6. How well did the candidate listen to you and/or others?
7. Did the candidate ask you any questions, and if so, how would you rate the questions?
8. What questions do you think we still need to ask this candidate?

9. Do you believe this candidate has what it takes to do the job? Why or why not?
10. Would you want to work with this candidate? Why or why not?

On a scale of 1–6 (1 is low and 6 is high), what is your overall rating of this candidate? __

CHAPTER 4

Twelve Emotional Intelligence Competencies[3]

Self-Awareness

- *Emotional self-awareness* means recognizing how personal emotions affect one's performance and relationships with others. People who have this competence know what they're feeling and why, and they use those insights as an ongoing guide for their behaviors.

Self-Management

- *Achievement orientation* addresses how much a person strives to meet or exceed a standard of excellence they and/or others have set. This competency means continuously looking for ways to do things better, set challenging goals, and take calculated risks.
- *Adaptability* focuses on flexibility in handling change. People with this competency willingly change their own ideas or approaches based on new information or changing needs. They juggle multiple demands with grace. Innovation and changes to the status quo are often seen as opportunities, not something to be avoided.
- *Emotional self-control* is about keeping one's disruptive emotions and impulses in check. Since we all have them from time to time, people who demonstrate this competency are able to maintain their effectiveness under stressful or even hostile conditions.
- *Positive outlook* focuses on persistence in pursuing goals despite obstacles and setbacks. These people see the positive in people, situations, and events far more often than the negative. They tend to have an abundant attitude toward life rather than an attitude of scarcity.

Social Awareness

- *Empathy* is sensing others' feelings and perspectives and taking an active interest in their concerns. It's paying attention and being "tuned in" to their frequency. People who demonstrate this competency are able to pick up cues and can truly "walk a mile in someone's shoes" even if they have not had a similar experience.
- *Organizational awareness* focuses on the dynamics among people. It's about reading a group's emotional currents and understanding the subtleties and power dynamics within relationships. People who demonstrate this competency sense and understand the interconnectedness of people and relationships throughout the organization, not just their part of it. They can accurately identify the influencers, the networks, and group dynamics.

Relationship Management

- *Conflict management* measures how well one negotiates and resolves conflict. People who demonstrate this competency bring disagreements into the open, effectively communicate the different positions, and help find solutions all can live with. They do not allow unresolved conflicts to create or sustain a dysfunctional environment.
- *Coach and mentor* means taking an active interest in others' development needs. It means spending time helping people via feedback, support, and assignments that will grow their skills and capabilities.
- *Influence* in emotional intelligence is about having a positive impact on others. People who demonstrate this competency persuade or convince others to gain support for an agenda. They are able to persuade others to get on board with a change, new idea, or plan of action.
- *Inspirational leadership* means the ability to inspire and guide individuals and groups. This is working to bring people together to get the job done. They bring out the best in others. People tend to follow the inspirational leader wherever they may go.
- *Teamwork* requires working with others toward a shared goal. It's about creating group synergy and group identity in pursuing collective goals. Teamwork is an orientation to work with others interdependently, not separately or competitively. Leaders with this competency understand that the whole is far greater than the sum of the parts, when and only when the whole is working well together.

A-H Factor Sample Questions

These questions are designed to help you understand the person who may be working with you in the near future and to help you decide if they are the right person. There is not a perfect or "right" answer to any of these questions. It will depend on your culture and what and who you are looking for. Behavioral questions go a long way to prevent "pat" or rehearsed answers.

A = Attitude: *Is the candidate passionate about the work and about helping others on their team succeed? Is their attitude one of abundance and a can-do, solution-oriented approach to work and challenges, or do they focus on scarcity, blame, and obstacles?*

1. Tell me about a failure. What was the situation, and how did you deal with it?
2. We all make mistakes. Tell me about a time you wish you'd handled a situation differently with another person.
3. When was a time you needed something from someone who wasn't helpful or responsive? What did you do?
4. Describe a time you had to work with a difficult person. What was the situation, and how did you handle it?
5. How would you describe the way you look at the world and life in general?
6. Describe what it takes for you to trust another person.

B = Brains: *Is the candidate capable of doing the job, or can the candidate learn how to do the parts of the job that are new in a reasonable time span? Can the candidate combine brainpower and execution?*

These are questions about the technical qualifications, knowledge, and experience required of the candidate for the specific job. Ask the candidate whatever is necessary for you to be certain you are being told the truth about those critical requirements. Here are some examples:

1. Describe a project that demonstrated your skills in _____.
2. Tell me about a time when you had to analyze information to make a recommendation. What was involved, and how did you go about doing that work?
3. I'd like to know about a time when you had to use all or many of your skills to solve a problem? First, how did you discover the problem? Second, what did you do to solve it?

4. Describe a time you had to make an immediate decision. What was it, and how did you decide what to do or say?
5. Share a story with us that will help us better understand the _____ skills you are bringing to this position.

C = Character: *What are the candidate's core values? Is the candidate trustworthy?*

1. Tell me about a time your integrity has been questioned. How did you feel, and what did you do?
2. Tell me about a time when you let your team or perhaps someone else down? What did you do about it?
3. Describe a situation where you could have done what someone wanted you to do without anyone knowing but, instead, you refused because you didn't believe it was right.
4. Explain how you deal with people you don't like or agree with at work and/or with someone who doesn't seem to like you. Give me an example.
5. Tell us about a time when you had to make a tough choice about a person. What was the situation, and how did you handle it?
6. Have you ever been part of a team where one or more people didn't get along? How did that affect you, and what did you do about it?
7. Describe a time when you had the choice between doing something well or going beyond good enough to great. What decision did you make and why?
8. What is the most difficult part of being a leader for you? What do you do about that?
9. What was your greatest achievement? What are you most proud of?

D = Drive: *Is the candidate self-motivated to achieve both personal goals and the goals of this position?*

1. What are the three things you want to learn in your first three months on the job?
2. Describe a problem you solved in a unique way. What was it, and why was your approach unique?
3. Share a time when your idea failed or you had a setback at work. How did you feel? What would you do differently?

4. Describe a time when you experienced rapid change. How do you approach change?
5. What makes you want to get up in the morning?
6. Imagine yourself in three years. What do you hope will be different about you then compared to now?
7. When have you gone above and beyond your job requirements to get something done?
8. What is an example of a time you took charge without having that role formally assigned to you? Why did you take charge? What did you do? How did it turn out?

E = Emotional Intelligence (EI): *What is the candidate's degree of self-awareness, and how well do they manage their own emotions? What is the candidate's social awareness and ability to manage relationships?*

1. Describe a time when you demonstrated empathy for someone.
2. How do you know what triggers you, and what do you do when that happens?
3. Describe a crisis situation in which you were involved. What was your response to it?
4. Describe how you choose to communicate at work. Is it different with different people? Why?
5. Do you trust first and then verify or verify first and then trust?
6. Remember the last time you were in a conflict with someone. What was your approach with that person?
7. Describe what happens for you when changes happen that you cannot control. How does it make you feel? What do you do about it?
8. Have you ever made an unpopular decision? What did you do, and how did you navigate others' reactions?
9. How do you work with and through others to get things done?
10. What stresses you the most? How do you manage your stress when it happens?

F = Fit: *Will the candidate be a fit within your mission, vision, values, and culture?*

1. Why are you attracted to our company/organization?
2. How do you see yourself and this position helping us accomplish our mission?

3. What questions do you have about our values?
4. How do you believe you can contribute the most to our team? Why do you believe that?
5. What have you learned about our culture? What questions do you have about it?
6. Describe why you believe you would be a great fit for this position.
7. How does this position differ from your previous one in terms of feeling like a "right fit" (if it does)?
8. What do you want your first 30 days on the job here to look like?

G = Gut: *What are your instincts telling you about this candidate? These are questions you ask of yourself, your Search Team, and other Interviewers*

1. What was my first reaction to this candidate? Why?
2. What biases might I have about this candidate (positive or negative)?
3. After getting to know the candidate better, have I changed my mind? Why?
4. What about this candidate do I need to learn to be sure about or perhaps change my feelings?
5. When all is said and done, what is my instinct telling me?
6. Are my experiences and gut feelings shared by anyone else on our team?
7. How heavily are my gut feelings weighing in on my "go or no-go" conclusion? And am I sure?
8. In weighing all the A–H factors, how does my "gut" factor align with everything else?

H = Heart: *What kind of a human being is this candidate? How grounded, other centered, well balanced, compassionate, and humble will this person be in the workplace?*

1. What has helped you most when it comes to building your confidence and self-esteem?
2. Can you describe a time when you went out of your way for someone? Why did you do that?
3. What behaviors do you expect from those you work with (peers, leaders, others)? How do you let them know what you expect?

4. What do you know to be true?
5. How do you currently integrate your time and energy for life and work? How do you think this position will impact that?
6. What makes you feel alive?
7. What, if anything, do you do to be centered, present, and grounded?
8. What gives you the most joy at work?
9. When have you taught or guided someone to learn something new?
10. Is there a time when you have gone to the "mat" for someone, even though you knew it could be detrimental to you?
11. How do you go about building trust with your colleagues? Give us a couple examples.

Additional questions for leadership roles:

1. Describe how you manage a high performer, a mid-performer, and a low performer.
2. What is your experience with delegation? How do you approach it?
3. How do you run your meetings? On a scale of 1–10 with 10 high, how do you think participants in your meeting would rate yours? Why?
4. How would you build a high-functioning team from a low-functioning one?
5. How would you keep a high-functioning team engaged and productive?
6. What do you think is the leader's most important responsibility? Second most important? Third most important?
7. What are some examples of the way you make decisions?
8. What presentations have you given and to whom? How did you prepare? How did they turn out?
9. How do you go about leading change?
10. How do you "manage up" to your own leader right now? How's that working for the two of you?
11. How do you inspire others to do their best work? What are some examples?

These are all examples to stimulate your thinking as you formulate your own questions to suit your purpose. For more questions that are behavioral in nature, TopEchelon.com,[4] a recruiting software company, is just one of many articles you can read about behavioral interview questions. They have a nice blog with 100 questions. Some questions are relevant to the A–H kinds of questions, and they go into more topics such as customer service, sales, and time management.

Sample Scenario: Budget Cut

This scenario is for a leadership position responsible for the budget of a large division that is facing big financial cutbacks.

For the Candidate: You are the Financial Director for a $250 million divisional operational budget with 2,000 employees, two-thirds of whom are unionized. You just received an e-mail from the COO that you must cut 7 percent of operating costs in the next budget, coming up in six months. If that weren't enough of a challenge, the COO wants to see that you have figured out how you'll make those cuts within the next three months.

Available to you in this 15-minute meeting are: your leader, the six department heads within your division (names provided) who are your peers, and the COO for the entire organization. Your task is to determine who will be in the meeting you've called and when they will be there. At the end of the meeting, you must make a recommendation to your leader about how to move forward.

For the Search Team: (rehearse ahead of time)

1. The divisional leader (name).
2. Assign a part for each department head to a member of the Search Team (playing themselves or not).
3. Determine what "attitude" each available person will demonstrate and role play (i.e., victim, critic, charge ahead, bystander, thoughtful, helpful, arrogant, etc.).
4. The COO part will be played with an attitude of "no possible change to the 7 percent charge," not helpful, not interested, and not creative.
5. The leader is looking for a recommendation from the candidate about *process, not specifics*, and, if need be, will press the candidate about how decisions should be made on the leadership team.

Sample Evaluation Sheet for Scenario Interviews

Based on the scenarios, these questions need to be tied directly to the quality of the answers *and* the behaviors demonstrated by the candidate as he or she is interacting with the Search Team during each of the scenario interviews. Fill out evaluations after each scenario while the interaction is fresh in your mind. Wait to compare evaluations with your team until *after* the candidate leaves the site.

Evaluation for Candidate _____ (Name)
Date _____ **Evaluator** _____
Scenario: Budget Cut

Score 1–10 with 10 high — Candidate Performance

Score _____ Who did the candidate ask to the meeting and why?

Score _____ Did this make sense to you? Why?

Score _____ How well did the candidate respond to and interact with the various attitudes demonstrated by role players?

Score _____ How well did the candidate manage the time and the people?

Score _____ How well did the candidate include peers in the upcoming budget change process?

Score _____ If the candidate included the COO, was that a good use of time?

Score _____ If the candidate included the leader before the end, was that a good use of time?

Score _____ How well did the candidate form and deliver a recommendation to the leader?

What impressed you about the candidate in this scenario?

What concerned you about the candidate in this scenario?

Overall Score for this candidate in this scenario _____ (1–10)

Based on this scenario, would you want to work with this candidate? Yes ___ Maybe ___ No ___ Why?

CHAPTER 5

Sample Offer Letter

If there are any contingencies for a final offer (e.g., reference checks, background checks, or drug tests), these must also be included.

Dear Name,   Date

It was delightful to speak with you on DATE about joining us as the Director of Finance and Budget for the Facilities Division at XYZ. We are certain your positive attitude, energy, skills, and experience will add a great deal to our team and are so pleased to offer you this position.

As we discussed, your starting date will be DATE with a starting salary of $---------- per year paid every two weeks on Friday. As you know, this is a professional, exempt from overtime position. In addition, we provide full medical coverage for you, your spouse or partner, and dependents. Our medical benefits are effective the first day of your employment. Eligibility for our 5 percent of base salary retirement plan begins 90 days after your start date. Additionally, we will match your retirement contributions up to an additional 5 percent of your base salary.

You will receive our flexible paid time off (PTO) plan that includes vacation, personal, and sick leave. Time off accrues at the rate of one and a half days per month for your first year and increases by two days more each year up to a maximum of 25 days per year.

If you choose to accept our job offer, please sign the second copy of this letter and return it to me at your earliest convenience by both e-mail and postal mail.

When your acceptance is received, we will send you the employee benefit enrollment forms, including direct deposit information (should you choose it) and a full set of details for our benefit and retirement plans. Any specific questions about the benefits we offer can be directed to Name, E-mail, Phone Number in our Talent and Development Human Resources Division who will provide you with employee portal access to sign up for your benefits.

We look forward to welcoming you to our team.

Please let me know if you have any questions or if I can provide any additional information.

Sincerely,
First Name Last Name

Title
XYZ
_____

I hereby accept the position of Director of Finance and Budget for the Division of XXXX at YYYY.

_____
Signature

_____
Date

CHAPTER 7

Individual Development Plan (IDP) Project Tracking Worksheet

Name
Supervisor
Date
Goal or Project:

_____
(list one item you want to accomplish)
Result Wanted:

_____

Target Completion Date: _____
Other People Involved (or team members): _____
Resources Needed: _____
Key Problems to Solve: _____

_____

Action Step: _____ By When: _____

Action Step: _____ By When: _____

Action Step: _____ By When: _____

Action Step: _____ By When: _____

Action Step: _____ By When: _____

Action Step: _____ By When: _____

Action Step: _____ By When: _____

Measurement Used to Evaluate Success: _____

Results: _____

_____

Things Learned or Other Comments: _____

Personal Goals Worksheet

For _____ **Date** _____

List one to three things you *really* want to accomplish within the next 12 months (personal, job related, or both). These might be related to your own desire to make something happen, or your personal dialogue (PD). They can be as different as "going back to college for a degree" to "keeping my work area organized" or changing a behavior or learning a skill. Keep them simple and clear. **Example:** "I want to learn how to give others *constructive feedback* and do it much more often."

_____

_____

When I am successful for each item above, I will . . . Example: "When I need to tell someone how I feel about something they say or do, I will do it in a timely and constructive way."

_____

_____

What do I have to do to make my goals happen? Example: "I will take a feedback course next spring and practice with someone who can help me get it right. I will start at home and then do it at work."

_____

_____

What can others, especially my supervisor, do to help me reach my goals? Example: "My supervisor's approval of course time and practicing this skill with me would be essential."

_____

_____

What are the biggest hurdles I need to get past to accomplish my goals? Example: "I need to overcome my fear of having a conflict when telling someone something they might not want to hear."

_____

_____

What dates do I want my goals to be accomplished? **Example:** "I will take the feedback course by June and practice at least four times by July."

_____

Employee Engagement Sample Survey Questions

Each organization may go about this differently and require a customized questionnaire, including breakdowns by leader or work group. Another option is to use well-tested group culture or employee engagement measurement instruments available on the market. These are 40 questions to choose from that address all four employee engagement factors.

1. My colleagues are committed to doing high-quality work.
2. I can be myself at work.
3. As a company/organization, XYZ demonstrates its values in word and action.
4. People at XYZ care about each other.
5. I trust my leader.
6. I am encouraged by my leader to continue my development.
7. I receive regular recognition or praise for doing good work from my leader.
8. In my job, I have the opportunity to do my best every day.
9. I believe my voice is heard and my opinions count.
10. XYZ promotes people fairly.
11. XYZ makes a positive difference in the world because of the work we do.
12. I feel emotionally safe at work.
13. I have fun at work.
14. Communication at XYZ is well managed.
15. Conflicts among colleagues at XYZ are dealt with quickly and fairly.
16. Meetings at XYZ are productive.
17. I work on a high-performing team.
18. I understand how decisions are being made that affect me and my work.
19. I feel my job is appreciated at XYZ.
20. Changes happen at XYZ in a thoughtful way.
21. I have good friends at work.
22. I have not experienced negative bias toward me at work.
23. We plan projects well at XYZ.
24. I am committed to XYZ.
25. I intend to stay at XYZ for a long time.

26. My team works well with other teams.
27. In the last year, I have had opportunities to learn and grow.
28. At XYZ, I can speak honestly without fear of repercussions.
29. I feel physically safe at work.
30. I have the resources I need to do my job well.
31. It's OK to make mistakes at XYZ as long as I share and learn from them.
32. I get the information I need to do my job well.
33. I receive constructive feedback that helps me develop and grow.
34. I know what is expected of me in my current position.

Open-Ended Questions:

35. What should we keep doing at XYZ?
36. What should we stop doing at XYZ?
37. What should we start doing at XYZ?
38. What should we keep doing on my team?
39. What should we stop doing on my team?
40. What should we start doing on my team?

CHAPTER 8

Personal Dialogue Questions

Adjust these questions to match the job at hand (i.e. if it is not a leadership position, replace question 9 with a question that is more appropriate to the person and position).

Part 1

1. Please note three to five things you have done especially well in your job in the past year.
2. How did you measure your own performance this year, and what were the results?
3. Please note three to five things you would like to have accomplished but didn't. Why? Are any of these a priority for the coming year?

4. What have you *liked most* about working here this year?
5. What have you *liked least* about working here this year?

Part 2

6. What goals and projects are most important to you in the year ahead? How will you know you've been successful? Are there any factors—personal, supervisory, or organizational—that might block you from accomplishing your goals?
7. What skills, education, experiences, or assistance (including from your supervisor) do you think would help you accomplish your goals and increase your job satisfaction?
8. What behaviors of yours *help you* in your interactions with others? What behaviors of yours *get in your way* in your interactions with others? Please give specific examples of each.
9. Who are you developing to succeed you in your position, and what is your succession plan?
10. What has gone well, and what needs to be improved in your relationship with your supervisor? Please be as specific as you can.

CHAPTER 9

Coaching Employees

Stage 1: The Coaching Agreement

- Establish mutual expectations and ground rules for how the process will work, including confidentiality.
- Build your agreement around the focus, scope, process, and/or specific outcomes for the coaching conversation to ensure clarity and transparency.
- Create a safe, supportive environment that produces ongoing mutual trust and respect.
- Both parties make joint decisions about the process.
- Hold the individual in *unconditional* positive regard.
- Ask the individual to explicitly identify their motivation and commitment for learning and change. What outcome do they want to achieve from the coaching process?

Stage 2: Attending to the Conversation

- The coach is prepared, centered, and fully present before beginning the conversation.
- The coach speaks no more than 25 percent of the time and pays close attention to body language, tone, words, emotions, and affect.
- Ask the individual what focus and what outcome (or outcomes) is desired for the coaching session.
- Ask permission to offer assessments of what the coach is noticing and then ask how the individual feels about that assessment.
- Offer choice points along the way.
- Ask powerful open-ended questions and together witness the experience of the individual when answering those questions. (See options for powerful questions following stage 4.)
- Respect the individual's learning style, perceptions, and resourcefulness.
- Use the individual's own words to reflect back what you hear.
- Use appropriate humor.
- Demonstrate flexibility, allowing time and space for an emergent process.
- Listen without evaluating or judging.
- Never advise, try to fix, or make the conversation about the coach.
- Pay attention to time, making sure the desired focus and the outcome(s) are attended to throughout the conversation.
- Pause to summarize with permission and without inserting opinions.
- Draw attention to what is happening in the conversation and relatedness to the individual's desired outcomes.

Stage 3: Learning

- Ask questions that create new understanding about a situation.
- Notice and reflect on any behavioral habits that emerge and offer assessments, based on the conversation, that offer new awareness and learning.
- Help the individual distinguish between their "story" and interpretations versus objective facts.
- Model self-awareness.
- Offer opportunities to reframe the individual's situation and perspective that open up new possibilities.

- Ask the individual what meaning they are deriving from a new awareness and what learning is happening for them.

Stage 4: Closure

- Review key points of the session to ensure common understanding.
- Identify specific actions and learning to practice or achieve between sessions. This should be relevant to the individual's learnings from the session and their commitment to integrate that learning.
- Affirm next steps and a positive relationship by commenting on the positive learning the coach observed during the coaching session.

Twenty-Five Powerful Coaching Openings and Questions

1. I'm curious . . . I'm wondering . . . I'd like to explore . . .
2. May I offer an assessment of what I'm noticing? How does that land with you?
3. I'd like to reflect what I hear you say to see if I got it right. Did I capture what you said? Is there more?
4. What are you feeling/thinking/experiencing right now?
5. What have you done so far to address this issue?
6. What might you start or stop that would shift this situation?
7. What is the ideal positive future if everything went perfectly?
8. What would reaching your goal mean to you?
9. How would reaching your goal feel?
10. What is your biggest challenge with . . . ?
11. How much longer are you willing to . . . ?
12. If you were to look at this situation from X's point of view, what might you see/think/notice?
13. How does doing/acting/feeling ABC serve you?
14. What is holding you back from _____?
15. What are you holding onto right now that is/is not serving you and your goal/commitment?
16. What needs to be different or to change for you to feel the way you want to feel?
17. What actions/steps are you willing to take to practice/move forward/be aligned with your goal/commitment/desired outcome?
18. How is this situation the same or different in other parts of your life/work/relationships?

19. What's at stake for you?
20. What sensations are you feeling in your body right now? What does that tell you?
21. How would you rather feel?
22. What are you noticing, and what meaning do you give it?
23. When have you been successful at ABC another time in your life?
24. Would you give that experience/sensation/feeling/emotion a plus, minus, or neutral rating?
25. What is the story you tell yourself about . . . ?

Mentoring Development Program and Benefits

There are a number of essential steps in building a robust mentoring program. There is a lot of detail behind each of the steps below. These are the key components.

- Customize XYZ's program.
- Identify senior-level and internal department head champions.
- Identify an appropriate Project Manager to work closely with the Consultant and/or Internal Executive Sponsor and oversee the development, implementation, and evaluation of the program.
- Identify and communicate the purpose of the program to all staff.
- Determine how success will be measured.
- Identify the intended mentors and mentees.
- Create a program implementation action plan.
- Create activities to support mentors and mentees.
- Develop a robust communications strategy.
- Train and educate the mentors and mentees.
- Implement and evaluate the program.
- Adjust as needed.

Benefits for the Mentor

- Gaining personal satisfaction in helping someone grow professionally.
- Building new relationships.
- Developing skills as a teacher—helping someone clarify career goals.
- Developing skills as a guide—helping someone navigate the waters of the company.

- Developing skills as an advisor—helping someone find their strengths and weaknesses.
- Receiving recognition.
- Putting knowledge and experience into action.
- Learning from the mentee.
- Being uplifted, engaged, and energized.
- Gaining an opportunity to leave a lasting legacy.

Benefits for the Mentee

- Learning from the valuable knowledge and experience of the mentor.
- Increasing competencies in areas of interest.
- Receiving knowledge about the "ins and outs" of the organization.
- Establishing valuable connections with more experienced staff and learning what it is like to be in a higher-level position.
- Having a sounding board to hear one's triumphs as well as frustrations.
- Getting a sharper focus on what's needed to grow professionally.
- Developing skills as a learner.
- Developing skills as a communicator in expressing expectations, goals, and concerns.
- Having an advocate within the organization.
- Getting honest feedback.

Leader Delegation Profile

Things I've Already Delegated	Things I Could Delegate	Things I'm Uncertain about Delegating	Things I Can't, or Believe I Can't, Delegate

Delegation Agreement

Delegated Projects / New Work / Assignments	Authority Level (1 = high; 3 = low)	Deadline

Performance Standards:

Comments:

_____   _____   _____
Delegator   Date   To Whom Delegated

Succession Planning Worksheets

Step 1: Identify business challenges and goals for the next one to five years.

Plan Worksheet

What do you know is happening inside and outside your organization that impacts your business?

Right Now?   The Near Future?   The Distant Future (1–5 years)?

Step 2: Identify the mission-critical positions that impact the success of your business, using the wisdom of key leaders and HR professionals.

Review both leadership and key individual contributor positions that are hard to or take a long time to fill. Evaluate the positions against strategic business goals and assign a vacancy risk factor to the current incumbent.

Position Worksheet

Position title _____

Position incumbent _____ or

Vacant (how long?) _____

Position impact on key business operations_____

_____

Risks: Vacancy _____

If not filled _____

Estimated time to fill a vacancy _____

Step 3: Identify competencies, skills, and knowledge that are critical to business success.

Once you have identified the mission-critical positions, particularly those that have a high vacancy risk or are vacant, identify what is needed in the successor to that position that you will either groom internally or hire externally.

Competency Worksheet

Position title _____

Core leadership and/or interpersonal competencies:

_____   _____   _____

_____   _____   _____

_____   _____   _____

Essential skills competencies:

_____   _____   _____

_____   _____   _____

Unique or preferred but not essential competencies:

_____   _____   _____

_____   _____   _____

Education: _____

Experience: _____

What is unique about this position (institutional knowledge, relationships, skill sets, etc.)? _____

_____

Who working here now could do this job? _____

Where and by whom is critical information and knowledge held currently?

_____

_____

What is the plan for sharing documentation and knowledge? (e.g., mentoring, job rotation, job shadowing, documentation on secure server, training, etc.)

_____

_____

Step 4: Identify high-potential employees for key positions over the next one to five years.

Who are current staff members or known external individuals who have the competencies required to assume the role and/or who have high potential and the motivation to grow into the role over a period of time?

High-Potential Employee Worksheet

Name: _____

Current position title: _____

Division/Department/Unit: _____

Years in current position: _____

Current leader: _____

Target position: _____

Core leadership and/or skill competencies needed for this position (take list from step 3): _____

What competencies/skills does this person need to develop to be ready for this position?:

_____   _____   _____

Readiness: Current ___ Within 6–12 months ___ Within 1–2 years ___ Within 3–5 years ___

Action plan for this high-potential employee:

_____

_____

Step 5: Create a targeted individual development plan (IDP) *with and for* each high-potential employee who wants to grow into a mission-critical position and whom you believe can do so.

Individual Development Planning Worksheet

(Or use version shown in chapter 7.)

Name: _____

Current position title: _____

Division/Department/Unit: _____

Current supervisor: _____

Succession position(s): _____

Current incumbent and incumbent's supervisor: _____

Division/Department/Unit: _____

Short-term goals: _____

Long-term goals: _____

Core competency, knowledge, and skill development plan:

Competency/Skill   Learning Plan   Dates   Costs   Outcome

CHAPTER 10

Termination and Resignation Checklist

Name of the Employee: _____

Employee's Position or Title: _____

Name of the Supervisor: _____

Date of the face-to-face meeting with the employee: _____

Date of termination or resignation: _____ Effective as of: _____

Communication of termination/resignation to appropriate staff, customers, clients, and others will be done by whom, by when, and how? _____

_____

_____

Type of Termination
Voluntary Resignation:

___ Received a written employee resignation letter (if the employee gave a verbal resignation, a written confirmation of resignation was given to the employee and management retained a copy)

___ Scheduled exit interview with _____. ___ Completed exit interview

___ This is a resignation ___ a retirement ___ an unpaid leave of absence ___ Other _____

Involuntary Termination:
Who will be present in the termination meeting? _____
_____

Is there any security risk to be considered? No _____ *Yes* _____ *If yes, what is the plan?*

_____

___ Provided employee with termination letter.

___ Provided employee with optional resignation letter.

___ Provided employee with severance agreement if offered.

___ Received signed severance agreement.

___ Provided employee with Worker Adjustment and Retraining Notification Act (WARN) / Older Workers Benefit Protection Act (OWBPA) notices (if applicable).

All Termination of Employment Situations, Voluntary or Involuntary:

Employee Benefits

___ Provided employee with employment insurance benefits information (COBRA, life insurance, supplemental insurance, etc.).

___ Checked the employee's Flexible Spending Arrangement (FSA) / Health Savings Account (HSA), if applicable, and informed employee of remaining funds and reimbursement deadlines (IRS approved).

___ Checked the employee's Dependent Care Assistance Plan (DCAP) if applicable, and informed employee of remaining funds and reimbursement deadlines.

___ Checked paid time off (PTO) balance and informed employee of any remaining PTO and how it will be processed at termination of employment.

___ Informed employee about retirement plan options, if applicable.

Employee Compensation

___ Reported any outstanding balances for money owed to the employer by the employee and how those funds will be collected.

___ Notified Payroll Department to process the employee's final paycheck including any earned PTO, bonuses, severance (and the method of paying severance), retirement, and instructions on how to deduct any money due the employer.

Employee Contracts and/or Legal Obligations

___ Provided letter reminding the employee of any legal obligations that continue post-employment (such as a nondisclosure agreement [NDA], a non-compete agreement, a confidentiality agreement, or an employment contract).

Immigration Status

___ Notified Human Resources (HR) or in-house attorney of the change in status for an employee with a valid work visa who is a non-citizen or not a permanent resident of the United States.

Recordkeeping

___ The employee's employment history and personnel file is filed properly as a termination or resignation. This includes all documentation related to the termination or resignation.

___ Provided written information about how the employer will respond to employment verification and/or referral requests.

___ Received written authorization from the employee to respond to employment verification and/or referral requests, if relevant and appropriate.

Information Technology

___ Deleted all of the involuntarily terminated employee's electronic and communication access including e-mail, intranet, key codes, phones, and voicemail.

___ Determined and communicated to the employee the terms and specifics of any continued access afforded for voluntary resignation, retirement, and possibly a layoff.

___ Removed employee's name from e-mail group distribution lists, internal phone lists, websites, and building directories, as appropriate.

Facilities/Office Manager

___ Disabled key and security codes for building and office access as appropriate.

___ Removed the employee's name from the door, desk, and mailbox.

___ Determined how and when the workspace of the departing employee will be cleared and by whom.

Collected the following items before the employee departs:

___ Keys and badges allowing access to : ___ offices ___ buildings ___ desks ___ file cabinets ___ other (list any other items here)

___ ID cards (with the possible exception of retiree and laid-off employee ID cards)

___ Building access card

___ Business cards

___ All employer-owned equipment and clothing (mobile phones, machinery, tools, uniforms, etc.)

___ Computer, workpad, and any other electronic equipment

___ Other _____

This Checklist was completed by:_____
Date: _____

Sample Confidential Exit Interview

Employee:	Date of Hire
Position	Last Day Worked
Supervisor	Department

- Why are you leaving?
- What led to the decision to leave?
- What did you like best about your job?
- What did you like least about your job?
- What changes would you recommend?
- If you had an opportunity, would you come back to work here? If yes or no, why?

Employee Signature	Date
Human Resources (HR) Manager	Date

If possible, ask the employee to fill out an Employee Engagement Survey as noted in chapter 7 or add questions to the exit interview. It will provide much more information.

Notes

INTRODUCTION

1. Louise Phipps Senft and William Senft, *Being Relational* (Deerfield Beach, FL: Health Communications, 2015), 11, 27.

2. Simon Sinek, "Simon Sinek Quotes," BrainyQuote, https://www.brainy quote.com/quotes/simon_sinek_418479.

3. Roberta Chinsky Matuson, "You're Kidding, Right? 50% of New Hires Fail," LinkedIn, April 14, 2017, https://www.linkedin.com/pulse/youre-kidding -right-50-new-hires-fail-roberta-chinsky-matuson.

4. Dr. John Sullivan, "Five Ugly Numbers That You Can't Ignore—It's Time to Calculate Hiring Failures," ERE, October 26, 2009, https://www .ere.net/five-ugly-numbers-that-you-cant-ignore-its-time-to-calculate-hiring -failures; Liz Kislik, "What to Do When You Realize You Made a Bad Hire," *Harvard Business Review*, August 22, 2018, https://hbr.org/2018/08/what-to -do-when-you-realize-you-made-a-bad-hire.

5. Jim Collins, *Good to Great* (New York: HarperCollins, 2001), 41.

6. Jan Johnson Osborn, "Do Managers Spend Too Much Time on Poor Performers at the Risk of Top Talent?" LinkedIn, August 18, 2014, https:// www.linkedin.com/pulse/20140818184227-16410391-do-managers-spend-too -much-time-on-poor-performers-at-the-risk-of-top-talent.

7. Megan Wells, "What Is the Average Employee Retention Rate by Industry?" *DailyPay* (blog), July 10, 2017, https://business.dailypay.com/blog/ employee-retention-rate.

8. Megan Wells, "What Are Turnover and Retention Rates for the Caregiver Industry?" *DailyPay* (blog), November 6, 2018, https://business.dailypay.com/blog/what-are-turnover-rates-in-the-caregiving-industry.

9. Gallup, "State of the American Workplace: Employee Engagement Insights for U.S. Business Leaders, 2013," https://news.gallup.com/opinion/gallup/170570/gallup-releases-new-findings-state-american-workplace.aspx.

10. Roxi Bahar Hewertson, *Lead Like It Matters . . . Because It Does* (New York: McGraw-Hill, 2014).

CHAPTER 1: CALL TO ACTION

1. Geoff Smart and Randy Street, *WHO: The A Method for Hiring* (New York: Ballantine Books, 2008).

2. Albert Einstein, "Albert Einstein Quotes," BrainyQuote, https://www.brainyquote.com/authors/albert_einstein.

3. Roberta Chinsky Matuson, "You're Kidding, Right? 50% of New Hires Fail," LinkedIn, April 14, 2017, https://www.linkedin.com/pulse/youre-kidding-right-50-new-hires-fail-roberta-chinsky-matuson.

CHAPTER 2: DIGGING FOR GOLD

1. Martin Zwilling, "10 Questions for Selecting a Recruiter to Attract the Best Talent to Your Business Team," *Inc.*, December 13, 2017, https://www.inc.com/martin-zwilling/how-to-find-best-hire-for-that-key-role-in-your-new-venture.html.

2. Atta Tarki and Ken Kanara, "How Recruiters Can Stay Relevant in the Age of LinkedIn," *Harvard Business Review*, February 8, 2019, https://hbr.org/2019/02/how-recruiters-can-stay-relevant-in-the-age-of-linkedin.

CHAPTER 3: GETTING TO KNOW YOU

1. Jonah Berger, *Contagious: Why Things Catch On* (New York: Simon & Schuster, 2013), 7–9.

2. Dawn Papandrea, "The Biggest Resume Lies to Avoid," Monster.com, https://www.monster.com/career-advice/article/the-truth-about-resume-lies-hot-jobs.

CHAPTER 4: UP CLOSE AND PERSONAL

1. Jack Welch, "How I Hire: The Must-Haves, the Definitely-Should-Haves and the Game Changer," LinkedIn, September 23, 2013, https://www.linkedin.com/pulse/20130923225948-86541065-how-i-hire-the-must-haves-the-definitely-should-haves-and-the-game-changer.
2. Oprah Winfrey, quoted in "66 Quotes to Live By," https://www.wow4u.com/quotestoliveby.
3. Daniel Goleman, *Emotional Intelligence* (New York: Bantam Books, 1995).
4. Annie McKee, "How to Hire for Emotional Intelligence," *Harvard Business Review*, February 5, 2016, https://hbr.org/2016/02/how-to-hire-for-emotional-intelligence.
5. Daniel Goleman and Richard Boyatizis, "Emotional and Social Competency Inventory (ESCI)," Korn Ferry (previously Hay Group), 2014, https://www.kornferry.com/insights/learning/trainings-and-certifications/esci-emotional-and-social-competency-inventory. All references to emotional intelligence (EI) are drawn from the "Emotional Intelligence Training Materials" supplied to certified EI professionals by Korn Ferry and are based on the work of Daniel Goleman, PhD, and Richard Boyatizis, PhD. Roxana Bahar Hewertson is a Korn Ferry–certified EI practitioner.
6. *New York Times* slogan since 1896.
7. Welch, "How I Hire."
8. Rod Napier, *The Power Interview* (Elkins Park, PA: Sunrise Press, 1990).

CHAPTER 5: THE INVITATION

1. Abraham Lincoln, quoted in "Character Quotes," BrainyQuote, https://www.brainyquote.com/topics/character-quotes.
2. Robert Half, "Check Your References," *Robert Half* (blog), March 11, 2019, https://www.roberthalf.com/blog/evaluating-job-candidates/check-your-references.
3. Robert Half, "Beyond the Paycheck: Employee Perks to Negotiate," *Robert Half* (blog), March 14, 2016, https://www.roberthalf.ca/en/blog/compensation-and-benefits/beyond-the-paycheck-employee-perks-to-negotiate.
4. Betterteam, "At-Will Employment," Betterteam, July 29, 2019, https://www.betterteam.com/at-will-employment.

CHAPTER 6: WELCOME ABOARD!

1. Vinay Koshy, "This Is How the Top Companies Onboard New Hires," *Hubstaff Blog*, April 16, 2018, https://blog.hubstaff.com/employee-onboarding -best-practices.

2. Madeline Laurano, "Onboarding 2013: A New Look at New Hires," Aberdeen Group, April 2013, http://deliberatepractice.com.au/wp-content/uploads/2013/04/Onboarding-2013.pdf.

3. Roy Maurer, "Onboarding Key to Retaining, Engaging Talent," Society for Human Resource Management, April 16, 2015, https://www.shrm.org/resourcesandtools/hr-topics/talent-acquisition/pages/onboarding-key-retaining -engaging-talent.aspx.

4. Joseph Michelli, *The Zappos Experience: 5 Principles to Inspire, Engage, and Wow* (New York: McGraw-Hill, 2012).

5. Kevin Martin and Justin Bourke, "Onboarding: The First Line of Engagement," Aberdeen Group, February 2010, http://www.hrzone.com/resources/onboarding-the-first-line-of-engagement-free-aberdeen-whitepaper.

6. Kathryn Vasel, "The Job Market Is So Good, New Hires Aren't Showing Up for Their First Day of Work," CNN Business, September 16, 2019, https://www.cnn.com/2019/09/16/success/ghosting-first-day-of-work/index.html.

7. Roxi Bahar Hewertson, *Lead Like It Matters . . . Because It Does* (New York: McGraw-Hill, 2014).

8. Maurer, "Onboarding Key to Retaining, Engaging Talent."

9. Andre Lavoie, "4 Ways to Get Truly Honest Feedback from Employees," *Entrepreneur*, May 26, 2015, https://www.entrepreneur.com/article/246556.

CHAPTER 7: HOW ARE YOU DOING?

1. Work Institute, "2019 Retention Report: Trends, Reasons and a Call to Action," https://info.workinstitute.com/hubfs/2019%20Retention%20Report/Work%20Institute%202019%20Retention%20Report%20final-1.pdf (free downloadable report).

2. Gallup, "Gallup Q^{12} Employee Engagement Survey," https://q12.gallup.com/Public/en-us/Features.

CHAPTER 8: WHERE DO WE GO FROM HERE?

1. VoiceGlance, "18 Quotes by Netflix's Talent Guru That Will Make You Rethink HR," VoiceGlance, March 6, 2015, https://voiceglance.com/18 -quotes-by-netflixs-talent-guru-that-will-make-you-rethink-hr.

2. Shawn Murphy, "The Annual Performance Review Is Insulting, Ineffective, and Outdated. Let It Die," *Slate*, January 20, 2016, https://slate.com/business/2016/01/kill-the-annual-performance-review.html.

3. Liz Ryan, "Let's Kill Performance Reviews in 2015," *Forbes*, February 19, 2015, https://www.forbes.com/sites/lizryan/2015/02/19/lets-kill-performance-reviews-in-2015.

4. Patty McCord, "How Netflix Reinvented HR," *Harvard Business Review*, January–February 2014, https://hbr.org/2014/01/how-netflix-reinvented-hr.

5. David Sturt and Todd Nordstrom, "10 Shocking Workplace Stats You Need to Know," *Forbes*, March 8, 2018, https://www.forbes.com/sites/davidsturt/2018/03/08/10-shocking-workplace-stats-you-need-to-know.

6. Stephen Covey, "Stephen Covey Quotes," BrainyQuote, https://www.brainyquote.com/quotes/stephen_covey_110198.

CHAPTER 9: GROWING YOUR PEOPLE

1. Teala Wilson, "8 Steps for Succession Planning," *Saba Blog*, November 23, 2015, https://www.saba.com/blog/8-steps-for-effective-succession-planning.

2. Sharlyn Lauby, *The Recruiter's Handbook: A Complete Guide for Sourcing, Selecting, and Engaging the Best Talent* (Alexandria, VA: Society for Human Resource Management, 2018), chapter 6.

3. Work Institute, "2019 Retention Report: Trends, Reasons and a Call to Action," https://info.workinstitute.com/hubfs/2019%20Retention%20Report/Work%20Institute%202019%20Retention%20Report%20final-1.pdf.

CHAPTER 10: WHEN IT'S REALLY OVER: PART 1

1. Robert I. Sutton, "Why I Wrote *The No Asshole Rule*," *Harvard Business Review*, March 17, 2007, https://hbr.org/2007/03/why-i-wrote-the-no-asshole-rule.

2. Betterteam, "Insubordination," Betterteam, July 29, 2019, https://www.betterteam.com/insubordination.

3. Dr. John Sullivan, "Ouch, 50% of New Hires Fail! 6 Ugly Numbers Revealing Recruiting's Dirty Little Secret," ERE, April 10, 2017, https://www.ere.net/ouch-50-of-new-hires-fail-6-ugly-numbers-revealing-recruitings-dirty-little-secret.

4. Jeff Hyman, "You Need to Fire More People," *Forbes*, June 12, 2019, https://www.forbes.com/sites/jeffhyman/2019/06/12/fire.

5. Greg McKeown, "Hire Slow, Fire Fast," *Harvard Business Review*, March 3, 2014, https://hbr.org/2014/03/hire-slow-fire-fast.

6. Wikipedia, "Worker Adjustment and Retraining Notification Act of 1988," last modified February 13, 2020, https://en.wikipedia.org/wiki/Worker_Adjustment_and_Retraining_Notification_Act_of_1988.

CHAPTER 11: WHEN IT'S REALLY OVER: PART 2

1. US Department of Labor, "Age Discrimination," https://www.dol.gov/general/topic/discrimination/agedisc.
2. Strategic HR, "Mandatory Retirement: Is It Legal?" April 25, 2017, https://strategichrinc.com/mandatory-retirement-guidelines.
3. US Department of Labor, "Family and Medical Leave Act," https://www.dol.gov/whd/fmla.

RESOURCES

1. Jacquelyn Smith, "New Research Shows Where Employers Find Their New Hires," *Forbes*, April 6, 2012, https://www.forbes.com/sites/jacquelynsmith/2012/04/06/new-research-shows-where-employers-find-their-new-hires.
2. Project Implicit, "Implicit Association Test," Harvard University, https://implicit.harvard.edu/implicit/takeatest.html.
3. Daniel Goleman and Richard Boyatizis, "Emotional and Social Competency Inventory (ESCI)," Korn Ferry (previously Hay Group), 2014, https://www.kornferry.com/insights/learning/trainings-and-certifications/esci-emotional-and-social-competency-inventory. All references to emotional intelligence are drawn from the "Emotional Intelligence Training Materials" supplied to certified EI professionals by Korn Ferry and are based on the work of Daniel Goleman, PhD, and Richard Boyatizis, PhD. Roxana Bahar Hewertson is a Korn Ferry certified EI practitioner.
4. Kaylee DeWitt, "100 Behavioral Interview Questions to Help You Find the Best Candidates," *Top Echelon* (blog), June 21, 2017, https://www.topechelon.com/blog/placement-process/top-behavioral-interview-questions-list-examples.

Bibliography

Berger, Jonah. *Contagious: Why Things Catch On*. New York: Simon & Schuster, 2013.

Betterteam. "At-Will Employment." Betterteam, July 29, 2019. https://www.betterteam.com/at-will-employment.

———. "Insubordination." Betterteam, July 29, 2019. https://www.betterteam.com/insubordination.

Collins, Jim. *Good to Great*. New York: HarperCollins, 2001.

Covey, Stephen. "Stephen Covey Quotes." BrainyQuote. https://www.brainyquote.com/quotes/stephen_covey_110198.

DeWitt, Kaylee. "100 Behavioral Interview Questions to Help You Find the Best Candidates." *Top Echelon* (blog), June 21, 2017. https://www.topechelon.com/blog/placement-process/top-behavioral-interview-questions-list-examples.

Einstein, Albert. "Albert Einstein Quotes." BrainyQuote. https://www.brainyquote.com/authors/albert_einstein.

Fair Labor Standards Act. "FLSA Coverage." FLSA Homepage. https://www.flsa.com/coverage.html.

Gallup. "Gallup Q^{12} Employee Engagement Survey." https://q12.gallup.com/Public/en-us/Features.

———. "State of the American Workplace: Employee Engagement Insights for U.S. Business Leaders, 2013." http://www.gallup.com/strategicconsulting/163007/state-american-workplace.aspx.

Goleman, Daniel. *Emotional Intelligence*. New York: Bantam Books, 1995.

Goleman, Daniel, and Richard Boyatizis. "Emotional and Social Competency Inventory (ESCI)." Korn Ferry (previously Hay Group), 2014. https://www

.kornferry.com/insights/learning/trainings-and-certifications/esci-emotional -and-social-competency-inventory.

Hewertson, Roxi Bahar. *Lead Like It Matters . . . Because It Does*. New York: McGraw-Hill, 2014.

Hyman, Jeff. "You Need to Fire More People." *Forbes*, June 12, 2019. https:// www.forbes.com/sites/jeffhyman/2019/06/12/fire.

Kislik, Liz. "What to Do When You Realize You Made a Bad Hire." *Harvard Business Review*, August 22, 2018. https://hbr.org/2018/08/what-to-do -when-you-realize-you-made-a-bad-hire.

Koshy, Vinay. "This Is How the Top Companies Onboard New Hires." *Hubstaff Blog*, April 16, 2018. https://blog.hubstaff.com/employee-onboarding -best-practices.

Lauby, Sharlyn. *The Recruiter's Handbook: A Complete Guide for Sourcing, Selecting, and Engaging the Best Talent*. Alexandria, VA: Society for Human Resource Management, 2018.

Laurano, Madeline. "Onboarding 2013: A New Look at New Hires." Aberdeen Group, April 2013. http://deliberatepractice.com.au/wp-content/uploads 2013/04/Onboarding-2013.pdf.

Lavoie, Andre. "4 Ways to Get Truly Honest Feedback from Employees." *Entrepreneur*, May 26, 2015. https://www.entrepreneur.com/article/246556.

Martin, Kevin, and Justin Bourke. "Onboarding: The First Line of Engagement." Aberdeen Group, February 2010. http://www.hrzone.com/resources/ onboarding-the-first-line-of-engagement-free-aberdeen-whitepaper.

Matuson, Roberta Chinsky. "You're Kidding, Right? 50% of New Hires Fail." LinkedIn, April 14, 2017. https://www.linkedin.com/pulse/youre-kidding -right-50-new-hires-fail-roberta-chinsky-matuson.

Maurer, Roy. "Onboarding Key to Retaining, Engaging Talent." Society for Human Resource Management, April 16, 2015. https://www.shrm.org/ resourcesandtools/hr-topics/talent-acquisition/pages/onboarding-key-retaining -engaging-talent.aspx.

McCord, Patty. "How Netflix Reinvented HR." *Harvard Business Review*, January–February 2014. https://hbr.org/2014/01/how-netflix-reinvented-hr.

McKee, Annie. "How to Hire for Emotional Intelligence." *Harvard Business Review*, February 5, 2016. https://hbr.org/2016/02/how-to-hire-for-emotional -intelligence.

McKeown, Greg. "Hire Slow, Fire Fast." *Harvard Business Review*, March 3, 2014. https://hbr.org/2014/03/hire-slow-fire-fast.

Michelli, Joseph. *The Zappos Experience: 5 Principles to Inspire, Engage, and Wow*. New York: McGraw-Hill, 2012.

Murphy, Shawn. "The Annual Performance Review Is Insulting, Ineffective, and Outdated. Let It Die." *Slate*, January 20, 2016. https://slate.com/ business/2016/01/kill-the-annual-performance-review.html.

Napier, Rod. *The Power Interview*. Elkins Park, PA: Sunrise Press, 1990.

Osborn, Jan Johnson. "Do Managers Spend Too Much Time on Poor Performers at the Risk of Top Talent?" LinkedIn, August 18, 2014. https://www.linkedin.com/pulse/20140818184227-16410391-do-managers-spend-too-much-time-on-poor-performers-at-the-risk-of-top-talent.

Papandrea, Dawn. "The Biggest Resume Lies to Avoid." Monster.com. https://www.monster.com/career-advice/article/the-truth-about-resume-lies-hot-jobs.

Project Implicit. "Implicit Association Test." Harvard University, https://implicit.harvard.edu/implicit/takeatest.html.

Robert Half. "Beyond the Paycheck: Employee Perks to Negotiate." *Robert Half* (blog), March 14, 2016. https://www.roberthalf.ca/en/blog/compensation-and-benefits/beyond-the-paycheck-employee-perks-to-negotiate.

———. "Check Your References." *Robert Half* (blog), March 11, 2019. https://www.roberthalf.com/blog/evaluating-job-candidates/check-your-references.

Ryan, Liz. "Let's Kill Performance Reviews in 2015." *Forbes*, February 19, 2015. https://www.forbes.com/sites/lizryan/2015/02/19/lets-kill-performance-reviews-in-2015.

Senft, Louise Phipps, and William Senft. *Being Relational*. Deerfield Beach, FL: Health Communications, 2015.

Sinek, Simon. "Simon Sinek Quotes." BrainyQuote. https://www.brainyquote.com/quotes/simon_sinek_418479.

Smart, Geoff, and Randy Street. *WHO: The A̲ Method for Hiring*. New York: Ballantine Books, 2008.

Smith, Jacquelyn. "New Research Shows Where Employers Find Their New Hires." *Forbes*, April 6, 2012. https://www.forbes.com/sites/jacquelynsmith/2012/04/06/new-research-shows-where-employers-find-their-new-hires.

Strategic HR. "Mandatory Retirement: Is It Legal?" April 25, 2017. https://strategichrinc.com/mandatory-retirement-guidelines.

Sturt, David, and Todd Nordstrom. "10 Shocking Workplace Stats You Need to Know." *Forbes*, March 8, 2018. https://www.forbes.com/sites/davidsturt/2018/03/08/10-shocking-workplace-stats-you-need-to-know.

Sullivan, Dr. John. "Five Ugly Numbers That You Can't Ignore—It's Time to Calculate Hiring Failures." ERE, October 26, 2009. https://www.ere.net/five-ugly-numbers-that-you-cant-ignore-its-time-to-calculate-hiring-failures.

———. "Ouch, 50% of New Hires Fail! 6 Ugly Numbers Revealing Recruiting's Dirty Little Secret." ERE, April 10, 2017. https://www.ere.net/ouch-50-of-new-hires-fail-6-ugly-numbers-revealing-recruitings-dirty-little-secret.

Sutton, Robert I. "Why I Wrote *The No Asshole Rule*." *Harvard Business Review*, March 17, 2007. https://hbr.org/2007/03/why-i-wrote-the-no-asshole-rule.

Tarki, Atta, and Ken Kanara. "How Recruiters Can Stay Relevant in the Age of LinkedIn." *Harvard Business Review*, February 8, 2019. https://hbr.org/2019/02/how-recruiters-can-stay-relevant-in-the-age-of-linkedin.

US Department of Labor. "Age Discrimination." https://www.dol.gov/general/topic/discrimination/agedisc.

———. "Family and Medical Leave Act." https://www.dol.gov/whd/fmla.

Vasel, Kathryn. "The Job Market Is So Good, New Hires Aren't Showing Up for Their First Day of Work." CNN Business, September 16, 2019. https://www.cnn.com/2019/09/16/success/ghosting-first-day-of-work/index.html.

VoiceGlance. "18 Quotes by Netflix's Talent Guru That Will Make You Rethink HR." VoiceGlance, March 6, 2015. https://voiceglance.com/18-quotes-by-netflixs-talent-guru-that-will-make-you-rethink-hr.

Welch, Jack. "How I Hire: The Must-Haves, the Definitely-Should-Haves and the Game Changer." LinkedIn, September 23, 2013. https://www.linkedin.com/pulse/20130923225948-86541065-how-i-hire-the-must-haves-the-definitely-should-haves-and-the-game-changer.

Wells, Megan. "What Are Turnover and Retention Rates for the Caregiver Industry?" *DailyPay* (blog), November 6, 2018. https://business.dailypay.com/blog/what-are-turnover-rates-in-the-caregiving-industry.

———. "What Is the Average Employee Retention Rate by Industry?" *DailyPay* (blog), July 10, 2017. https://business.dailypay.com/blog/employee-retention-rate.

Wikipedia. "Worker Adjustment and Retraining Notification Act of 1988." Last modified February 13, 2020. https://en.wikipedia.org/wiki/Worker_Adjustment_and_Retraining_Notification_Act_of_1988.

Wilson, Teala. "8 Steps for Succession Planning." *Saba Blog*, November 23, 2015. https://www.saba.com/blog/8-steps-for-effective-succession-planning.

Work Institute. "2019 Retention Report: Trends, Reasons and a Call to Action." https://info.workinstitute.com/hubfs/2019%20Retention%20Report/Work%20Institute%202019%20Retention%20Report%20final-1.pdf.

Zwilling, Martin. "10 Questions for Selecting a Recruiter to Attract the Best Talent to Your Business Team." *Inc.*, December 13, 2017. https://www.inc.com/martin-zwilling/how-to-find-best-hire-for-that-key-role-in-your-new-venture.html.

Index

About the Author

Leadership expert **Roxi Bahar Hewertson** brings more than three decades of practical experience from the worlds of higher education, business, and nonprofits. She is an organizational consultant, executive leadership coach, motivational speaker, and author of the acclaimed book *Lead Like It Matters . . . Because It Does*. She taught at Cornell University's School of Industrial and Labor Relations where she received her master's degree. Roxi has coached more than a hundred senior leaders and taught her award-winning leadership courses to thousands more.

Roxi has spent her entire career being a leader and has helped both emerging and expert leaders boost quantifiable job performance to achieve or exceed personal and organizational goals. As a certified Presence-Based® and International Coaching Federation coach, she invites leaders to create their best lives and share the powerful journey that one-on-one executive leadership coaching can offer.

At the core of Roxi's passion is her desire to inspire and empower leaders on their journey of: honing interpersonal effectiveness, increasing emotional intelligence, and sharpening their capacity to create great results with their teams. Roxi offers her practical, commonsense, and proven solutions to complex leadership and organizational problems, making her advice and counsel in high demand.

Roxi is the CEO of Highland Consulting Group Inc. based in Brevard, North Carolina.